Josephus David Wijnkoop

Manual of Hebrew syntax

Josephus David Wijnkoop

Manual of Hebrew syntax

ISBN/EAN: 9783337735654

Printed in Europe, USA, Canada, Australia, Japan

Cover: Foto ©ninafisch / pixelio.de

More available books at **www.hansebooks.com**

MANUAL OF HEBREW SYNTAX

BY

REV. J. D. WIJNKOOP

Litt. Hum. Cand. in the University of Leyden,
Rabbi of the Jewish Congregation in
Amsterdam.

TRANSLATED FROM THE DUTCH

BY

REV. DR. C. VAN DEN BIESEN

Prof. of Theology at St. Joseph's Foreign Missionary College,
Mill-Hill.

LONDON:
LUZAC & Co.
PUBLISHERS TO THE INDIA OFFICE.
46, GREAT RUSSELL STREET.
1897.

LETTER OF COMMENDATION

FROM

HIS EMINENCE CARDINAL VAUGHAN
Archbishop of Westminster.

My dear Dr. Van den Biesen.

You have followed the example of the great St. Jerome who acquired his knowledge of the Hebrew tongue by becoming a learner under Jewish doctors, and now you are about to render assistance to others by translating the work on Hebrew Syntax drawn up by your Hebrew master the Rev. J. D. Wijnkoop, Rabbi at Amsterdam.

You tell me that this Syntax promises great linguistic merits. I much regret that upon this point I can myself form no opinion. But I have confidence in your judgment on such a matter. And of this I am certain that you will be rendering a great public service to the Church in England if you help to promote the study of the Bible languages, especially the Hebrew. One of the pressing needs of the Church in England is a Catholic school abreast of the times and of the latest researches in all that concerns Biblical science. This I have a strong hope to see established. There are many growing up like yourself, enamoured of these studies. It is for you who possess knowledge to do all that you can to promote the formation of such a Catholic school.

Believe me
Your faithful & devoted servant,
HERBERT CARDINAL VAUGHAN.

AUTHOR'S PREFACE.

By publishing a Dutch Manual of Hebrew Syntax I believe I am corresponding with the wish of many of my countrymen. At least I have heard several complaints of the want of such a book. I had moreover in my Manual of Hebrew Grammar (Edition Joachimsthal, Amsterdam 1888) promised to undertake the composing of a Syntax.

As regards the plan I have adopted in my Manual of Syntax I should like to draw attention to the following points. I need scarcely remark that I have consulted and utilised existing works bearing on the subject. Yet in the treatment of certain chapters I have thought it necessary to work independently for reasons which on comparison would be obvious.

This applies in the first place to my treatment of the infinitive and participle of the verb. As I could not accept the existing opinions concerning them, I have preferred to adopt a simpler theory arising from their unique twofold character of *verbum* and *nomen*.

Further, the connecting of two verbs into one idea

appeared to me to require a more or less original treatment, while in the manner of dealing with the *status constructus* and ה׳ הַיְדִיעָה certain alterations seemed to me desirable.

The terminology, moreover, for naming the cases, such as we find in the classic and modern languages, has in so far it was possible been intentionally avoided. This plan I adopted, because in Hebrew scarcely any trace can be found of the so called flexion of the *nomina*, by which the various cases are expressed. The *status constructus* which most of all would remind us of them, on the one hand differs from them because of the alteration of vowels, and the abbreviation instead of prolongation of words, and on the other hand it is capable of expressing so many cases, that it cannot well be identified with one or more of them.

Finally, it should be observed that I have ventured to divide this Manual in a manner different to that usually adopted, by first considering the different parts of the sentence, and then its construction.

J. D. WIJNKOOP.

TRANSLATOR'S PREFACE.

This volume, as the title indicates, is not intended to be a complete or exhaustive work on Hebrew Syntax. By treating of its primary principles, its aim is to initiate students into its more difficult problems and to prepare them for more profound and comprehensive works.

The Manual is based upon the Hebrew text as determined by the Massorah, irrespective of the demands of textual criticism.

The translation of this Manual has been undertaken from motives of gratitude for the valuable instruction received from the author in time past, and from a desire to introduce to English students a Hebrew Syntax, the work of one so eminently qualified for the task, the author having been Professor of Hebrew at the Israelitish Seminary in Amsterdam for upwards of 25 years, besides giving proof of his Hebrew scholarship in his three essays "The signification of the word עתה" "The signification of the adverb אז" and "דרכי הנסיגה sive Leges de accentus Hebraicae linguae ascensione", the latter of which was published both in Latin and Hebrew.

For the defects in translation and any errors that may have crept into this little work, the translator trusts to the kind indulgence of the reader, and will be grateful for corrections.

C. VAN DEN BIESEN.

CONTENTS.

	Page
Letter of Commendation from Cardinal Vaughan.	V
Author's Preface	VII
Translator's Preface	IX
Contents	XI

PART I. — NOMEN.

CHAPTER I. The noun.

§ 1. Gender of the noun 1
§ 2. Number of the noun 2

CHAPTER II. Determination of the noun.

§ 3. ה׳ הַיְדִיעָה 7
§ 4. The adjective 12
§ 5. Status Constructus 16
§ 6. Apposition 19
§ 7. Other means of connecting two nouns . 21
§ 8. Comparative and Superlative 22
§ 9. Numerals 24

CHAPTER III. Pronouns.

§ 10. Personal pronouns and pronominal suffixes 27
§ 11. Demonstrative and Interrogative pronouns 31

CONTENTS.

	Page
§ 12. Relative pronoun	33
§ 13. Pronouns for which the Hebrew has no proper words.	35

PART II. — VERBUM.

CHAPTER IV. The verbal forms.

§ 14. The use of the עָבַר	38
§ 15. The use of the עָתִיד	40
§ 16. The עָבַר and עָתִיד with ו conversive	42
§ 17. The cohortative and jussive	44
§ 18. The use of the imperative	47
§ 19. Persons of the verb	49
§ 20. Modifications of the verbal idea	52
§ 21. Connection of two verbs	52

CHAPTER V. The nominal forms.

§ 22. The Infinitive	57
§ 23. Use of the Participle.	61

PART III. — THE PARTICLES.

CHAPTER VI. Adverbs and Adverbial expressions.

§ 24. Adverbs	65
§ 25. Words expressing negation.	66

CHAPTER VII. Interrogative particles.

§ 26. Interrogative words and sentences	73

CHAPTER VIII. The remaining particles.

§ 27. Prepositions	80
§ 28. Conjunctions	94
§ 29. Interjections	114

PART IV. — Construction of the Sentence.

Chapter IX. Nominal sentences.

§ 30. Subject and Predicate 115
§ 31. Expression of the copula in nominal sentences 119

Chapter X. Verbal sentences.

§ 32. Object of the verb 120
§ 33. Verbs with a twofold object 128
§ 34. Construction of the Passive 130
§ 35. Connection of the noun with the verb through addition of letters or words . 132

Chapter XI. The influence of the subject upon the predicate as regards gender and number.

§ 36. Constructio ad Synesin 135
§ 37. Construction of sentences in which the predicate precedes the subject. . . . 138
§ 38. Compound subjects 141

Chapter XII. Sequence of the different parts of the sentence.

§ 39. Place of the subject and predicate . . . 144
§ 40. The places of the other parts of the sentence. 147
§ 41. Case Absolute 149
Index of passages quoted 153

ERRATA.

Page	3	line	21	*for*	Zech. 13,9	*read* 3,9
,,	24	,,	14	,,	occurence	,, occurrence
,,	89	,,	22	,,	,,	,, ,,
,,	38	,,	7	,,	relative and	,, and relative
,,	38	,,	15	,,	Fulturum	,, Futurum
,,	46	,,	23	,,	wit-hout	,, with-out
,,	49	,,	29	,,	a the third	,, the third
,,	100	,,	11	,,	someti-mes	,, some-times
,,	127	,,	11	,,	prophetise	,, prophesy

HEBREW SYNTAX.

PART I.

NOMEN.

CHAPTER I — THE NOUN.

§ 1 Gender of the noun.

1) With living beings, the feminine gender is either formed through the appending of a feminine termination to a masculine noun, as פָּרָה *cow* from פַּר *ox*, or expressed by a different word, as אָב *father* אֵם *mother*. (See author's grammar § 54, Spelling and derivation of nouns.)

There also are nouns (*communia*) which remain unchanged when used as feminine, the gender of which, therefore, can be distinguished only by the construction; e. g. חֲמִשָּׁה בָקָר (masc.) *five oxen* Ex. 21, 37; הַבָּקָר עָלוֹת (fem.) *the herd giving suck* Gen. 33, 13; גְּמַלִּים בָּאִים (masc.) *camels coming* Gen. 24, 63; גְּמַלִּים מֵינִיקוֹת (fem.) *milch camels* Gen. 32, 16.

2) The gender of other nouns again cannot even be distinguished by the construction. These always have the

same gender whether they are used for masc. or fem. (*epi-coena*); e. g. דוֹב שַׁכּוּל *a bear bereaved of her whelps* Hos. 13, 8; Prov. 17, 12; אַלּוּפֵינוּ מְסֻבָּלִים *our cows are with young* Ps. 144, 14. In this manner כֶּלֶב *dog*, זְאֵב *wolf*, are always constructed as masc., but אַרְנֶבֶת *hare*, חֲסִידָה *stork*, יוֹנָה *dove*, as fem.

Rem. 1 דֹּב *she bear* is once found *fem.* in construction: וַתֵּצֶאנָה שְׁתַּיִם דֻּבִּים *and there came forth two she bears* 2 Kings 2, 24.

Rem. 2 Even in cases where a proper word exists to express the *fem.*, the *masc.* is sometimes used instead of the *fem.* e. g. חֲמוֹר *she ass* 2 Sam. 19, 27; אַיָּל *hind* Ps. 42, 2. An example of this in the case of a human being occurs once Gen. 23, 4, where מֵת refers to a woman.

3) Besides those instances, in which the feminine form is required, there are others where it is used by preference:

(*a*) to express an abstract idea by means of an adjective used as substantive; e. g. רָעָה *calamity*; נְכוֹנָה *steadfastness* Ps. 5, 10. This often occurs especially in the plur.; as גְּדוֹלוֹת *grandeur, haughtiness* Ps. 12, 4; רַבּוֹת *much* Ps. 40, 6; הָאֹתִיּוֹת *the future* Jes. 41, 23; (The pronouns זֹאת, הִיא are frequently used for the indefinite *this, that*.)

(*b*) to express a collective idea; e. g. דָּג *a fish* דָּגָה *fish*, אֹרַח *a traveller* אֹרְחָה *a caravan*, עֵץ *a tree* עֵצָה *timber* Jer. 6, 6; גּוֹלָה *exiles*, יוֹשֶׁבֶת *inhabitants* Jes. 12, 6; אֹיְבָה *enemies* Michah 7, 8, 10.

Hence we find the poetic forms: בְּנֵי צִיּוֹן = בַּת צִיּוֹן; בְּנֵי' = בַּת עַמִּי; בְּנֵי' = בַּת צוּר; בְּנֵי' = בַּת יְהוּדָה

§ 1. GENDER OF THE NOUN.

Rem. 3 With certain words, on the contrary, we find just the opposite, viz. that the *fem.* denotes an *individual* object while the *masc.* is used in a *collective* sense; e. g. שַׂעֲרָה *a hair* שֵׂעָר *hair*; אֳנִיָּה *a ship* אֳנִי *a fleet* 1 Kings 9, 26.

4) The following are usually construed as *fem.*:

(*a*) names of countries and towns, and in general names which denote *land, town, court, way* etc.; e. g. אֶרֶץ *land*, תֵּבֵל *earth*, עִיר *town*, דֶּרֶךְ *road*, חָצֵר *court*, צָפוֹן *north*, שְׁאוֹל *hades*.

Rem. 4 But since the names of *countries* refer in the first place to the people who live in them, they are occasionally constructed as *masc.*; e. g. וַיֹּאמֶר אֵלָיו אֱדוֹם *and Edom said unto him* Num. 20, 18; יְהוּדָה נָפָל *Jehudah is fallen* Jes. 3, 8.

Yet even in these cases the *fem.* construction is not excluded; e. g. וַתֶּחֱזַק מִצְרַיִם *and the Egyptians urged* Ex. 12, 33; נָחָה אֲרָם *Syria resteth* Jes. 7, 2.

(*b*) names of members or parts of the body, both of men and animals, as רֶגֶל *foot*, בֶּטֶן *womb* etc.

Rem. 5 Some names however of this class are usually constructed as *masc.*; e. g. פֶּה *mouth*, צַוָּאר *throat*, עֹרֶף *neck*, אַף *nose*, and others occasionally, as לָשׁוֹן *tongue* Ps. 22, 16; יָד Ez. 2, 9; עַיִן Zech. *f* 3, 9.

(*c*) names of the powers of nature, as אֵשׁ *fire*, רוּחַ *wind*.

Rem. 6 Yet שֶׁמֶשׁ *sun*, אוֹר, *light*, mostly occur as masc., perhaps because the fem. nouns חַמָּה, *heat*, and אוֹרָה *light* also exist.

(*d*) names of instruments, as חֶרֶב *sword*, נַעַל *shoe*.

§ 2 Number of the noun.

1) To express plurality the Hebrew language employs beside the ordinary plural-ending:

(*a*) for *animate beings*, sometimes a totally different noun with a collective meaning; e. g. שֶׂה *a sheep*, אַרְבַּע צֹאן *four sheep* Ex. 21, 37; שׁוֹר *an ox*, חֲמִשָּׁה בָקָר *five oxen* ibid.

(*b*) for several nouns, the fem. form with a collective meaning. See § 1, 3 *b*.

(*c*) for certain other nouns, the singular form, which then serves as a collective: אִישׁ *a man* and *men*, עֵץ *a tree* and *trees*, רֶכֶב *a chariot* and *chariots*.

Rem. 1 Concerning הֹ׳הַיְדִיעָה (definite article) with this class of *singularia* see § 3, 4.

2) *Dualia* and *pluralia* (*dualia* and *pluralia tantum*) are often employed where in other languages the *singular* is generally used:

(*a*) for ideas of *space*, as שָׁמַיִם *heaven*, מַיִם *water*, מַרְגְּלוֹת *place at the feet*, מְרַאֲשׁוֹת *place at the head*.

(*b*) for certain parts of the body which express *extension* or *surface*, פָּנִים *face*, צַוָּארִים (as well as צַוָּאר) *throat*.

(*c*) for ideas of *time*, as חַיִּים *life*, זְקֻנִים *old age*, נְעוּרִים *youth*.

(*d*) for *states* or *conditions of persons or things*, as סַנְוֵרִים *blindness*, שִׁכּוּלִים *childlessness*.

Rem. 2 *Pluralia* of this kind especially occur in poetry e. g. עִוְעִים *perverseness* Jes. 19, 14; חֲשֵׁכִים (*tenebrae*) *darkness* Jes. 50, 10; אֲמָנִים

faithfulness Jes. 26, 2 הַתַּעֲנוּגִים (*deliciae*) *delight* Mich. 1, 16; חֶרְפּוֹת *reproach* Ps. 69, 11.

(*e*) for ideas of *power, dominion, majesty* (pluralis majestatis) e. g. בְּעָלִים *possessor*, Ex. 21, 29; אֲדֹנִים *lord* Jes. 19, 4; עֹשִׂים *creator* Ps. 149, 2; תְּרָפִים *penates*, קְדֹשִׁים *the Holy One* Hos. 12, 1; Pr. 9, 10 (cf. Jos. 24, 19).

Rem. 3 All these nouns however (except תְּרָפִים) are found also in the singular. Concerning the construction of these *plurals* with adjectives see § 4, 13; and with verbs § 36, 3.

3) Of two ideas, joined into one by the *status constructus*, only the *nomen regens* (main idea) is placed in the plural; e. g. אִישׁ חַיִל *a courageous man*, אַנְשֵׁי חַיִל *courageous men*, בֶּן יְמִינִי *Benjamite*, בְּנֵי יְמִינִי *Benjamites*.

Rem. 4 Both words of the *st. constr.*, are very rarely found in the plural e. g. בָּתֵּי כְלָאִים *prisons* Jes. 42, 22; and of yet rarer occurence are the instances where the *nomen rectum* (subordinate idea) alone is placed in the plural, e. g. בֵּית אָבוֹת *families, tribes* Num. 1, 2.

4) When a noun with a plural suffix refers in the mind of the writer or speaker to each of the individuals designated by that suffix, it may as in English be placed in the singular; e. g. לְבַבְכֶם *your heart*, יְמִינָם *their right hand*.

(5) With כָּל (*st. constr* of כֹּל) = *all*, the noun belonging to it either stands in the sing. or plur.; e. g. כָּל אִישׁ, כָּל הָאֲנָשִׁים *all men*, or is repeated in the sing.; e. g. כָּל אִישׁ וְאִישׁ *all men* (see § 4, 6; 13, 2.)

The same signification however is also obtained by

repetition of the noun in the sing. without כָּל (and this with or without ו copulative) e. g. אִישׁ אִישׁ or אִישׁ וְאִישׁ *all men*, דּוֹר דּוֹר or דּוֹר וָדוֹר *all generations*.

6) The repetition of a noun (in the sing. or plur.) sometimes produces a distributive sense; e. g. עֵדֶר עֵדֶר *every drove* Gen. 32, 17; גֵּבִים גֵּבִים *full of trenches* 2 Kings 3, 16; and if necessary even with the *st. constr.* בֶּאֱרֹת בֶּאֱרֹת חֵמָר *slime pits after slime pits* Gen. 14, 10 (§ 13, 2.)

7) The repetition of a singular noun without כָּל but with ו *copulative* may denote a diversity of kind; e. g. אֶבֶן וָאֶבֶן *a double weight*, לֵב וָלֵב *a double heart*.

8) *Names of materials* when placed in the plural designate either portions of such materials or things composed of them, as כֶּסֶף, *silver*; כְּסָפִים, *silver coins*, חִטָּה, *wheat*; חִטִּים, *grains of wheat*. In like manner דָּם, *blood*, when considered as an organic unity, in the plur. is דָּמִים *blood that is shed, blood spots*; hence its meaning *blood guiltiness*.

9) The *plural form* is occasionally employed to express an indefinite singular, עַל הָרֵי אֲרָרָט *on one of the summits of Ararat* Gen. 8, 4; בְּעָרֵי גִלְעָד *in one of the cities of Gilead* Judges 12, 7.

Rem. 5 Concerning the plur. with לְ *distributive* see § 18, 2.

CHAPTER II — DETERMINATION OF THE NOUN.

§ 3 הַיְדִיעָה ה׳

1) ה׳ הַיְדִיעָה generally takes the place of our definite article and is used to determine a noun.

It is however also used where nothing definite is intended:

(a) before names of well known materials, objects or classes of objects; e. g. בְּמִקְנֶה בַּכֶּסֶף וּבַזָּהָב *on (the) cattle, on (the) silver, on (the) gold* Gen. 13, 2. In like manner we always say שָׂרַף בָּאֵשׁ *he burned it in (the) fire.*

(b) frequently in comparisons; e. g. כַּשֶּׁלֶג כַּשָּׁנִים כַּתּוֹלָע *as (the) snow as (the) wool as (the) scarlet* Jes. 1, 18; בַּסֵּפֶר *as a book.*

When however the noun is determined by an adjective ה׳ הַיְדִיעָה is omitted e. g. כְּפֶגֶר מוּבָס *as a carcase trodden under foot* Jes. 14, 19; כְּצִפּוֹר נוֹדֶדֶת *as a wandering bird* Pr. 27, 8.

(c) frequently also with abstract ideas, or in the case of physical or moral evils; e. g. בַּסַּנְוֵרִים *with (the) blindness* Gen. 19, 11; הַחֹשֶׁךְ יְכַסֶּה אֶרֶץ *(the) darkness covereth the earth* Jes. 60, 2, or also when such evils are personified by a living being; e. g. הָאַרְיֵה *a lion* 1 Kings 20, 36; הָאֲרִי *a lion* Amos 3, 12.

(d) in the well known expression וַיְהִי הַיּוֹם *it happened one day*, which is sometimes even more emphatically determined, וַיְהִי כְּהַיּוֹם הַזֶּה Gen. 39, 11.

2) ה׳ הַיְדִיעָה is used moreover to change in a certain sense

a *nomen appellativum* into a *nomen proprium*, as אָדָם *man*, הָאָדָם *the first man*; אֱלֹהִים *God*, הָאֱלֹהִים *the (eternal) God*; נָהָר *river*, הַנָּהָר *the Euphrates*.

3) Hence, ה׳ הַיְדִיעָה is placed before names of mountains, towns, and rivers, of which the derivation is still so clear, that they can be thought of as *nomina appellativa*; e. g. הַלְּבָנוֹן *(the white mountain, the snow mountain) (the) Lebanon*; הָעַי *(the heap of ruins) Ai*; הַגִּבְעָה *(the hill) Gibea*; הַיַּרְדֵּן *(the river) Jordan*.

4) Further, ה׳ הַיְדִיעָה is used before a singular noun with a collective sense to designate all the individuals implied by it; e. g. הַכְּנַעֲנִי, *the Canaanites* Gen. 13, 7; הָאִשָּׁה *the women* Eccles. 7, 26; מְשַׁל הַקַּדְמֹנִי *the proverb of the ancients* 1 Sam. 24, 14. (see § 2, 1 c).

5) Finally, ה׳ הַיְדִיעָה is employed where a person or object is addressed, as הַקָּהָל *Ye congregation* Num. 15, 15; הַזְּקֵנִים *Ye elders* Joel 1, 2.

6) On the contrary ה׳ הַיְדִיעָה is often omitted in poetry before names of objects which are unique in their kind, as אֶרֶץ, שָׁאוֹל, תְּהוֹם. This also occurs in prose in certain well known and frequently used expressions as וּגְבֻל *and the border*, אֹהֶל מוֹעֵד *the tent of meeting*.

7) Nouns which are already rendered definite by the *st. constr.* or by a suffix, do not take ה׳ הַיְדִיעָה. But if a noun, already definite by a *st. constr.* is to be further determined, the ה׳ הַיְדִיעָה then is placed before the *nom. rectum*; e. g. דְּבַר אֱלֹהִים *a word of God* דְּבַר הָאֱלֹהִים *the word of God*; לֻחֹת אֶבֶן *stone tables*, לֻחֹת הָאֶבֶן *the stone tables*.

Rem. 1 ה׳ הַיְדִיעָה is found in a few instances before the *nom. regens* of the *st. constr.* e. g. הַמִּזְבַּח הַנְּחֹשֶׁת *the brazen altar* 2 Kings 16, 14; and sometimes also before a noun that has a suffix; e. g. הָאֹהֱלִי *my tent* Jos. 7, 21; הַמַּכֵּהוּ *he that smote them* Jes. 9, 12.

8) ה׳ הַיְדִיעָה placed before the *nom. rectum* alone, serves also for those instances in which both ideas of the *st. constr.* have to be determined; e. g. דְּבַר הַמֶּלֶךְ *the word of the king*.

Rem. 2 In this case also ה׳ הַיְדִיעָה is sometimes repeated before the *nom. regens*; e. g. הַיָּתֵד הָאֶרֶג *the pin of the weaver's beam* Jud. 16, 14, and the *st. constr.* occasionally even omitted; e. g. הָאָרוֹן הַבְּרִית *the ark of the covenant* Jos. 3, 14 (Such expressions, however, are by authoritative commentators considered as pregnant e. g. הָאָרוֹן אֲרוֹן הַבְּרִית (Conf. § 3, 4) [1]).

9) The *nomen regens*, however, not unfrequently takes ה׳ הַיְדִיעָה, when the *nomen rectum* is a *nomen proprium*, which cannot have ה׳ הַיְדִיעָה; e. g. הָאֵל בֵּית־אֵל *the God of Bethel* Gen. 31, 13; הַגֶּפֶן שִׂבְמָה *the vine of Sibma* Jer. 48, 32; or when for other reasons the *nomen rectum* cannot have ה׳ הַיְדִיעָה; e. g. הַקֶּבֶר אִישׁ הָאֱלֹהִים *the grave of the man of God* 2 Kings 23, 17; הַלְּשָׁכוֹת בֵּית ה׳ *the chambers of the house of the Lord* Ezra 8, 29.

10) Compound names of nations are considered as two nouns in the *st. constr.*; e. g. בֶּן הַיְמִינִי *the Benjamite* בֵּית הַלַּחְמִי *the Bethlehemite*.

Rem. 3 Since כָּל is the *st. constr.* of כֹּל it follows the rule of n° 7;

---

1) Confer also Dr. Driver's "Hebrew Tenses" § 190 Obs. (*Translator*).

e. g. כָּל הָאָדָם *all men*. If, however, its meaning is indefinite, e. g. *all kinds*, *any*, or *distributive*, as *every*, ה׳ הַיְדִיעָה is omitted before the *nomen rectum*; e. g. כָּל יוֹם *every day* Ps. 7, 12; כָּל עֵץ *all kinds of trees*.

11) If a noun, which is already definite either by ה׳ הַיְדִיעָה or by the *st. constr.* or by a pronominal suffix, is to be connected with an attributive adjective or with another word used as an adjective or with an attributive pronoun or number, then the latter also must be determined by ה׳ הַיְדִיעָה; e. g. דְּבַר הַמֶּלֶךְ הַגָּדוֹל *the great word of the king*; הַדָּבָר הַזֶּה; דְּבָרוֹ הַגָּדוֹל; הַדָּבָר הָאֶחָד. The same rule applies to the case of a definite noun followed by a series of qualifications; e. g. הַמַּרְאֶה הַגָּדוֹל הַזֶּה *this great vision* Ex. 3, 3; הָאֵל הַגָּדוֹל הַגִּבּוֹר וְהַנּוֹרָא *the great, mighty and terrible God* Deut. 10, 17.

Rem. 4 Sometimes, however, ה׳ הַיְדִיעָה is found before the adjective while it is omitted before the noun; e. g. פָּרוֹת הַטּוֹבֹת *the good kine* Gen. 41, 26; בּוֹר הַגָּדוֹל *the great well* 1 Sam. 19, 22; לְאִישׁ הֶעָשִׁיר *unto the rich man* 2 Sam. 12, 4; הָרִים הַגְּבֹהִים *the high mountains* Ps. 104, 18; בְּאֶרֶץ הָרְחָבָה וְהַשְּׁמֵנָה *in the large and fat land* Neh. 9, 35. This is of special occurrence with *numeralia ordinalia*; e. g. יוֹם הַשִּׁשִּׁי *the sixth day* Gen. 1, 31; וּפַר הַשֵּׁנִי *and the second bullock* Judges 6, 25. ²).

---

2) Expressions such as בְּדֶרֶךְ הַטּוֹבָה וְהַיְשָׁרָה *in the way of virtue and righteousness* 1 Sam. 12. 23; שַׁעַר הַפָּנִים *the corner gate* Zech. 14, 10, should not be reckoned in this class of exceptions, because the words הַפָּנִים and הַיְשָׁרָה הַטּוֹבָה may be considered as nouns connected with דֶּרֶךְ and שַׁעַר in the *st. constr*.

§ 3. ה׳ הידיעה

Rem. 5 The instances on the contrary where הַ֫הֲיְדִיעָה is omitted before the qualification following a definite noun are very rare, and generally occur when the qualification is a demonstrative pronoun; e. g. דִּבָּתָם רָעָה *the evil report of them* Gen. 36, 2; הַגּוֹיִם רַבִּים *(the) many nations* Ez. 39, 27; בַּלַּ֫יְלָה הוּא *in that night* Gen. 19, 33; מְשֻׁבָעָתִי זֹאת *this my oath* Gen. 24, 8; אֹתֹתַי אֵ֫לֶּה *these my signs* Ex. 10, 1.

The demonstrative pronoun זוּ always remains without the article; e. g. הַדּוֹר זוּ *this generation* Ps. 12, 8.

In the expression אֲחִיכֶם אֶחָד *one of your brethren* Gen. 42, 19 ה׳ הַיְדִיעָה is left out before אֶחָד to signify that in the speaker's mind it was indifferent which of the two brethren should remain behind. The passages Gen. 43, 14 אֲחִיכֶם אַחֵר *your other brother*; and Num. 28, 4 אֶת הַכֶּ֫בֶשׂ אֶחָד *one of the two sheep* may be taken as a further illustration of this remark (see however Talmud Babyl. Tract. Megilla f° 28ᵃ).

Rem. 6. It should be observed that Rule n° 11 applies exclusively to the *attributive adjectives*, for *the predicative adjectives*, do not take ה׳ הַיְדִיעָה, except to express a contrast in a very forcible manner; e. g. ה׳ הַצַּדִּיק וַאֲנִי וְעַמִּי הָרְשָׁעִים *the Lord is just but I and my people are sinners* Ex 9, 27; or when ה׳ הַיְדִיעָה has the force of אֲשֶׁר; e. g. פִּי הַמְדַבֵּר *it is my mouth that speaketh* Gen. 45, 12 (Conf. n° 13).

12) In certain expressions ה׳ הַיְדִיעָה has the force of a demonstrative pronoun, as הַיּוֹם *this day (hodie)*; הַפַּ֫עַם *this time*.

13) When joined to a verb ה׳ הַיְדִיעָה has, (especially in later Hebrew) the signification of a relative pronoun; e. g. וְכָל הַהִקְדִּישׁ *and all that he had dedicated* 1 Chr. 26, 28. The same signification ה׳ הַיְדִיעָה often has when placed before a participle; e. g. הַמְלַמֵּד *who teacheth* Ps. 144, 1. One instance occurs of ה׳ הַיְדִיעָה connected with a pre-

position הָעָלֶיהָ = אֲשֶׁר עָלֶיהָ (τὸ ἐπ' αὐτῆς) *and that which was upon it* 1 Sam. 9, 24.³).

§ 4 The adjective.

1) The adjective is either *attributive*, i. e. restricting the idea of its noun to those individuals possessing the qualification expressed by it, or *predicative*, i. e. affirming of its noun a certain property; e. g. *the gold of that land is good* Gen. 2, 12.

2) In comparison with its richness in nouns, the Hebrew language possesses but few adjectives. For example those denoting materials are almost wholly wanting, and the few instances which occur have the form of a passive participle, e. g. אָרוּז *cedrine* Ez. 27, 24 (derived from אֶרֶז *cedar*); נָחוּשׁ *brazen* Job. 6, 12 (from נְחֻשֶׁת *brass*). In order to supply this defect nouns are substituted.

3) When a noun takes the place of an attributive adjective, it is connected with the noun to be qualified in the *st. constr.*; e. g. כְּלִי כֶסֶף (*vessels of silver*) *silver vessels*; אֲרוֹן עֵץ (*a chest of wood*) *a wooden chest*; אֲחֻזַּת עוֹלָם (*a possession of lasting duration*) *an everlasting possession* Gen. 17, 8; מְתֵי מִסְפָּר (*men of number*) *numerable men, a few men* viz. such as can easily be counted Gen. 34, 30; אֶבֶן חֵן (*a stone which finds favour, a stone of beauty*) *a precious stone* Pr. 17, 8.

---

3) Concerning the last named example and Gen. 18, 21; 46, 27; Jes. 51, 10; Gen. 21, 3; 1 Kings 11, 9 see Driver, "Notes on the Hebrew text of Samuel" 1 Sam. 9, 24. (*Translator*).

§ 4. THE ADJECTIVE.

4) In like manner the negation of an attribute may be expressed by means of a noun with לֹא, e. g. בֹּקֶר לֹא עָבוֹת *a cloudless morning* 2 Sam. 23, 4; וּזְרֹעַ לֹא עֹז *a powerless arm* Job 26, 2.

5) Nouns however are also employed in cases where suitable adjectives exist, e. g. בְּגָדִים קְדֹשִׁים = בִּגְדֵי קֹדֶשׁ *sacred vestments* Ex. 28, 2; צִיצָה נֹבֶלֶת = צִיצַת נֹבֵל *a withering flower* Jes. 28, 4; תַּהְפֻּכוֹת רָעוֹת = תַּהְפֻּכוֹת רָע *evil deceits* Pr. 2, 14; אִשָּׁה רָעָה = אֵשֶׁת רָע *an evil woman* Pr. 6, 24; the noun רָע is often so used.

6) In all these instances the noun which is qualified is *nomen regens*, and that which serves as adj. *nomen rectum*. Sometimes however, especially in poetry, this order is reversed; e. g. רֹעַ מַעַלְלֵיכֶם, *your evil deeds*, Jes. 1, 16; מִשְׁמַן בְּשָׂרוֹ, *his fat body*, Jes. 17, 4; see also Jes. 37, 24. This last named construction is always employed with כֹּל, *all* (See § 2, 5).

7) The connecting of two nouns by means of the *st. constr.* is of course only possible with *attributive* adjectives. Yet the use of a noun instead of a *predicative* adjective also occurs; e. g. וְהָאָרֶץ הָיְתָה תֹהוּ וָבֹהוּ (*and the earth was a waste and a wilderness*) *and the earth was waste and void*, Gen. 1, 2; especially when the property implied is to be emphasised; e. g. הַיּוֹם הַהוּא יְהִי חֹשֶׁךְ *let that day be dark (darkness)*. In like manner שָׁלוֹם *peace, prosperity* often serves as an adjective; e. g. הֲשָׁלוֹם אֲבִיכֶם הַזָּקֵן *is your aged father well?* Gen. 43, 27; אֲנִי שָׁלוֹם. *I am peaceful* Ps. 120, 7. (Concerning the last example see Rem. 2).

Rem. 1 Sometimes a predicative adjective is found expressed by a noun with a preposition; e. g. קוֹל ה׳ בַּכֹּחַ *the voice of the Lord is with power* i. e. *powerful* Ps. 29, 4.

8) Adjectives denoting a permanent state or condition are often expressed by a noun, possessing the quality of the adjective, connected with the *st. constr.* of אִישׁ, בֶּן, בַּעַל, and of their feminine and plural forms; e. g. אִישׁ דְּבָרִים, אַנְשֵׁי חַיִל, אֵשֶׁת חַיִל, אִישׁ חַיִל *an orator* Ex. 4, 10; אִישׁ שֵׂעָר (= אִישׁ בַּעַל שֵׂעָר) Gen. 27, 11) *a hairy man* 2 Kings 1, 8; בַּת בְּלִיַּעַל *a worthless woman* 1 Sam. 1, 16.

The same occurs in poetry even with inanimate beings קֶרֶן בֶּן שָׁמֶן *a fruitful height* (hill) Jes. 5, 1; בֶּן לַיְלָה *in one night* Jon. 4, 10; בֶּן קֶשֶׁת *an arrow* Job. 41, 20.

Rem. 2 אִישׁ or בֶּן are sometimes boldly omitted e. g., וַאֲנִי תְפִלָּה = וַאֲנִי אִישׁ תְּפִלָּה. *but, I was praying* Ps. 109, 4; חֲמוּדוֹת אָתָּה = אִישׁ חֲמוּדוֹת אָתָּה *thou art greatly beloved* Dan. 9, 23 (conf. *scelus = scelestissimus*,) see Abn Esra on Ps. 85, 14.

9) Adjectives, on the other hand, denoting a *permanent attribute* are sometimes used instead of the nouns possessing this attribute; e. g. נָשִׂיא (= נָשׂוּא *lifted up*) *a prince*; אַבִּיר (*strong*) *a bull*, Ps. 22, 13; *a horse* Jer. 50, 11; אָבִיר (*powerful*) *God* Gen. 49, 24; קַל (*swift*) *a horse* Jes. 30, 16; לְבָנָה (*white*) *the moon*; פֻּרִיָה (*fruitful*) *a fruit tree* Jes. 17, 6 (conf. *merum = vinum*; ὑγρόν, *the sea*).

10) The proper place of an attributive adjective is *after* the noun to which it belongs, and if this noun is in the *st. constr.*, after the *nomen rectum*, as אִישׁ גָּדוֹל, *a great man*; סֵפֶר הַתּוֹרָה הַזֶּה *this book of doctrine* Deut. 29, 20.

§ 4. THE ADJECTIVE.

Rem. 3 In a few cases it is found before the noun, as רַבִּים עַמִּים *many nations* Ps. 89, 51; רַבּוֹת עִתִּים *many times* Neh. 9, 28; especially when it serves as a *subst.*, and is connected in the *st. constr.* with the noun determined by it; e. g. חַלְקֵי אֲבָנִים (*those that are smooth amongst the stones*) *Smooth stones* 1 Sam. 17, 40 = אֲבָנִים חַלָּקִים. In the other cases where it precedes the noun it is *predicative*.

11) The adjective agrees with its noun in *number* and *gender*. If however a feminine noun is followed by more than one adjective, not unfrequently the first adjective alone agrees with the noun; e. g. רוּחַ גְּדוֹלָה וְחָזָק *a great and strong wind* 1 Kings 19, 11.

12) With a dual noun the adjective stands in the plural; e. g. עֵינַיִם רָמוֹת *haughty eyes* Ps. 18, 28.

13) With a noun in the *plur. majestatis* (§ 2, 2) the adjective usually stands in the singular; e. g. אֲדֹנִים קָשֶׁה *a hard lord* Jes. 19, 4.

Rem. 4 We however always say אֱלֹהִים חַיִּים *the living God*.

14) With collectives the adjective generally stands in the singular; e. g. גּוֹי גָּדוֹל *a great people*; sometimes, however, also in the plural; e. g. גָּלוּת יְהוּדָה הַבָּאִים *the exiles of Jehudah who came* Jer. 28, 4; הָעָם הַנִּמְצָאִים *the people that were found present* Esther 1, 5.

15) The adjective is also occasionally connected in the *st. constr.* with a noun for the purpose of further determination; e. g. אִשָּׁה יְפַת מַרְאֶה *a woman of fair appearance* Gen. 12, 11. If in this case it requires ה' הַיְדִיעָה it follows the rule of § 3, 7; e. g. הַפָּרֹת רָעוֹת הַמַּרְאֶה וְדַקֹּת הַבָּשָׂר *the ill favoured and leanfleshed kine* Gen. 41, 4.

Rem. 5 Concerning ה׳ הַיְדִיעָה with the adj. see § 3, 11.

§ 5. Status Constructus.

1) If the main idea (*nomen regens*) is to be connected with more than one subordinate idea (*nomen rectum*), the main idea is repeated in the *st. constr.*; e. g. כֶּסֶף אָשָׁם וְכֶסֶף חַטָּאוֹת *the money for the guilt offerings and sin offerings* 2 Kings 12, 17.

Rem. 1 Sometimes however this repetition is omitted; e. g. מֶלֶךְ סְדֹם וַעֲמֹרָה *the kings of Sodom and Gomorra* Gen. 14, 10; נֶדֶר אַלְמָנָה וּגְרוּשָׁה *the vow of a widow, or of her that is divorced* Num. 30, 10 [1]).

2) If on the contrary more than one main idea is to be connected with a *nom. rect.*, the first idea alone is connected in the *st. constr.* with the *nom. rect.*, while the other main ideas follow the *nom. rect.* by means of another construction; e. g. אֶל תְּפִלַּת עַבְדְּךָ וְאֶל תַּחֲנוּנָיו *to the prayer and supplication of thy servant* Dan. 9, 17 (Conf. § 7, 1).

Rem. 1 Exceptions to this rule are rare and only occur when the main ideas are synonymous, or at least very closely affiliated, as מִבְחַר בְּרֹשָׁיו וְטוֹב לְבָנוֹן *the choicest and best of Lebanon* Ez. 31, 16; דַּעַת וְיִרְאַת יה׳

---

[1]) The passage נֶפֶשׁ בָּנָיו וּבְנוֹתָיו *the souls of his sons and his daughters* Gen. 46, 15 can hardly be considered as an exception, for בָּנָיו וּבְנוֹתָיו form one idea (*his children*). The same also applies to Jes. 11, 2 רוּחַ עֵצָה וּגְבוּרָה, חָכְמָה וּבִינָה, דַּעַת וְיִרְאַת ה׳ *the spirit of counsel and strength, of wisdom and understanding, of knowledge and of fear for God;* and to other similar expressions, e. g. תְּסַפֵּר בְּאָזְנֵי בִנְךָ וּבֶן בִּנְךָ *that thou mayest tell in the ears of thy son and of thy son's son.* Ex. 10, 2.

§ 5. STATUS CONSTRUCTUS.

knowledge and fear of the Lord Jes. 11, 2 [1]). In this case the conjunction is sometimes omitted, e. g. מִסְפַּר מִפְקַד הָעָם *the sum (and) the numbering of the people* 2 Sam. 24, 9. [2])

3) The *nom. rect.* as main idea may in turn be connected in the *st. constr.* with a noun following, and this again with another subsequent noun. Thus one finds e. g., five nouns following one another in the *st. constr.*, as וּשְׁאָר מִסְפַּר קֶשֶׁת גִּבּוֹרֵי בְנֵי קֵדָר *the residue of the number of bows of the mighty men of the children of Kedar* Jes. 21, 17.

Rem. 3. In these cases, however, the chain of *nomina regentia* is sometimes broken and one of them is placed in the *st. abs.* e. g. גִּבּוֹרֵי חַיִל מְלֶאכֶת עֲבוֹדַת בֵּית הָאֱלֹהִים *able men for the work of the service of the house of God* 1 Chr. 9, 13. (See § 7, 1).

4) The *st. constr.* is used to express all possible relations between two nouns or ideas; e. g. חַטֹּאת אָבִיו *the sins of his father (genitive of subject)* 1 Kings 15, 3; חֲמַס אָחִיךָ *injustice against your brother (gen. of object)* Obadja 10; שְׁבֻעַת יה' *an oath sworn by the Lord* Ex. 22, 10; מֵי מָתְנַיִם *water that reached to the loins* Ez. 47, 4; שָׁבֵי פֶשַׁע *those that turn from transgression* Jes. 59, 20; יוֹרְדֵי הַיָּם *they that go down to the sea* Ps. 107, 23; דֶּרֶךְ הַיָּם *the way to the sea* Jes. 8, 23.

---

1) רַעַת may also be considered as a *status absolutus*; the prophet then identifies *true knowledge* with *piety*.

2) This passage may also be translated: *the sum of (= obtained through) the numbering of the people*, for מִסְפַּר may be considered as connected in the *st. constr.* with מִפְקַד.

Further than this, a single noun may be connected in the *st. constr.* with a whole sentence; e. g. מְקוֹם לֹא יָדַע אֵל *the place which knoweth not God* Job. 18, 21 (מְקוֹם אֲשֶׁר לֹא =); and this even where אֲשֶׁר is expressed, as (בַּמָּקוֹם אֲשֶׁר =) מְקוֹם אֲשֶׁר אֲסִרֵי הַמֶּלֶךְ אֲסוּרִים *the place where the king's prisoners were bound* Gen. 39, 20; and also with or without אֲשֶׁר instead of the *st. abs.* with ה' הַיְדִיעָה; e. g. כָּל הַיָּמִים אֲשֶׁר =) כָּל יְמֵי אֲשֶׁר הַנֶּגַע בּוֹ) *all the days that the plague is in him* Lev. 13, 46; יִתְרַת עָשָׂה *the abundance (which) he has gotten* Jer. 48, 36 (see § 12, 5).

5) In cases where the *st. constr.* does not express the simple genitive of object or subject, another construction which alone would be sufficient to express the idea, is sometimes used along with it; e. g. יֹשְׁבֵי בָאָרֶץ (יֹשְׁבִים בָּאָרֶץ) or יֹשְׁבֵי אֶרֶץ =) *they that dwelt in the land* Jes. 9, 1; יוֹרְדֵי אַבְנֵי בוֹר (= יוֹרְדֵי אֶל אַבְנֵי בוֹר) or יוֹרְדִים א'א') *they that go down to the stones of the pit* Jes. 14, 19; גְמוּלִים מֵחָלָב) or גְמוּלֵי חָלָב (= גְמוּלֵי מֵחָלָב) *they that are weaned from the milk* Jes. 28, 9; יֹשְׁבֵי עַל מִדִּין (יוֹשְׁבִים עַל מִדִּין or יוֹשְׁבֵי מִדִּין=) *Ye that sit on carpets* Judg. 5, 10; מְשַׁחֲרֵי טָרֶף =) מְשַׁחֲרִים לַטָּרֶף) *seeking for prey* Job. 24, 5.

Rem. 4 The *st. constr.* occasionally occurs where we would expect the *st. abs.*, e. g. שִׁכְרַת וְלֹא מִיָּיִן (= שִׁכְרָה) *drunken, but not with wine* Jes. 51, 21; נֵפֶל אֵשֶׁת (= אִשָּׁה) *the untimely birth of a woman* Ps. 58, 9 [3]). In like manner אַחַד frequently occurs instead

---

[3]) The opinion however that such fem. forms may be considered as collateral forms of the *st. abs.* is not improbable.

of אֶחָד, as כְּאַחַד מִמֶּנּוּ *like one of us* Gen. 3, 22; once, Jes. 27, 12, we find both forms together לְאַחַד אֶחָד *one to another*. (In cases of apposition see § 6, 3).

On the other hand, the *st. abs.* sometimes occurs where the *st. constr.* would have been expected, as מַיִם לַחַץ (= מֵי לַחַץ) *water of affliction* 1 King. 22. 27, i. e. *a small measure of water*.⁴)

Rem. 5 Proper names also occur sometimes in the *st. constr.* e. g. אֲרַם נַהֲרַיִם *Mesopotamia (Aram between the two rivers.)*

Rem. 6 With reference to the appending of suffixes to nouns connected by the *st. constr.* see § 10, 6 and Rem. 1. As to the plur. of nouns connected by the *st. constr.* see § 2, 3 and Rem. 4. And as to ה׳ הַיְדִיעָה before nouns in the *st. constr.* see § 3, 7—11. and Rem. 2 and 3.

§ 6. Apposition.

1) A noun may be determined by another noun following it without the *st. constr.* (apposition); e. g. אֲנָשִׁים אַחִים *men (namely) brethren* Gen. 13, 8; זְבָחִים שְׁלָמִים *offerings (namely) peace offerings* Ex. 24, 5.

Rem. 1 In the case of proper names the apposition may either precede or follow, as אֶת אָחִיו אֶת הָבֶל *his brother Abel* Gen. 4, 2; שָׂרַי אִשְׁתּוֹ *Sarai his wife* Gen. 12, 5. In certain expressions the apposition always precedes, as הַמֶּלֶךְ דָּוִד; הַמֶּלֶךְ שְׁלֹמֹה (once only, 2 Sam. 13, 39, we find דָּוִד הַמֶּלֶךְ).

2) Apposition is pretty frequently used with nouns denoting either the material of which a thing is composed,

---

4) Certain authors prefer to consider such expressions as instances of apposition (§ 6, 2) while other authors regard them as pregnant constructions; e. g. מַיִם מֵי לַחַץ (§ 3 Rem. 2; § 10 footnote 1).

or the nature or attribute which a thing possesses; e. g.
טוּרִים אֶבֶן *rows (of) stone* Ex. 28, 17; מַדּוֹ בַד *his measure (of) linen* (= *his linen garment*) Lev. 6, 3; אֲמָרִים אֱמֶת *words (of) truth* Pr. 22, 21.

3) Often, however, the noun to be qualified is connected in the *st. constr.* with the qualifying noun; e. g. טוּרֵי אֶבֶן Ex. 39, 10 (conf. § 4, 3); אֵשֶׁת בַּעֲלַת אוֹב *a woman possessing a familiar spirit* 1 Sam. 28, 7 (conf. § 5 Rem. 4, and footnote 4); חַכְמֵי יֹעֲצֵי פַרְעֹה *the wise* (*men namely*) *the counsellors of Pharaoh* Jes. 19, 11.

Rem. 2 With appellatives the order of placing the words is sometimes reversed; e. g. פֶּרֶא אָדָם *a wild* (lit. *a wild ass*) *man* Gen. 16, 12; כְּסִיל אָדָם *a foolish man* (*a fool of a man*) Prov. 15, 20; 21, 20. Such passages however may also be regarded as instances of the *st. constr.* Conf. נְסִיכֵי אָדָם *princely* (*princes*) *men* Micha 5, 4.

4) All prepositions and particles prefixed to the first noun are repeated before the second noun; e. g. אֶת אָחִיו אֶת הָבֶל *his brother Abel* Gen. 4, 2; בְּאֶרֶץ מוֹלַדְתּוֹ בְּאוּר כַּשְׂדִּים *in the land of his nativity, in Ur of the Chaldees* Gen. 11, 28; מִיַּד אָחִי מִיַּד עֵשָׂו *from the hand of my brother from the hand of Esau* Gen. 32, 12; לְעַבְדְּךָ לְיַעֲקֹב *of thy servant Jacob* Gen. 32, 19.

Rem. 3 Sometimes, however, they are omitted before the second noun; e. g. אֶת שָׂרַי אִשְׁתּוֹ *Sarai his wife* Gen. 12, 5; אֶל חֲתָנָיו לֹקְחֵי בְנֹתָיו *to his sons in law who were to marry his daughters* Gen. 19, 14.

5) If the first noun is determined (by a pronom. suff., st. constr., etc.), the apposition also should be deter-

mined; e. g. אֲדֹנִי הַמֶּלֶךְ (conf. § 3, 11), unless it be a proper name.

Rem. 4 With adjectives also instances of apposition occur, as פָּרָה אֲדֻמָּה תְּמִימָה *a perfectly red heifer* Num. 19, 2.

§ 7. Other means of connecting two nouns.

1) Two nouns may be connected by placing אֲשֶׁר לְ between them.

This construction is chiefly used for the genitive of possession, and especially when two or more subsequent nouns would otherwise have to be placed in the *st. constr.*, as שַׂר צְבָא אֲשֶׁר לְשָׁאוּל (= שַׂר צְבָא שָׁאוּל) *captain of Saul's host* 2 Sam. 2, 8 (conf. however § 5, 3); or when more than one main idea is dependent on another idea, as (הַמַּשְׁקֶה וְהָאֹפֶה אֲשֶׁר לְמֶלֶךְ מִצְרַיִם =) מַשְׁקֵה מֶלֶךְ מ׳ וְאֹפוֹ *the butler and the baker of the king of Egypt* Gen. 40, 5 (§ 5, 2).

In ordinary cases, however, this construction is rarely used instead of the *st. constr.*; e. g. הַצֹּאן אֲשֶׁר לְאָבִיהָ (= צֹאן אָבִיהָ) *her father's sheep* Gen. 29, 9.

Rem. 1 In the subsequent development of the Hebrew language אֲשֶׁר became contracted into שֶׁ־, and אֲשֶׁר לְ combined into the one word שֶׁל; e. g. Cant. 1, 6; 3, 7 conf. Jonas 1 v. 8 with v. 7. — In Mischna and Talmud שֶׁל is the usual expression for the genitive of possession.

2) A second means of connecting two nouns is to prefix לְ (without אֲשֶׁר) to the second noun. This construction also is used instead of the genitive of possession:

(a) when the first idea is to be expressed indefinitely; e. g. עֲבָדִים לְשָׁאוּל servants of Saul 1 Sam. 17, 8 (עַבְדֵי שָׁאוּל would mean the servants of Saul); שְׁנֵי עֲבָדִים לְשִׁמְעִי two servants of Shimei 1 Kings 2, 39 (שְׁנֵי עַבְדֵי שִׁמְעִי would mean the two servants of Shimei).

Rem. 2 It is seldom employed when the main idea is definite; e. g. (צֹפֵי שָׁאוּל =) הַצֹּפִים לְשָׁאוּל the guards of Saul 1. Sam. 14, 16.

(b) to prevent accumulation of words in the *st. constr.* e. g. רָאשֵׁי אֲבוֹת מַטּוֹת (= רָאשֵׁי הָאָבוֹת לְמַטּוֹת בְּנֵי יִשְׂרָאֵל בְּנֵי יִשְׂרָאֵל) the heads of the fathers' houses of the tribes of the children of Israel Jos. 19, 51.

(c) for numbers; e. g. בְּאֶחָד לַחֹדֶשׁ on the first day of the month Num. 1, 1.

§ 8. Comparative and Superlative.

1) The *comparative* is formed in Hebrew by prefixing מִן or מִ־ to the word with which comparison is made. It is indifferent whether the thing compared is expressed by a verb or adj. e. g. רַב וְעָצוּם מִמֶּנּוּ *more numerous and mightier than we* Ex. 1, 9; וַיַּעֲצִמֵהוּ מִצָּרָיו *and he made it stronger than its enemies* Ps. 105, 24.

2) When two objects or classes of objects are contrasted with each other, then their opposite qualities are expressed without מִן or מִ־; e. g. — אֶת הַמָּאוֹר הַגָּדוֹל וְאֶת הַמָּאוֹר הַקָּטֹן *the greater light — and the lesser light* Gen. 1, 16; לָתֵת הַצְּעִירָה לִפְנֵי הַבְּכִירָה *to give the younger before the firstborn* Gen. 29, 26.

3) The comparative with מִן or מִ־ has in Hebrew

§ 8. COMPARATIVE AND SUPERLATIVE. 23

also the meaning of *too* with the positive, and may therefore be used when there is no object with which comparison is made; e. g. גָּדוֹל עֲוֹנִי מִנְּשׂוֹא *mine iniquity is too great for me to bear* Gen. 4, 13; קָטֹן מֵהָכִיל *too small to contain* 1 Kings 8, 64; הַמְעַט מִכֶּם *is it too small a thing for you?* Numb. 16, 9.

Rem. 1 In poetry the qualitative word is sometimes omitted, so that it has to be supplied from the context; e. g. וּפְסִילֵהֶם מִירוּשָׁלָיִם *their idols are (more numerous) than (those) in Jerusalem* Jes. 10, 10.

4) The *superlative* is expressed:

(*a*) in the same manner as the comparative, except that בָּל is added to the word with which comparison is made; e. g. וַיֶּחְכַּם מִכָּל הָאָדָם *and he was the wisest of all men* 1 Kings 5, 11; אָהַב אֶת יוֹסֵף מִכָּל בָּנָיו *he loved Joseph most of all his children* Gen. 37, 3.

(*b*) by prefixing בְּ to the plural of the word with which comparison is made; e. g. הַיָּפָה בַּנָּשִׁים *the fairest amongst women* Cant. 6, 1.

(*c*) by connecting the singular form of a noun in the *st. constr.* with the plural form of the same noun; e. g. קֹדֶשׁ הַקֳּדָשִׁים *the most holy*.

(*d*) by connecting an adj. or particip. in the *st. constr.* with the noun with which comparison is made; e. g. חַכְמוֹת שָׂרוֹתֶיהָ *the wisest of her princesses* Jud. 5, 29; נִכְבַּדֵּי אָרֶץ *the most honourable of the earth* Jes. 23, 8; וְאֶבְיוֹנֵי אָדָם *the most needy amongst men* Jes. 29, 19; עֲשִׁירֵי עָם *the richest amongst the people* Ps. 45, 13.

§ 9. Numerals.

1) The cardinal numbers from 1—10 may be connected with the noun to which they belong in a threefold manner, viz.:

(a) by placing the number before the noun in the *st. constr.*, as שֵׁשֶׁת יָמִים *six days.*

(b) by placing it before the noun in the *st. abs.*, as שִׁשָּׁה יָמִים *six days.*

(c) by placing it after the noun, as יָמִים שִׁשָּׁה *six days.*

With these (1—10) the noun stands in the plural, and exceptions are rare, as שְׁמֹנֶה שָׁנָה *eight years* 2 Kings 22, 1.

2) With the cardinal numbers from 11—19 nouns of very frequent occurence (such as שָׁנָה, יוֹם, אִישׁ) are made to follow in the sing; e. g. תִּשְׁעָה עָשָׂר אִישׁ *nineteen men*; אַרְבָּעָה עָשָׂר יוֹם *fourteen days*; שְׁתֵּים עֶשְׂרֵה שָׁנָה *twelve years.* They rarely occur in the plur. e. g. שְׁנֵים עָשָׂר אֲנָשִׁים *twelve men* Deut. 1, 23.

Nouns however which are not so often used either follow or precede in the plur.; e. g. שְׁנֵים עָשָׂר מַטּוֹת *twelve tribes* שְׁנֵים עָשָׂר אֵלִים *twelve rams* Num. 7, 87.

3) The tens from 20—90 are construed in a twofold manner:

(a) generally with the noun following in the sing.; e. g. עֶשְׂרִים יוֹם *twenty days* שִׁשִּׁים עִיר *sixty cities;* rarely in the plur. חֲמִשִּׁים צַדִּיקִים *fifty just men* Gen. 18, 24; שִׁשִּׁים בָּנוֹת *sixty daughters* 2 Chr. 11, 21.

(b) less frequently with the noun preceding, but then always in the plur.; e. g. אַמּוֹת שִׁשִּׁים 60 *cubits* 2 Chr.

3, 3; וּפִילַגְשִׁים שִׁשִּׁים *sixty concubines.* 2 Chr. 11, 21.

4) As regards מֵאָה *hundred*, one may say just as well מֵאָה שָׁנָה as מְאַת שָׁנָה *a hundred years.* In both cases the noun may stand also in the plur.; e. g. מֵאָה שְׁעָרִים *a hundred fold (hundred measures)* Gen. 26, 12; מְאַת אֲדָנִים *hundred sockets* Ex. 38, 27.

The same constructions may be used with the plural forms of מֵאָה, and with אֶלֶף and its plural forms.

Here also certain words of common occurrence, are usually made to follow in the sing.; e. g. אַלְפַּיִם אַמָּה *two thousand cubits.*

5) With numerals composed of units and tens or hundreds, the noun stands either in the *sing.* and *after* the number; e. g. שְׁלֹשִׁים וְחָמֵשׁ שָׁנָה or חָמֵשׁ וּשְׁלֹשִׁים שָׁנָה *thirty five years* (rarely in plur. עֶשְׂרִים וְאַרְבָּעָה פָרִים *twenty four heifers* Num. 7, 88); or in the *plur.* and *before* the number; e. g. שִׁבְעִים שִׁשִּׁים וּשְׁנַיִם *sixty two weeks* Dan. 9, 26; אֵילִים תִּשְׁעִים וְשִׁשָּׁה *ninety six rams* Ezra 8, 35; כְּבָשִׂים שִׁבְעִים וְשִׁבְעָה *seventy seven sheep* (Ibid).

Frequently however the noun is repeated, viz. with the units in the plur., with the tens and hundreds in the sing.; e. g. חָמֵשׁ שָׁנִים וְשִׁבְעִים שָׁנָה *seventy five years* Gen. 12, 4; מֵאָה שָׁנָה וְעֶשְׂרִים שָׁנָה וְשֶׁבַע שָׁנִים *a hundred and twenty seven years* Gen. 23, 1.

6) The Ordinals from 1—10 are adjectives (see Grammar § 77, 1) and are treated as such.

Instead of the ordinals above ten the cardinals are used, and as before, either with the noun preceding in the *st. constr.*; e. g. בִּשְׁנַת שְׁמֹנֶה עֶשְׂרֵה *in the eigh-*

teenth year (in which case the noun may be repeated after the number, as בִּשְׁנַת שְׁתֵּים עֶשְׂרֵה שָׁנָה *in the twelfth year* 2 Kings 8, 25); or with the noun following; e. g. בְּאַרְבָּעִים שָׁנָה *in the fortieth year*.

Rem. 1 In numbering years or the days of the month cardinals are not unfrequently used instead of the ordinals from 1—10; e. g. בִּשְׁנַת שָׁלוֹשׁ *in the third year* Est. 1, 3; בְּאֶחָד לַחֹדֶשׁ *on the first day of the month* Num. 1, 1. Yet the ordinals are not altogether excluded, as שְׁנַת הַשְּׁבִיעִית *the seventh year* Esra 7, 8.

7) When the cardinals are used as nouns, they may, like nouns take הַשְּׁלֹשָׁה וְהַשִּׁבְעִים וְהַמָּאתַיִם; e. g. ה׳ הַיְדִיעָה *the two hundred and seventy three* Num. 3, 46.

The ordinals naturally follow the rules of the adjective as to ה׳ הַיְדִיעָה.

Rem. 2 Nouns of *measure*, *weight* and *time* are sometimes omitted after the numerals; e. g. עֶשְׂרִים כָּסֶף *twenty (shekels of) silver*; בָּעֲשִׂירִי *in the tenth (month)*; בַּשֵּׁנִי *on the second (day)*.

Rem. 3 Instead of אַמָּה we often find בְּאַמָּה; e. g. אַלְפַּיִם בָּאַמָּה *two thousand cubits* Num. 35, 5. The best explanation of this expression is to admit an ellipsis of words (e. g. בְּאַמַּת אִישׁ) as appears from Deut. 3, 11 תֵּשַׁע אַמּוֹת אָרְכָּהּ וְאַרְבַּע אַמּוֹת רָחְבָּהּ בְּאַמַּת אִישׁ *nine cubits was the length thereof, and four cubits the breadth of it, after the cubit of a man*.

8) The distributive numerals are expressed:

(a) by repetition of the noun with its cardinal; e. g. אִישׁ אֶחָד אִישׁ אֶחָד לַשָּׁבֶט *one man for each tribe* Jos. 3, 12; sometimes with the addition of לְאֶחָד, as שֵׁשׁ כְּנָפַיִם שֵׁשׁ כְּנָפַיִם לְאֶחָד *each had six wings* Jes. 6, 2.

(b) by repetition of the cardinal number alone; e. g.

§ 10. PERSONAL PRONOUNS. 27

שְׁנַיִם שְׁנַיִם *two and two* Gen. 7, 9; sometimes with ו copulative prefixed to the second; e. g. שֵׁשׁ וָשֵׁשׁ *six and six* (= *on every hand six*) 2 Sam. 21, 20.

(c) without repetition, but by prefixing לְ to the noun; e. g. אִישׁ אֶחָד לַשָּׁבֶט *one man for each tribe* Deut. 1, 23; or in a more simple manner by means of the so called לְ *distributive*; e. g. לְמֵאוֹת וְלַאֲלָפִים *by hundreds and by thousands* 2 Sam. 18, 4 (conf. § 13, 2.)

9) The cardinals may sometimes be used as adverbs (*adverbia numeralia*) to determine a verb by omitting the word פַּעַם; e. g. וְהִכֵּיתִי אֶתְכֶם שֶׁבַע (= שֶׁבַע פְּעָמִים) *I will smite you seven times* Lev. 26, 24.

Certain numeral adverbs may be expressed by a cardinal in the dual, as שִׁבְעָתַיִם *seven times* Gen. 4, 15; אַרְבַּעְתָּיִם *four times* 2 Sam. 12, 6.

The ordinal שֵׁנִית is occasionally used as a numeral adverb in the sense of *a second time*.

CHAPTER III — PRONOUNS.

§ 10. Personal pronouns and pronominal suffixes.

1) The personal pronoun (see Grammar § 71, Rem. 3) is sometimes used to repeat the pronominal suffix in a separate form for the purpose of emphasis. This occurs as well with the suffixes of nouns and particles as with those of verbs; e. g. בָּרְכֵנִי גַם אָנִי *bless me, even me also* Gen. 27, 34; הוֹדַעְתִּיךָ הַיּוֹם אַף אָתָּה *I have made it known to thee this day, even to thee* Pr. 22, 19; וּפְנֵיכֶם אַתֶּם

but as for you, your carcases Num. 14, 32; הָעֵת לָכֶם אַתֶּם *is it now time for you yourselves* Hagg. 1, 4; כִּי אֲנִי *upon me, upon me* 1 Sam. 25, 24; עָלָיו גַּם הוּא *upon him also* 1 Sam. 19, 23. It even occurs when no suffix but only a noun precedes; e. g. לְשֵׁת גַּם הוּא *to Seth, to him also* Gen. 4, 26.

Still more emphasis is given to the sentence when the personal pronoun is made to precede; e. g. אַתָּה יוֹדוּךָ אַחֶיךָ *thee, thy brethren shall praise* Gen. 49, 8; אֲנִי יָדַי נָטוּ שָׁמַיִם *I, even mine hands have stretched out the heavens* Jes. 45, 12.

2) The pronominal suffix with a verb is occasionally used to express not the *passive* object, but the object *interested* in the act; e. g. לֹא תִנָּשֵׁנִי *thou shalt not be forgotten of me* Jes. 44, 21; הֲצוֹם צַמְתָּנִי *did ye fast for me?* Zech. 7, 5. Hence נָתַן is now and then found with a double accusative of object, as אֶרֶץ הַנֶּגֶב נְתַתָּנִי *thou hast given me a barren land* (lit. *the land of the south*) Jos. 15, 19.

3) The personal pronoun as object of a verb is to be translated by means of אֵת with a suffix:

(*a*) when it stands with special emphasis before the verb; e. g. אֹתְךָ הָרַגְתִּי *I had slain just thee* Num. 22, 33.

(*b*) when the verb is already connected with another personal suffix as its object; e. g. וְהִרְאַנִי אֹתוֹ *and he will show himself to me* 2 Sam. 15, 25.

4) The construction of אֵת with a suffix is used by preference in case of an infinitive with a verbal meaning,

§ 10. PERSONAL PRONOUNS.

as וָּבְחוּר אֹתוֹ *and I chose him* 1 Sam. 2, 28 (conf. § 22, 5).

5) The pronominal suffix of a noun may, like the *st. constr.* denote the genitive of object or the genitive of subject; e. g. וּמוֹרַאֲכֶם וְחִתְּכֶם *the fear and dread of you* Gen. 9, 2; יִרְאָתוֹ *his fear* (i. e. *fear for him*) Ex. 20, 20.

6) When the compound idea expressed by two nouns connected in the *st. constr.* is to have a pronominal suffix, this is appended not to the main idea (nom. regens), but to the subordinate idea (nom. rectum). (Compare the analogous rule for ה' הַיְדִיעָה § 3, 7) e. g. בֵּית תְּפִלָּה *house of prayer* בֵּית תְּפִלָּתִי *my house of prayer*; אֱלִילֵי כֶסֶף *silver idols* אֱלִילֵי כַסְפּוֹ *his silver idols.*

Rem. 1 Sometimes this is more accurately expressed by the repetition of the first noun; e. g. גְּבִיעִי גְּבִיעַ הַכֶּסֶף (= גְּבִיעַ כַּסְפִּי) *my silver cup* Gen. 44, 2.

7) If however the *nom. rectum* cannot have a suffix the latter is then appended to the *nom. regens*; e. g. בְּרִיתִי יַעֲקוֹב *my covenant with Jacob* Lev. 26, 42; בְּרִיתִי הַיּוֹם *my covenant with the day* Jer. 33, 20; שֹׂנְאַי חִנָּם (= שֹׂנְאַי חִנָּם with suffix 1st pers. sing.) *my haters without cause* Ps. 69, 5.

Rem. 2 The suffix is sometimes appended to the *nom. regens* even without this reason; e. g. חֲבֹלָתוֹ חֹב (= תַּבֻלַּת חֹבוֹ) *the pledge of his debt* Ez. 18, 7; אֹיְבַי שֶׁקֶר (= אֹיְבֵי שִׁקְרִי) *my enemies without cause* Ps. 35, 19.

Rem. 3 The passages, however, where the second noun is the predicate, should be considered as elliptical; e. g. כִּסְאֲךָ אֱלֹהִים (= כִּסְאֲךָ כִּסֵּא אֱלֹהִים) *thy throne is a throne of God* Ps. 45, 7 [1]).

Rem. 4 Now and then the suffix is appended to both nouns; e. g. רָאשֵׁיכֶם שִׁבְטֵיכֶם (= רָאשֵׁי שִׁבְטֵיכֶם) *your tribal chiefs* Deut. 29, 9.

Rem. 5 With the personal pronouns and especially with the pronominal suffixes the *masculine* is sometimes used instead of the *feminine*; e. g. שִׁשִּׁים הֵמָּה מְלָכוֹת (= שִׁשִּׁים הֵנָּה מְלָכוֹת) *there are sixty queens* Cant. 6, 8; מִקְנֵה אֲבִיכֶם (= מִקְנֵה אֲבִיכֶן) *the cattle of your father* (viz. of Rachel's and Leah's father) Gen. 31, 9 (Conf. § 18 Rem. and § 19, 1).

Rem. 6 The personal pronoun as object of a verb is sometimes omitted, when it can be easily supplied from what precedes; e. g. וַיִּקַּח בֶּן בָּקָר ...... וַיִּתֵּן אֶל הַנַּעַר *he took a calf* ...... *and gave (it) to his servant* Gen. 18, 7; עַד שַׁלְּחֶךָ *till thou send (it)* Gen. 38, 17.

Rem. 7 On the other hand, the noun to which a pronominal suffix refers is sometimes added to it as apposition (conf. n° 1); e. g. וַתִּרְאֵהוּ אֶת הַיֶּלֶד *she saw him* (viz.) *the boy* Ex. 2, 6.

This occurs also, when the suffix is appended not to the verb but to some other part of speech; e. g. וְכֹל אֲשֶׁר יִקְרָא־לוֹ הָאָדָם נֶפֶשׁ חַיָּה *and whatsoever name the man gave it (namely) the living creature* Gen. 2, 19; sometimes with repetition of the preposition, e. g. אֲנִי נֹתֵן לָהֶם לִבְנֵי יִשְׂרָאֵל *which I do give to them (namely) to the children of Israel* Jos. 1, 2; הִנֵּה מִטָּתוֹ שֶׁלִּשְׁלֹמֹה *his litter (namely that) of Solomon* Cant. 3, 7; and occasionally for the sake of explanation; e. g. שִׁיתֵמוֹ נְדִיבֵמוֹ *make them (namely) their nobles* Ps. 83, 12.

Rem. 8 The suffix sometimes refers to indefinite persons; e. g. דְּגָנָם וְתִירוֹשָׁם *their corn and their new wine* Ps. 4, 8.; וְאֵין־לְחָם לוֹ *but there is none warm* Hagg. 1, 6.

---

[1]) Several commentators consider this construction in general as elliptical.

§ 11. DEMONSTR. AND INTERROG. PRONOUNS.

§ 11. The Demonstrative and Interrogative pronouns.

1) The personal pronoun of the third person הוּא, when used as a demonstrative (conf. grammar § 72, 4), differs from the demonstrative pronouns זֶה, זֹאת and אֵלֶּה, as *that* (Lat. *is*) differs from *this* (Lat. *hic*); e. g. הַיּוֹם הַזֶּה *this day*, viz. the day on which one speaks; הַיּוֹם הַהוּא *that day*, the day of which the narrator has already spoken; הָעֵת הַזֹּאת the time in which one speaks; הָעֵת הַהוּא the time of which one is speaking.

Rem. 1 In certain fixed expressions, however, this rule is sometimes neglected. We always say הַדָּבָר הַזֶּה and הָאֵלֶּה הַדְּבָרִים even where one would have expected הַדָּבָר הַהוּא and הַדְּבָרִים הָהֵם. On the contrary generally בַּיָּמִים הָהֵם instead of בַּיָּמִים הָאֵלֶּה.

2) זוּ which usually possesses also a relative signification, is more than once employed as a relative pronoun (= אֲשֶׁר); e. g. בְּרֶשֶׁת־זוּ טָמָנוּ *in the net which they had hidden* Ps. 9, 16. Yet also זֶה and זוּ are sometimes used in like manner; e. g. אֶל מָקוֹם זֶה יָסַדְתָּ לָהֶם *unto the place which thou hast founded for them* Ps. 104, 8 (conf. gram. § 72).

3) זֶה and זֹאת may be used adverbially:

(*a*) referring *to place*; e. g. זֶה הַיָּם *yonder is the sea* Ps. 104, 25.

(*b*) referring *to time*; e. g. זֶה פַעֲמַיִם *already twice* Gen. 27, 36.

(*c*) for the purpose of strengthening questions, e. g. מַה זֹּאת עָשִׂיתָ *what is this thou hast done?* Gen. 3, 13; אַתָּה זֶה בְּנִי *is it thou my son Esau?* Gen. 27, 24;

לָמָּה זֶה שְׁלַחְתָּנִי *why is it that thou hast sent me?*
Ex. 5, 22 (Conf. § 26, 7).

הוּא also is sometimes used in the same manner; e. g.
מִי הוּא זֶה וְאֵי זֶה הוּא *who is he, and where is he?* Esther
7, 5.

4) מִי occasionally refers to *things* when the idea of *persons* is implied (Conf. grammar § 74); e. g. מִי שְׁכֶם *what is Shechem?* Judges 9, 28. This chiefly occurs after מִי has already been used in reference to persons; e. g. מִי אָנֹכִי וּמִי חַיַּי *who am I and what is my life?* 1 Sam. 18, 18; מִי אָנֹכִי וּמִי בֵיתִי *who am I and what is my house?* 2 Sam. 7, 18.

Although מִי may refer to several persons, yet one sometimes says in that case מִי וָמִי; e. g. מִי וָמִי הַהֹלְכִים *who are they that shall go?* Ex. 10, 8.

5) As מִי and מָה are used as substantives, they naturally occur sometimes as dependent on a *nomen regens*; e. g. בַּת מִי *whose daughter?* Gen. 24, 23 וְחָכְמַת מֶה לָהֶם *knowledge of what have they?* Jer. 8, 9.

For the same reason they may also be connected with a *prefix* or separate *preposition*; e. g. אֶת מִי *whom?*; לְמִי *to whom?*; אַחֲרֵי מִי *after whom?* עַל־מָה (= לָמָּה) (*for what reason*) *why?*

Rem. 2 מָה and מֶה with בְּ are written בַּמָּה and בַּמֶּה, with כְּ כַּמָּה and כַּמֶּה, and with לְ generally לָמָּה, sometimes לָמֶה.

Rem. 3 מִי and מָה are sometimes used indefinitely in the sense of *whosoever, whatsoever*; e. g. מִי אֲשֶׁר חָטָא Ex. 32, 33); e. g. מִי אֲשֶׁר יָרֵא (= מִי יָרֵא וְחָרֵד Ex. 24, 14; מִי בַעַל דְּבָרִים *whosoever hath a cause* *whosoever is fearful and trembling* Judg. 7, 3; וִיהִי מָה *come what may* 2 Sam. 18, 22.

With the same meaning מִי is once found following the predicate namely 2 Sam. 18, 12 שָׁמְרוּ מִי *beware whosoever ye be*[1]).

§ 12. The Relative pronoun.

1) אֲשֶׁר often serves merely to give a relative meaning to demonstrative words, and is generally separated from them by the other words of the sentence; e. g. הָאִישׁ אֲשֶׁר אַתָּה נֹשֶׁה בוֹ (= אֲשֶׁר בּוֹ) *the man to whom thou dost lend* Deut. 24, 11. Less frequently they stand together, as אֲשֶׁר בּוֹ נֶפֶשׁ חַיָּה *wherein there is life* Gen. 1, 30; אֲשֶׁר לָהֶם הָרִיב *between whom the controversy is* Deut. 19, 17.

Rem. 1 A preposition is very seldom placed before אֲשֶׁר as a relative pronoun, or joined with it so as to form one word; e. g. עִם אֲשֶׁר תִּמְצָא (= אֲשֶׁר תִּמְצָא עִמּוֹ) *with whomsoever thou findest* Gen. 31, 32; בַּאֲשֶׁר יָגַעַתְּ (= אֲשֶׁר יָגַעַתְּ בָּהֶם) *wherein thou hast laboured* Jes. 47, 12; בַּאֲשֶׁר חָפַצְתִּי (= אֲשֶׁר חָפַצְתִּי בוֹ) *the things that pleased me* Jes. 56, 4.

2) The demonstrative word to which אֲשֶׁר belongs, is sometimes entirely omitted; e. g. אֲשֶׁר אֲמַרְתֶּם (= אֲשֶׁר לוֹ אֲמַרְתֶּם) *of whom ye have spoken* Gen. 43, 27; אֲשֶׁר אֵין חָרִישׁ (= אֲשֶׁר בָּהֶם אֵין חָרִישׁ) *in which there shall be no ploughing* Gen. 45, 6.

3) As אֲשֶׁר may refer to all persons, objects, genders, and numbers, and is moreover indeclinable, it is evi-

---

1) Pr. Driver in his "Hebrew notes on Samuel" suggests, as probably right, the reading שָׁמְרוּ לִי because of the Pesh. and Sept. φυλάξατέ μοι. (*Translator*).

dent, that the respective person, object, gender and number should be indicated by a demonstrative word, (a construction which is quite contrary to the English mode of expression); e. g. אֲנִי יוֹסֵף אֲשֶׁר מְכַרְתֶּם אֹתִי *I am Joseph whom ye have sold* Gen. 45, 4 (אֹתִי cannot be translated); אָנֹכִי אֲתֹנְךָ אֲשֶׁר רָכַבְתָּ עָלַי *I am thine ass upon which thou hast ridden* Num. 22, 30 (עָלַי remains untranslated); אֲנִי יְהֹוָה אֲשֶׁר לֹא יֵבֹשׁוּ קֹוָי *I am the Lord whose faithful ones shall not be put to shame* Jes. 49, 23.

The same applies to the pronominal suffixes of a verb; e. g. אַתָּה יַעֲקֹב אֲשֶׁר בְּחַרְתִּיךָ *thou art Jacob whom I have chosen* Jes. 41, 8. (The suffix remains again untranslated).

<small>Rem. 2 This construction may perhaps be further explained by supplying after אֲשֶׁר a verb such as *to say, to declare*; e. g. In the instance quoted Gen. 45, 4 *I am Joseph (of whom I say* = אֲשֶׁר) *ye have sold me*; Jes. 41, 8 "*thou art Jacob (of whom I said* = אֲשֶׁר) *I have chosen thee*".</small>

4) אֲשֶׁר, like זוּ, not unfrequently has the signification of a demonstrative followed by a relative; e. g. וַיֹּאמֶר לַאֲשֶׁר עַל בֵּיתוֹ *he said to him that was appointed over his house* Gen. 43, 16; אֲשֶׁר לֹא סֻפַּר רָאוּ *that which they had not heard they saw* Jes. 52, 15; בְּיַד אֲשֶׁר שָׂנֵאתָ *into the hand of him whom thou hatest* Ez. 23, 28.

5) In all these constructions אֲשֶׁר may also be omitted; e. g. (בְּאֶרֶץ אֲשֶׁר לֹא לָהֶם =) בְּאֶרֶץ לֹא לָהֶם *in a land that is not theirs* Gen. 15, 13; (בְּיַד אֲשֶׁר תִּשְׁלָח =) בְּיַד תִּשְׁלָח *by the hand of him whom thou wilt send* Ex. 4, 13; בְּיָדִי לֹא

§ 13. REMAINING PRONOUNS.

בִּידֵי אֲשֶׁר לֹא אוּכַל קוּם (= אוּכַל קוּם) *into the hands of them from whom I am not able to rise up* Lam. 1, 14.

§ 13. Pronouns for which the Hebrew has no proper words.

1) *Each, everyone*, when used as substantives are expressed either by אִישׁ; e. g. אִישׁ צְרוֹר כַּסְפּוֹ *everyone's bundle of money* Gen. 42, 35; or by אִישׁ אִישׁ and אִישׁ וָאִישׁ (אִישׁ וָאִישׁ in pausa); e. g. אִישׁ אִישׁ מִמְּלַאכְתּוֹ *everyone from his work* Ex. 36, 4; אִישׁ וְאִישׁ יֻלַּד בָּהּ *everyone that was born in her* Ps. 87, 5; כִּרְצוֹן אִישׁ וָאִישׁ *according to everyone's pleasure* Esther 1, 8.

2) *Each, everyone* when used as adjectives are expressed either by כָּל followed by a noun without ה' הַיְדִיעָה; e. g. כָּל רֹאשׁ *every head* Jes. 1, 5; or by repetition of the noun; e. g. בַּבֹּקֶר בַּבֹּקֶר *every morning*; or by placing the noun in the plural; e. g. לַבְּקָרִים *every morning* Lam. 3, 23; לִרְגָעִים *every moment* Job. 7, 18. (Conf: § 2, 5).

2) *Anyone, someone* are expressed:

(a) by אִישׁ; e. g. אִם יִתֵּן אִישׁ *if anyone gave* Cant. 8, 7. Hence אִישׁ with a negation = *no one*; אַל יֵצֵא אִישׁ *let no one go out* Ex. 16, 29.

(b) by אָדָם; e. g. אָדָם כִּי יַקְרִיב *when anyone offereth* Lev. 1, 2.

(c) by אֶחָד connected in the *st. constr.* with another noun; e.g. אַחַד הָעָם *someone of the people* Gen. 26, 10. Hence the use of אֶחָד with a negation; e. g. אֵין אֶחָד, לֹא אֶחָד = *no one*.

(d) sometimes without any proper word, but simply

by the third person; e. g. וַיִּתֶּן־יָד֒ *and one put forth his hand* Gen. 38, 28.

(e) by adding to the verb a participle of the same stem as the subject; e. g. וְכִי יָמוּת מֵת *if any man die* Num. 6, 9. (Conf. § 23, 5.)

Rem. 1 The indefinite *a certain man* is expressed by אִישׁ אֶחָד, e. g. Sam. 1, 1.

4) *Something*, *anything* are expressed by דָּבָר; e. g. הֲיִפָּלֵא מֵיְהֹוָ֑ה דָּבָר *is anything too wonderful for the Lord* Gen. 18, 14; or by כָּל דָּבָר; e. g. בְּכָל דָּבָר טָמֵא *anything unclean* Lev. 5, 2. Hence דָּבָר with a negation = *nothing*; e. g. אַל תַּעֲשׂוּ דָבָר *do nothing* Gen. 19, 8; אֵין דָּבָר *it is nothing* [1]).

Further by מְאוּמָה, sometimes by מָה; e. g. וִיהִי מָה *come what may* 2 Sam. 18, 22; וּדְבַר מַה יַּרְאֵנִי *and whatsoever he showeth me* Num. 23, 3; or by מִן; e. g. אִם יִפֹּל מִשַּׂעֲרַת רֹאשׁוֹ *there shall not a hair of his head* (lit. *anything of the hair of his head*) *fall to the ground* 1 Sam. 14, 45. Conf. 1 Sam. 3, 19.

Rem. 2 The sentence becomes still more indefinite when *anyone*, *anything* is not indicated at all; e. g. הַעוֹד עִמָּךְ *is there yet any (corpse) with thee?* Amos 6, 10; אֵין כָּמוֹךָ *there is none like unto thee* Ps. 86, 8.

5) *Self:*

(a) refering to persons, is expressed by placing הוּא, הִוא etc. after the noun to which it belongs; e. g.

---

1) דָּבָר is sometimes connected in the *st. constr.* with another noun; e. g. דְּבַר בְּלִיַּעַל *something wicked* Ps. 41, 9; or another noun in the *st. constr.* with דָּבָר; e. g. עֶרְוַת דָּבָר *something shameful* Deut. 23, 15.

§ 13. REMAINING PRONOUNS.

הַלֵּוִי הוּא *the Levite himself* Num. 18, 23; הַיְּהוּדִים הֵמָּה *the Jews themselves* Esth. 9, 1 (Conf. grammar § 70, 2).

(*b*) refering to things, by placiug עֶצֶם before the noun; e. g. כְּעֶצֶם הַשָּׁמַיִם *as heaven itself* Ex. 24, 10.

6) *The same:*

(*a*) in reference to persons is expressed by הוּא, הוּא etc. placed after the noun to which it belongs; e. g. וְאַתָּה הוּא *but thou art the same* Ps. 102, 28.

(*b*) in reference to things, by עֶצֶם before the noun; e. g. בְּעֶצֶם הַיּוֹם הַזֶּה *on the same day*.

7) *The one ..... the other* (*alter ..... alter*) is expressed:

(*a*) by זֶה ..... זֶה; e. g. וְקָרָא זֶה אֶל זֶה *and one cried unto the other* Jes. 6, 3.

(*b*) by אֶחָד ..... אֶחָד; e. g. וַיַּכּוּ הָאֶחָד אֶת הָאֶחָד *but the one smote the other* 2 Sam. 14, 6.

(*c*) by אִישׁ followed by אָחִיו or רֵעֵהוּ, and for the feminine by אִשָּׁה followed by אֲחוֹתָהּ or רְעוּתָהּ, in reference both to persons and things; e. g. חֲמֵשׁ הַיְרִיעוֹת תִּהְיֶיןָ חֹבְרֹת אִשָּׁה אֶל אֲחֹתָהּ Ex 26, 3.

The last named construction is also used for the reflexive *one another*; e. g. וַיִּפָּרְדוּ אִישׁ מֵעַל אָחִיו *and they separated from one another* Gen. 13, 11 (Conf. gram. § 70, 2 (*a*)).

8) *Some* is expressed by the plural of the noun to wich it belongs; e. g. יָמִים *some days* Gen. 24, 55; while אֲחָדִים is sometimes added; e. g. וְיָשַׁבְתָּ עִמּוֹ יָמִים אֲחָדִים *and thou shalt remain with him some days* Gen. 27, 44.

Occasionally it is expressed by יֵשׁ אֲשֶׁר; e. g. יֵשׁ אֲשֶׁר

אֹמְרִים *some said* Neh. 5, 2; or also by מָן; e. g. יָצְאוּ מִן
הָעָם *some of the people went out* Ex. 16, 27; מִזִּקְנֵי יִשְׂרָאֵל
some of the elders of Israel Ex. 17, 5; sometimes even
by מִן with a singular word, as מִמְּךָ לִי יֵצֵא *out of thee some
shall go forth* Michah 5, 1. Conf. Ps. 132, 11; 2 Kings
10, 10; Dan. 11, 7.

Rem. 2 Concerning the possessive‚ reflexive and ˊ pronouns see gram.
§§ 62—64, and § 70, 2.

PART II

VERBUM.

CHAPTER IV — THE VERBAL FORMS.

§ 14 The use of the עָבַר (*actio perfecta*).

The עָבַר is used in the first place for events which
belong to the past; viz. to express the *Perfect*, *Pluperfect* and *Future Perfect* (Futurum Exactum); e. g.
בָּאוּ אֶל נֹחַ בַּאֲשֶׁר צִוָּה אֱלֹהִים *they came unto Noah as God
had commanded* Gen. 7, 9; אֲשֶׁר גָּנְבוּ עַבְדֵי אֲבִימֶלֶךְ *which the
servants of Abimelech had stolen* Gen. 21, 25; כַּאֲשֶׁר
שָׁכֹלְתִּי שָׁכָלְתִּי *and if I shall have been bereaved of my
children, I shall be bereaved* Gen. 43, 14; אִם רָחַץ ה׳
when the Lord shall have washed away Jes. 4, 4.

2) The עָבַר is further employed where in English we use
the present; viz., in those instances which imply a similar
action to have taken place in the past, or which are
based upon it. The עָבַר consequently serves to express:

(*a*) an enduring act, already in operation; e. g.

§ 14. THE USE OF THE עָבַר

שָׂנֵאתִי הַשֹּׁמְרִים הַבְלֵי שָׁוְא *I hate them who seek for vain things* Ps. 31, 7; יָדַעְתִּי בְנִי יָדַעְתִּי *I know it, my son I, know it* Gen. 48, 19; לֹא שָׁקַטְתִּי וְלֹא שָׁלַוְתִּי וְלֹא נָחְתִּי *I have no rest, nor peace, nor a moment of ease* Job 3, 26;

(*b*) solemn declaration, promises, decrees and similar acts; e. g. בִּי נִשְׁבַּעְתִּי *I swear by myself* Gen. 22, 16; סָלַחְתִּי כִּדְבָרֶיךָ *I forgive according to thy word* Num. 14, 20.

Prophetic predictions (the so called *perfectum propheticum*) belong to this rule.

(*c*) actions of frequent recurrence; e. g. אַשְׁרֵי הָאִישׁ אֲשֶׁר לֹא הָלַךְ *blessed the man that walketh not in the counsel of the wicked* Ps. 1, 1 (Conf. § 15, 5).

3) In case of an hypothesis, of which one knows that it is not, or will not be fulfilled, the עָבַר is used both in the main sentence (*apodosis*), and in the hypothetical clause (*protasis*); e. g. לוּלֵי אֱלֹהֵי אָבִי הָיָה לִי כִּי עַתָּה רֵיקָם שִׁלַּחְתָּנִי *if the God of my fathers had not been with me thou hadst sent me away empty* Gen. 31, 42; אוּלַי נָטְתָה מִפָּנַי כִּי עַתָּה גַּם אֹתְכָה הָרַגְתִּי וְאוֹתָהּ הֶחֱיֵיתִי *if she had not turned aside from me, surely I should have slain thee and saved her alive* Num. 22, 33.

If on the contrary one does not know this, other verbal forms may be used; e. g. לוּ חָכְמוּ יַשְׂכִּילוּ *if they were wise they would understand* Deut. 32, 29; לוּ עַמִּי שֹׁמֵעַ לִי ..... כִּמְעַט אוֹיְבֵיהֶם אַכְנִיעַ *if my people would hearken to me ..... I would quickly bow down their enemies* Ps. 81, 14, 15.

§ 15 The use of the עָתִיד (*actio imperfecta*).

1) The עָתִיד naturally is used for actions which have to take place in the future; e. g. כִּי שָׁמְעוּ כִּי שָׁם יֹאכְלוּ לֶחֶם *for they heard that they should take their meal there* Gen. 43, 25; וְאַחֲרֵי כֵן יְשַׁלַּח אֶתְכֶם *and after that he will let you go* Ex 3, 20; לֹא תָקוּם וְלֹא תִהְיֶה *it shall not stand, neither shall it come to pass* Jes. 7, 7.

2) Hence the עָתִיד is used in sentences (*final sentences*) which express the object (*finis*), after conjunctions such as בַּעֲבוּר, לְמַעַן (*ut, for the end that*) פֶּן (*ne, lest*); e. g. וּבַעֲבוּר תִּהְיֶה יִרְאָתוֹ עַל פְּנֵיכֶם לְבִלְתִּי תֶחֱטָאוּ *that the fear of him may restrain you that ye sin not* Ex. 20, 20; אֲשֶׁר לֹא יִשְׁמְעוּ *that they may not understand* Gen. 11, 7; פֶּן תִּנָּקֵשׁ *that ye may not be ensnared* Deut. 12, 30; also after וְ when it has the meaning of a final conjunction; e. g. וְהָיוּ לְאֹתוֹת *that they may be for signs* Num. 17, 3.

3) For the same reason it is used to express *a wish* (instead of the cohortative or jussive form); e. g. יֵרָאֶה אֶל עֲבָדֶיךָ פָעֳלֶךָ *may thy work be seen by thy servants* Ps. 90, 16; וְלִבְּךָ תָּשִׁית לְדַעְתִּי *take thou my plan unto thy heart* Prov. 22, 17.

Especially where the cohortative has no proper form the עָתִיד is employed with נָא = *I pray*; e. g. יְדַבֶּר נָא עַבְדְּךָ *let thy servant, I pray thee, speak* Gen. 44, 18.

4) The עָתִיד is further used to express a prohibition with לֹא or אַל, (by preference of course with the jussive); e. g. לֹא תַעֲשֶׂה לְךָ פֶסֶל *thou shalt not make unto thee a graven image* Ex. 20, 3; לֹא תִשָּׂא שֵׁמַע שָׁוְא *thou shalt not take up a false report* Ex. 23, 1; אַל תַּבִּיט אַחֲרֶיךָ *look*

not behind thee Gen. 19, 17; אַל־תָּשֶׁת יָדְךָ עִם־רָשָׁע *put not thine hand with the wicked* (= *be no partner with the wicked*) Ex 23, 1.

5) The עָתִיד moreover usually serves to express the forms of our present tense; e. g. מַה־תְּבַקֵּשׁ *what seekest thou* Gen. 37, 15; אוֹדְךָ *I thank thee* Ps. 118, 21; and it often denotes also a continuing or frequently recurring action, when that which has happened in the past is not thought of, or at least is not uppermost in the mind of the speaker or writer (Conf. § 14, 2 *a* and *c*); וּמִשָּׁם יִפָּרֵד *and from hence it was parted* Gen. 2, 10 עַל־כֵּן יַעֲזָב־אִישׁ *therefore a man leaveth his father* Gen. 2, 24; לֹא יֵעָשֶׂה כֵן בִּמְקוֹמֵנוּ *it is not so done in our place* Gen. 29, 26; וּמְעִיל קָטֹן תַּעֲשֶׂה־לּוֹ אִמּוֹ *and his mother used to make a little robe for him* I Sam. 2, 19.

6) The עָתִיד further serves to express ideas equivalent to *I can, I may, it ought* etc.; e. g. אָכֹל תֹּאכֵל *may ye eat* Gen. 2, 16; מַעֲשִׂים אֲשֶׁר לֹא־יֵעָשׂוּ *deeds that ought not to be done* Gen. 20, 9; הֲיָדוֹעַ נֵדַע *could we know this?* Gen. 43, 7; מִי יַעֲמֹד *who can exist* Ps. 130, 3.

7) Finally the עָתִיד is usually employed after the conjunctions אָז *then*, and טֶרֶם *before, not yet*, even where in English we use a past tense; אָז יָשִׁיר מֹשֶׁה *then sang Moses* Ex. 15. 1; אָז תִּפְשַׁע לִבְנָה *then did Libnah revolt* 2 Kings 8, 22; וְכָל־עֵשֶׂב הַשָּׂדֶה טֶרֶם יִצְמָח *and no herbs of the field had yet sprung up.* Gen. 2, 5.

§ 16. The עָבַר and עָתִיד with ו conversive.

1) The עָבַר with ו conversive is used to continue a

sentence which commenced with עָתִיד or with any other form of expression designating the action as future; e. g. פֶּן יִשְׁלַח יָדוֹ וְלָקַח גַּם מֵעֵץ הַחַיִּים וְאָכַל וָחַי לְעֹלָם *lest he put forth his hand and take also of the tree of life aud eat and live for ever* Gen. 3, 22 (conf. Gen. 24, 40; 41, 34); עוֹד מְעַט וּסְקָלֻנִי *they be almost ready to stone me* Ex. 17, 4; אִם אֶת הַדָּבָר הַזֶּה תַּעֲשֶׂה וְצִוְּךָ אֱלֹהִים וְיָכָלְתָּ עֲמֹד *if thou shalt do this thing then shall God give thee his commandments, and thou shalt be able to endure* Ex. 18, 23; צַו אֶת בְּנֵי יִשְׂרָאֵל וְאָמַרְתָּ אֲלֵיהֶם *command the children of Israel and say to them* Num. 28, 2.

2) Without a preceding word referring to something future, הָיָה with וְ conversive is used to introduce a future action (conf. n° 5), which action then follows expressed by עָתִיד, or by עָבַר with וְ conv., or by the Imperative; e. g. וְהָיָה כָל מֹצְאִי יַהַרְגֵנִי *and it shall come to pass, that whosoever findeth me shall slay me* Gen. 4, 14; וְהָיָה בַּיּוֹם הַהוּא יִתָּקַע בְּשׁוֹפָר גָּדוֹל *and it shall come to pass in that day that a great trumpet shall be blown* Jes. 27, 13; וְהָיָה כִּי יִרְאוּ אֹתָךְ הַמִּצְרִים וְאָמְרוּ אִשְׁתּוֹ זֹאת וְהָרְגוּ אֹתִי וְאֹתָךְ יְחַיּוּ *and it shall come to pass when the Egyptians shall see thee, that they shall say: this is his wife and they will kill me, but they will save thee alive* Gen. 12, 12; וְהָיָה כִּי יְבִיאֲךָ ה' ...... הִשָּׁמֶר לְךָ *and it shall be when the Lord shall bring thee into the land ..... then beware lest* Deut. 6, 10—12; וְהָיָה אִם שָׁמֹעַ תִּשְׁמְעוּ ..... וְנָתַתִּי *and it shall come to pass if ye shall hearken diligently unto my commandments ..... that I will give ye* Deut. 11, 13. 14.

§ 16. THE עָבַר AND עָתִיד WITH ו CONVERSIVE

3) The עָתִיד with ו conversive serves to continue a narrative which commenced with a past tense. The first verb therefore of the narrative should properly stand in the עָבַר. Yet this generally happens only when an entirely new subject is introduced; e. g. Gen. 1, 1; 25, 19; Ex. 3, 1; 19, 1; 1 Kings 5, 1. If, however, this is not the case, then the first verb frequently stands in the עָתִיד with ו conv. Hence it is that a narrative so often commences with וַיְהִי. וַיְדַבֵּר. וַיֹּאמֶר.

Sometimes it even happens that the first verb of the narrative has to be mentally supplied; e. g. שֵׁם בֶּן מְאַת שָׁנָה וַיּוֹלֶד (= שֵׁם הָיָה) *Shem (was) a hundred years old when he begat;* or *Shem begat at the age of a hundred years* Gen. 11, 10; וַיְהִי) בַּיּוֹם הַשְּׁלִישִׁי וַיִּשָּׂא אַבְרָהָם אֶת עֵינָיו (*It happened) on the third day when Abraham lifted up his eyes;* or, *on the third day Abraham lifted up his eyes* Gen. 22, 4.

4) The עָתִיד with ו conv. is in certain cases regularly used in the main sentence, viz:

(*a*) after a preceding causal sentence; e. g. יַעַן מָאַסְתָּ אֶת דְּבַר ה' וַיִּמְאָסְךָ מִמֶּלֶךְ *because thou hast rejected the word of the Lord, He hath also rejected thee from being king* 1 Sam. 15, 23.

(*b*) when the subject or object of the sentence for some reason or other precedes; e. g. וּפִלַגְשׁוֹ וּשְׁמָהּ רְאוּמָה וַתֵּלֶד גַּם הִוא *and his concubine whose name was Reumah, she also bare* Gen. 22, 24; וְתוֹרָתִי וַיִּמְאָסוּ בָהּ *and as for my doctrine, they despised it* Jer. 6, 19.

5) Just as וְהָיָה is used to introduce a future action

(conf. n° 2), וַיְהִי frequently serves to introduce a narrative; e. g. Gen. 14, 1; 15, 17; 22, 1. 20; 29, 25; Jos. 5, 1. 13 etc.

6) The עָתִיד with ו conv. is sometimes used instead of the present; e. g. וַתְּכַבֵּד *and thou honourest* 1 Sam. 2, 29; וַיִּתְאַבֵּל *and he grieveth* 2 Sam. 19, 2; וַיַּעֲנֵנִי *and he heareth me* Ps. 3, 5. In like manner it is used for future events especially in prophecies; e. g. וַיִּשְׂגַּב ה׳ *and the Lord shall exalt* Jes. 9, 10; וְיוֹרֶד *and He shall cause the rain to come down* Joel 2, 23; וַיַּעֲבֹר מַלְכָּם *and their king shall pass on* Mich. 2, 13.

7) The ו conv. both of the עָבַר and of the עָתִיד finally serves to express all the different conjunctions; e. g. וּקְרָאָהוּ אָסוֹן וְהוֹרַדְתֶּם אֶת שֵׂיבָתִי *and if any mischief befall him, then shall ye bring down my gray hairs with sorrow* Gen. 42, 38; מָה אֱנוֹשׁ וַתֵּדָעֵהוּ *what is man that thou takest knowledge of him?* Ps. 144, 3.

Rem. 1 Sometimes a עָתִיד is found which is still under the influence of a preceding ו conv.; e. g. וַיֹּאכְלוּ וַיִּשְׂבְּעוּ מְאֹד וְתַאֲוָתָם יָבִא לָהֶם *they ate and they were filled, and he gave them what they lusted after* Ps. 78, 29; and sometimes under that of one following; e. g. יַסַּע קָדִים בַּשָּׁמַיִם וַיְנַהֵג בְּעֻזּוֹ תֵימָן *he caused the east wind to blow in the heaven; and guided the south wind by his power* Ps. 78, 26.

§ 17. The cohortative and jussive besides the other modes of speech for expressing a wish.

1) The cohortative (a prolonged form of the עָתִיד by appendig הָ) rarely occurs except with the first person (Conf. gram. § 45, 1—3), and is used to express:

§ 17. COHORTATIVE AND JUSSIVE.

(a) an ardent wish or supplication; e. g. וַאֲסַפְּרָה כָּל יִרְאֵי אֱלֹהִים *come and hear and let me declare all ye that fear God* Ps. 66, 16; נַעְבְּרָה נָּא בְאַרְצֶךָ *let us pass, I pray thee, through thy land* Num. 20, 17.

(b) a resolution which is uttered with some excitement or animation; e. g. אֵלְכָה נָּא וְאָשׁוּבָה וְאֶרְאֶה *I will go, and return to my brethren and see* Ex. 4, 18; נָּרוּצָה *we will run after thee* Cant. 1, 4.

Rem. 1 It follows from rules *a* and *b* that the cohortative may be used with or without נָא. Where no proper from of the cohortative exists, the עָתִיד is used with נָא (conf. § 15, 3).

(c) sometimes also an hypothesis, with or without אִם; e. g. אִם אֲדַבְּרָה ..... וְאַחְדְלָה *if I speak my grief is not assuaged, and if I forbear* Job. 16, 6; אֶרְדְּפָה אוֹיְבַי וָאַשְׁמִידֵם *if I pursue mine enemies, I overtake them* 2 Sam. 22, 38.

2) The forms of the cohortative are sometimes used with ו conversive, with the consequence that the original meaning of the cohortative is lost; e. g. וָאֶשְׁלְחָה *and I sent* Gen. 32, 6; וָאִישָׁנָה *and I slept* Ps. 3, 6.

3) The jussive (abbreviated form of עָתִיד Conf. gram. § 45, 4—7) is used:

(a) to express a command or wish; e. g. יְהִי רָקִיעַ *let there be a firmament* Gen. 1, 6; לוּ יְהִי כִדְבָרֶךָ *may it be according to thy word* Gen. 30, 34; וְיָשֵׂם לְךָ שָׁלוֹם *may he give thee prosperity* Num. 6, 26; וְתֵעָשׂ *it shall be done* Esther 7, 2.

(b) to express a prohibition with a negative, usually with אַל; e. g. אַל תֵּפֶן אֶל מִנְחָתָם *respect not their offering* Num. 16, 15; אַל מַשְׁחֵת עַמְּךָ *destroy not thy people* Deut. 9, 26; and sometimes with לֹא; e. g. רַק אֶת בְּנִי לֹא תָשֵׁב שָׁמָּה *only thou mayest not bring my son thither again* Gen. 24, 8.

(c) not unfrequently also in conditional sentences; e. g. תָּשֶׁת חֹשֶׁךְ וִיהִי לָיְלָה *if thou makest darkness, it becometh night* Ps. 104, 20; יַךְ וְיַחְבְּשֵׁנוּ *if he smiteth, he will again heal us* Hos. 6, 1.

4) In addition to the ordinary forms of the cohortative and jussive, a wish may be further expressed:

(a) in the form of a question; e. g. מִי יְשִׂמֵנִי שֹׁפֵט *Oh that I were appointed judge* 2 Sam. 15, 4; מִי יִתֵּן אֶת הָעָם הַזֶּה בְּיָדִי *Oh, that this people were given into my hand* Judges 9, 29.

The expression מִי יִתֵּן subsequently became a phrase which has lost its original meaning and only serves to introduce a wish; e. g. מִי יִתֵּן עֶרֶב *would that it were evening* Deut. 28, 67; מִי יִתְּנֵנִי בַמִּדְבָּר *would that I were in the desert* Jer. 9, 1. In this signification it may also be constructed with the infinitive; e. g. מִי יִתֵּן מוּתֵנוּ *would that we had died* Ex. 16, 3; מִי יִתֵּן אֱלוֹהַּ דַּבֵּר *Oh that God would speak* Job 11, 5; or with a *verbum finitum* with or without ו conjunctive; e. g. מִי יִתֵּן וְהָיָה לְבָבָם זֶה לָהֶם *would that they had such a heart* Deut. 5, 26; מִי יִתֵּן אֵפוֹא וְיִכָּתְבוּן מִלָּי *Oh that my words were written down* Job. 19, 23; מִי יִתֵּן יָדַעְתִּי *Oh that I knew* Job 23, 3.

(b) by the particles אִם and לוּ with the עָתִיד or with a participle; e. g. יִשְׂרָאֵל אִם תִּשְׁמַע לִי *Oh Israel that thou*

§ 18. IMPERATIVE.   47

wouldst hearken unto me Ps. 81, 9; אִם תִּקְטֹל אֱלוֹהַּ רָשָׁע *Oh that thou wouldst slay the wicked, o God* Ps. 139, 19; לוּ עַמִּי שֹׁמֵעַ לִי *Oh that my people would hearken to me* Ps. 81, 14.

In one instance אִם is found beside לוּ with the imperative; אַךְ אִם אַתָּה לוּ שְׁמָעֵנִי *Oh that thou, I pray thee, wouldst listen to me* Gen. 23, 13.

Rem. 2 When לוּ is followed by a verb in the עָבַר it expresses a wish which has not been fulfilled (just as לוּלֵא conf. § 14, 3); e. g. לוּ מַתְנוּ *would that we had died* Numb. 14, 2; לוּא הִקְשַׁבְתָּ לְמִצְוֹתָי *Oh that thou hadst hearkened unto my commandments* Jes. 48, 18.

§ 18. The use of the Imperative.

1) The most ordinary use of the imperative is to express a command; e. g. זֹאת עֲשׂוּ *do this* Gen. 45, 19; צַו אֶת בְּנֵי יִשְׂרָאֵל *command the children of Israel* Num. 28, 2.

2) The imperative moreover is frequently used to express:

(a) a petition, especially with נָא; e. g. אִמְרִי נָא *say, I pray thee* Gen. 12, 13.

(b) a wish; e. g. לוּ שְׁמָעֵנִי *Oh that thou wouldst listen to me* Gen. 23, 13.

(c) a promise; e. g. וְאִכְלוּ אֶת חֵלֶב הָאָרֶץ *and ye shall eat the fat of the land* Gen. 45, 18.

3) When the imperative has the meaning of a promise, it generally is the result of a preceding wish expressed in the form of an imperative; e. g. זֹאת עֲשׂוּ וִחְיוּ *do this and then you shall live* Gen. 42, 18; זִרְעוּ

וְקִצְרוּ וְנִטְעוּ כְרָמִים וְאָכְלוּ פֶרְיָם *sow ye, and reap, and plant vineyards, and you shall eat the fruit thereof* Jes. 37, 30; רְאֵה דְרָכֶיהָ וַחֲכָם *consider her ways and thou shalt be wise* Prov. 6, 6.

Such a preceding wish, however, may also be expressed by the עָתִיד; e. g. וְיִתְפַּלֵּל בַּעַדְךָ וֶחְיֵה *and may he pray for thee and then thou shalt live* Gen. 20, 7; אִיעָצְךָ נָא עֵצָה וּמַלְּטִי אֶת נַפְשֵׁךְ *let me, I pray, give thee counsel and thou shalt save thy life* 1 Kings 1, 12.

Rem. With the imperative the masculine is sometimes used instead of the feminine; e. g. וַיֹּאמֶר אֵלֶיהָ עֲמֹד (= עִמְדִי) *and he said unto her: stand in the door of the tent* Judges 4, 20; רְתֹם.... יוֹשֶׁבֶת לָכִישׁ (= רִתְמִי) *bind the chariot unto the swift steed, oh inhabitant of Lachish* Michah 1, 13; חֶרְדוּ שַׁאֲנַנּוֹת (= חֲרַדְנָה) *tremble ye women that are at ease* Jes. 32, 11. (Conf. § 10 Rem. 5 and § 19, 1).

4) When more words than one refer to the subject addressed by the imperative, the suffix of the third person, and not that of the second, is generally used; e. g. שִׂימוּ אִישׁ חַרְבּוֹ עַל יְרֵכוֹ *place ye everyone your swords upon your thigh* Ex. 32, 27; קְחוּ לָכֶם מַחְתּוֹת קֹרַח וְכָל עֲדָתוֹ (not עֲדָתְךָ. Conf. however ibid. vers 11) *take ye censers, Korah, and all your company* Num. 16, 6; שִׁמְעוּ עַמִּים כֻּלָּם (not כֻּלְּכֶם) *hear ye nations, all of you* 1 Kings 22, 28.

This construction is once found with עָתִיד, and in such a manner that the suffix of the third person is made even to precede; e. g. כֻּלָּם תָּשׁוּבוּ *return ye, all of you* Job. 17, 10.

§ 19. PERSONS OF THE VERB.

§ 19. Persons of the Verb.

1) In the use of the persons of the verb the masc. affix is now and then used instead of the fem. (*enallage*); e. g. וַתִּכְרָת *and thou* (i. e. *the harlot* v. 3) *hast made thee a covenant* Jes. 57, 8; נּתוּכָל after וַתַּעֲשִׂי *thou* (i. e. *the harlot*) *hast done evil things, and thou hast had thy way* Jer. 3, 5; וִידַעְתֶּם *and ye* (i. e. *adulterous women*) *shall know* Ez. 23, 49; אַל תִּירְאוּ בַּהֲמוֹת שָׂדַי *be not afraid ye beasts of the field* Joel 2, 22; אִם תָּעִירוּ וְאִם תְּעוֹרְרוּ *that ye* (i. e. *daughters of Jerusalem*) *stir not up nor awaken love* Cant. 2, 7; בַּאֲשֶׁר עֲשִׂיתֶם *as ye* (i. e. *daughters of Naami*) *have dealt with the dead* Ruth 1, 8; הַנָּשִׁים יִתְּנוּ *the wives shall give* Esther 1, 20 (Conf. § 10 Rem. 5 and § 18 Rem.)

2) The impersonal is expressed by the third person sing. masc. as is evident from the frequently occurring expression וַיְהִי *and it was, it came to pass*, or also by the third pers. fem.; ex. g. לֹא תָקוּם וְלֹא תִהְיֶה *it shall not stand neither shall it come to pass* Jes. 7, 7; לְךָ יָאָתָה *for to thee it doth appertain* Jer. 10, 7; נִשְׂעֲרָה מְאֹד *and round about him it is very tempestuous* Ps. 50, 3; תָּבוֹא אֵלֶיךָ *but now it is come to thee* Job 4, 5. In like manner the third person fem. is used by preference when something indefinite takes the place of the subject; e. g. כֹּל אֲשֶׁר הָיְתָה לְמֶלֶךְ מִצְרָיִם *all that belonged to the King of Egypt* 2 Kings 24, 7; וְלֹא עָלְתָה עַל לִבִּי *neither came it into my mind* Jer. 19, 5.

3) The impersonal form on the other hand is not unfrequently used where the third person is meant; e. g.

וַיֵּצֶר לוֹ (lit. *strait was to him*) *and he was afraid* Gen. 32, 8; וְרָפָא לוֹ (lit. *lest there be healing for them* i. e. *the people*) *lest they be healed* Jes. 6, 10. In this case also the fem. form is sometimes used; e. g. וַתֵּצֶר לְדָוִד (lit. *and strait was to David*) *and David was afraid* 1 Sam. 30, 6.

4) The indefinite *one*, *they* are expressed:

(*a*) by the 3rd person sing. masc.; e. g. קָרָא שְׁמָהּ *they called her name* Gen. 11, 9; יִשָּׂא אֶת חֵיל דַּמֶּשֶׂק *they shall carry away the riches of Samaria* Jes. 8, 4.

(*b*) by the 3rd person plur. masc.; e. g. וַיִּקְרְאוּ שְׁמוֹ *and they called his name* Gen. 25, 25; וַיַּשְׁקוּ *they watered the flock* Gen. 29, 2; וַיְרִיצֻהוּ *and they brought him hastily out of the dungeon* Gen. 41, 14; יְבַקְשׁוּ *let there be sought* 1 Kings 1, 2.

(*c*) by the passive; e. g. אָז הוּחַל *then began men to call* Gen. 4, 26.

(*d*) by the 2nd person; e. g. בֹּאֲכָה *as one goeth* Gen. 10, 19. 30; תִּשָּׂרְפֶנּוּ *it shall be burned* Lev. 13, 55. 57 conf. v. 52 (perhaps also בְּעֶרְכְּךָ *according to ones estimation* Lev. 27, 2.)

(*e*) by אִישׁ; e. g. יְחַיֶּה אִישׁ *one shall nourish a young cow* Jes. 7, 21; but rarely by הָאִישׁ; e. g. כֹּה אָמַר הָאִישׁ *thus they said* 1 Sam. 9, 9.

(*f*) by repeating the verb in the form of a participle; e. g. כִּי יִפֹּל הַנֹּפֵל *if a man fall from thence* Deut. 22, 8 (seldom however in the plur.; e.g. נָטְעוּ נֹטְעִים *they shall plant* Jer. 31, 5), or by adding a noun derived from a word which forms an integral part of the sentence; e. g. אַל יִתְהַלֵּל חָכָם בְּחָכְמָתוֹ *let no one glory in his wisdom* Jer. 9, 22.

Rem. 1 On the contrary, in certain cases, the 3rd person plur. is to be translated as passive; e. g. מִנּוּ לִי *and wearisome nights are appointed to me*; viz. *by God*, Job 7, 3; יִסָּחוּ מִמֶּנָּה *they shall be rooted out of it* Pr. 2, 22. (conf. וְהוֹדְעוּן *that the interpretation may be made known to the king* Dan. 2, 30; הַנְפָּקוּ *that were taken out of the temple* Dan. 5, 3).

5) When the subject is to be emphasised, it is placed separately as a personal pronoun before its predicate; e. g. אֲנִי הֶעֱשַׁרְתִּי *I, I have made Abram rich* Gen. 14, 23; conf. Gen. 9, 7; 15, 15; Deut. 3, 24; Judg. 15, 18; 1 Kings 21, 7; Ps. 2, 6; 139, 2; occasionally also after the predicate; e. g. פֶּן תִּפְגְּעוּן בִּי אַתֶּם *that ye will not kill me yourselves* Judg. 15, 12. In later Hebrew it is found after the verb without adding any emphasis; e. g. וְדִבַּרְתִּי אֲנִי *I said within my heart* Eccles. 1, 16; Conf. 2, 11 ff.; וְשִׁבַּחְתִּי אֲנִי *and I commended mirth* Eccl. 8, 15.

Rem. 2 In the writings of the poets and prophets we sometimes find a sudden transition from one person into another; e. g. וַיִּשְׁמַן יְשֻׁרוּן ...... שָׁמַנְתָּ *Jeshurun waxed fat ..... yea, thou art waxen fat* Deut. 32, 15; conf. Deut. 32, 17; Jes. 1, 29; 5, 8; 22, 16; 61, 7; Mal. 2, 15; Job. 16, 7; וַאֲנִי כְּרָקָב אֶבְלֶה = וְהוּא כְּרָקָב יִבְלֶה *though I waste away as a rotten thing* Job 13, 28.

N. B. This transition should not be confounded with that from *the oratio abliqua* into the *oratio recta*; e. g. Gen. 26, 7.

§ 20. Modifications of the verbal idea.

Modifications of the original sense of a verb, (such as

are found in other languages e. g. *ire, inire, exire, redire, transire*), by composition with prepositions and other words, do not exist in Hebrew, but are expressed:

(*a*) by different verbal stems; e. g. הָלַךְ *to go*, בָּא *to go in*; יָצָא *to go out*, שָׁב *to go back* etc.

(*b*) by constructing a verb with different prepositions; e. g. הָלַךְ *to go*; הָלַךְ אַחֲרֵי *to go after, to follow* (German *nachgehen*) קָרָא *to call*; קָרָא לְ *to call to* (*zurufen*); קָרָא אַחֲרֵי *to call after* (*nachrufen*); קָרָא בְ *to call upon to invoke* (*anrufen*); נָפַל *to fall*; נָפַל עַל *to fall upon, to attack* (*anfallen*); נָפַל לִפְנֵי *to fall down before, to prostrate* (*niederfallen*); רָאָה *to see*; רָאָה בְ *to look on, to behold* (*ansehen*) viz. *with pleasure or with revenge*. The further particulars of this rule belong to the sphere of the Lexicon.

(*c*) by connecting the verb with other words; e. g. עָשָׂה כָלָה *to destroy, to consume*; נָתַן בְּיַד *to give up, to deliver up*.

§ 21. Connection of two verbs into one idea.

1) Adverbs in Hebrew are frequently expressed by *verba finita*, which follow the same construction as that of the verbs with a relative meaning (the so called *Auxiliary verbs of mood*, as *I can, I will, I begin*).

2) A verb expressing the main action is connected with the verb serving as adverb:

A. in the form of an infinitive; e. g. וְיָכָלְתָּ עֲמֹד *thou shalt be able to endure* Ex. 18, 23; לֹא נִסְּתָה כַף רַגְלָהּ הַצֵּג *she dared not to set the sole of her foot upon*

§ 21. CONNECTION OF TWO VERBS.

the ground Deut. 28, 56; נִלְאֵיתִי נְשֹׂא *I am weary to bear them* Jes. 1, 14; לֹא אָבוּ בִדְרָכָיו הָלוֹךְ *they would not walk in his ways* Jes. 42, 24; הִסְכַּלְתָּ עָשׂוֹ *thou hast done foolishly* Gen. 31, 28; וַיּוֹסִפוּ עוֹד שְׂנֹא אֹתוֹ *they hated him still more* Gen. 37, 5; אָחֵל תֵּת (lit., *I will begin to put*, etc.) *this day will I for the first time put the dread of thee* etc., Deut. 2, 25; וְהַצְנֵעַ לֶכֶת *to walk humbly* Michah 6, 8.

B. more frequently in the form of an infinitive with לְ; e. g. מִהַרְתָּ לִמְצֹא *thou hast found quickly* Gen. 27, 20; נַחְבֵּאתָ לִבְרֹחַ *thou didst flee secretly* Gen. 31, 27; וַיֹּאֶל לָלֶכֶת *and he assayed to go* 1 Sam. 17, 39; הִקְשִׁיתָ לִשְׁאוֹל *thou hast asked a great thing* 2 Kings 2, 10.

Rem. 1. This construction is nearly always used in prose with the verbs, הֵחֵל, הוֹאִיל *to commence*, הוֹסִיף *to continue*, מִהֵר *to hasten*, הִרְחִיק *to remove*, הֶעֱמִיק *to make deep*, הִפְלִיא *to make wonderful* (even with the infinitive passive לְהֵעָזֵר 2 chr. 26, 15), חָדַל, כִּלָּה *to cease*, תַּם *to be ready, completed*, הֵיטִב *to find good, to approve*, הִרְבָּה *to multiply* (and other similar verbs), אָבָה, חָפֵץ *to will, to desire*, מֵאֵן *to refuse*, בִּקֵּשׁ *to seek*, יָכֹל, יָדַע *to be able*, לָמַד *to learn*, נָתַן, נָטַשׁ *to permit*.

This is moreover the usual construction with nomina which imply a verbal idea; e. g. אֵין לָבוֹא (lit. *there is no entering*) *no one may enter* Esther 4, 2; עָתִיד לַכִּידוֹר *ready to seize upon* Job 15, 24.

Rem. 2. This construction is seldom found reversed, viz. that the infinitive is made to express the adverbial idea; e. g. עָשֹׂה לְהַפְלִיא *who has acted wondrously* Joel 2, 26.

Rem. 3. In poetry however the לְ is, in all these cases, frequently omitted before the infinitive; e. g. אֵין עָרֹךְ *there is nothing to be com-*

pared unto thee Ps. 40, 6. הָעֲתִדִים עֹרֵר *who will* (lit. *are ready*) *rouse up leviathan* Job 3, 8.

C. in the form of a *verbum finitum*, viz.

α in such a manner that both verbs agree as to the *tempus*, *modus*, *genus* and *numerus*, and are connected with ו conjunctive; e. g. וַיָּחֶל נֹחַ וַיִּטַּע *and Noah began to plant* Geg. 9, 20; וַיֹּסֶף אַבְרָהָם וַיִּקַּח *and again Abram took a wife* Gen. 25; וַתְּמַהֵר וַתּוֹרֶד *and she let down quickly* Gen. 24, 18; הוֹאֶל נָא וְלִין *do I pray thee tarry all night* Judg. 19, 6; וְשָׁבָה וְהָיְתָה *it shall be again unto destruction* Jes. 6, 13; חָמַדְתִּי וְיָשַׁבְתִּי (lit. *I desired and I sat down*) *I sat down with pleasure* Cant. 2, 3.

β in such a manner that they agree in every thing except as to the *tempus*; viz. in the following order:

1) first the *actio imperfecta* and then the *actio perfecta*; e. g. וּלְמַעַן יִלְמְדוּ וְיָרְאוּ *that they may learn to fear* Deut. 31, 12; אָשׁוּב וְלָקַחְתִּי *I will take back* Hosea 2, 11; תָּשׁוּב וְנִבְנְתָה *it shall be built again* Dan. 9, 25.

2) first the *actio perfecta* and then the *actio imperfecta*; e. g. וְלוּ הוֹאַלְנוּ וַנֵּשֶׁב *would that we had been content to dwell* Jos. 7, 7; יָדַעְתִּי וְאֶמְצָאֵהוּ *shall I be able to find it* Job. 23, 3; וְשַׁבְתִּי אֲנִי וָאֶרְאֶה *and again I saw* Eccl. 4, 1. 7.

γ in such a manner that they agree in all things except as to the *modus*; e. g. תָּשׁוּבוּ וּבֹאוּ נָא *return ye again, I pray* Job. 17, 10.

δ in such a manner that they agree in all points, but are not connected by ו conjunctive (*asyndeton*); e. g. הָחֵל רָשׁ *commence to possess it* Deut. 2, 24; הֶרֶב

§ 21. CONNECTION OF TWO VERBS. 55

כַּבְּסֵנִי הֶרֶב wash me still more Ps. 51, 4; הוֹאִילוּ פְנוּ be pleased to look upon me Job 6, 28; אָשׁוּבָה אֶרְעֶה I will again feed thy flock Gen. 30, 31; אַל תַּרְבּוּ תְדַבְּרוּ talk no more 1 Sam. 2, 3; קִרְאוּ מַלְאוּ cry ye aloud Jer. 4, 5; הַשְׁפִּילוּ שֵׁבוּ sit ye down low Jer. 13, 18; הֶעְמִיקוּ שִׁחֵתוּ they have deeply corrupted themselves Hos. 9, 9; מִהֲרוּ שָׁכְחוּ they soon forgot Ps. 106, 13; פִּזַּר נָתַן he giveth liberally Ps. 112, 9.

Rem. 4 The construction *with* ו conjunctive is the usual one in prose, and that *without* ו conjunctive the usual one in poetry. The latter however, is now and then also found in prose; e. g. הוֹאִיל מֹשֶׁה בֵּאֵר *and Moses began to declare* Deut. 1, 5; תַּמּוּ נִכְרָתוּ *they were wholly cut off* Jos. 3, 16; הֶחֱרָה הֶחֱזִיק *he earnestly repaired* Neh. 3, 20; נִפְרְצָה נִשְׁלְחָה *let us send abroad every where unto our brethren* 1 Chr. 13, 2.

Rem. 5 Also in the construction without ו conjunctive it may happen that both verbs differ as to the *tempus*; e. g. וְשִׁלַּשְׁתָּ תֵּרֵד *and on the third day thou shalt go down* 1 Sam. 20, 19; לֹא יָדַעְתִּי אֲכַנֶּה *I cannot give titles* Job. 32, 22. In this case the first verb is sometimes expressed by a participle; e. g. מַשְׁכִּימֵי בַבֹּקֶר שֵׁכָר יִרְדֹּפוּ *who early in the morning seek for strong drink* Jes. 5, 11; חָפֵץ ...... יַגְדִּיל *it pleased him to magnify* Jes 42, 21.

Rem. 6 It is a bold and unusual construction when the two verbs differ in *person* and *number*; e. g. אוּלַי אוּכַל נַכֶּה בּוֹ *we shall perhaps be able to smite them* (lit. *I shall perhaps prevail that we may smite them*) Num. 22, 6; לֹא תוֹסִיפִי יִקְרְאוּ לָךְ *thou shalt no more be called* (lit. *thou shalt not continue that they call thee*) Jes. 47, 1. [1])

---

[1]) This place in Jes. may, however, be also explained according to § 19, 4 rem. 1.

D. in the form of a participle or of a verbal adjective; e. g. הֵחֵלּוּ כֵהוֹת *had begun to wax dim* 1 Sam. 3, 2; יוֹדֵעַ מְנַגֵּן *who is able to play* (as regards the participle יוֹדֵעַ conf. Rem. 5) 1 Sam. 16, 16; כַּהֲתִימְךָ שׁוֹדֵד *when thou shalt have ceased to spoil* Jes. 33, 1 ¹).

3) The verb expressing the main action is not unfrequently entirely omitted, so that it must be supplied from the context; e. g. מַהֲרִי וּקְחִי = מַהֲרִי (*take*) *quickly* Gen. 18, 6; וַיֶּחֶרְדוּ לִרְאוֹת = וַיֶּחֶרְדוּ *and they regarded one another trembling* Gen. 42, 28; וַיִּתְמְהוּ לִרְאוֹת = וַיִּתְמְהוּ *and they regarded one another with astonishment* Gen. 43, 33 (Conf. Jes. 13, 8); יִדְרְשׁוּ לִשְׁאוֹל = יִדְרְשׁוּ *they shall anxiously inquire* Jes. 11, 10 (Conf. 8, 19); פָּסַח וַיִשְׁלָחֵם = פָּסַח *that sent not its prisoners home in freedom* Jes. 14, 17; הַחֲרִישׁוּ = הַחֲרִישׁוּ וָבֹאוּ *come hear me in silence* Jes. 41, 1; הַחֲרִישׁוּ וּצְאוּ מִמֶּנִּי = מִמֶּנִּי *depart from me in silence* Job 13, 13; עֲנִיתָנִי וְהִצַּלְתַּנִי = עֲנִיתָנִי *and from the horns of the wild-oxen deliver me in answer to my prayer* Ps. 22, 22. ²)

Hence one always says מִלֵּא לָלֶכֶת אַחֲרֵי = מִלֵּא אַחֲרֵי *to follow sincerely*.

---

1) שׁוֹדֵד may be also considered as an infinitive, and would then belong to the examples of A.

2) It is not necessary, however, to reckon as belonging to this rule such places as Ps. 74, 7; and 89, 40, where חִלֵּל may be the פִּעֵל of a denominativum of חָלָל *slain*, with the signification *to cast down*, *to destroy*.

CHAPTER V — THE NOMINAL FORMS.

§ 22. The Infinitive.

1) The use of the infinitive in Hebrew is exceedingly frequent, and since it is a verbal substantive it belongs as well to nouns as to verbs, forming a transition from the one to the other, and following the construction of both.

2) One consequence of this is that it follows the construction of the noun and at the same time governs an object, as if it were a *verbum finitum*; e. g. בְּלִדְתָּהּ אֹתָם *when she bare them* (lit. *in baring them*) Gen. 25, 26; בְּפִגְעוֹ בוֹ *when he met him* (lit. *in his meeting him*) Num. 35, 19; מָלְאָה הָאָרֶץ דֵּעָה אֶת ה' *the earth is full of the knowledge of the Lord* (lit. *of knowing the Lord*) Jes. 11, 9; לֹא נִסְּתָה כַף־רַגְלָהּ הַצֵּג עַל הָאָרֶץ *who would not venture to set the sole of her foot upon the earth* Deut. 28, 56; בְּחֶמְלַת ה' עָלָיו *the Lord being merciful unto them* Gen. 19, 16; בְּשִׂנְאַת ה' אֹתָנוּ *because the Lord hated us* Deut. 1, 27; וּבְיוֹם הָקִים אֶת הַמִּשְׁכָּן *and on the day that the tabernacle was reared up* Numb. 9, 15; הֲלוֹא הִיא הַדַּעַת אֹתִי *was not this knowing me?* Jer. 22, 16.

3) The infinitive occurs also as a pure substantive, without governing an object, taking the place of a *nomen regens* or *nomen rectum*, of the subject, object, or attribute, or is connected with pronominal suffixes or prepositions; in a word, it is entirely constructed as if it were a noun without the grammatical cha-

racter of a verb; e. g. לֹא טוֹב הֱיוֹת הָאָדָם לְבַדּוֹ *it is not good that man should be alone* Gen. 2, 18; עֵת הֵאָסֵף הַמִּקְנֶה *the time that the cattle should be gathered together* Gen. 29, 7; וְאֵין מַיִם לִשְׁתּוֹת הָעָם *there was no water for the people to drink* Ex. 17, 1; גַּם עֲנוֹשׁ לַצַּדִּיק לֹא טוֹב *also to punish the righteous is not good* Prov. 17, 26; עַל אָמְרֵךְ *because thou sayest* Jer. 2, 35; וַתִּכְהֶיןָ עֵינָיו מֵרְאוֹת *and his eyes were dim so that he could not see* Gen. 27, 1.

4) Further, the infinitive is frequently used as object of a *verbum finitum* or *participium* of the same stem, and is then placed either before or after it. Thus it generally serves to modify or emphasise the action (conf. § 28, 6), or to express a repetition or continuation; e. g. הֲמָלֹךְ תִּמְלֹךְ עָלֵינוּ *wouldst thou perhaps reign over us* Gen. 37, 8; הָלֹךְ הָלַכְתָּ כִּי נִכְסֹף נִכְסַפְתָּה *and now thou art gone away because thou sore longedst* Gen. 31, 30; הָעֵד הֵעִד בָּנוּ הָאִישׁ *the man has expressely warned us* Gen. 43, 3; הוֹרֵישׁ לֹא הוֹרִישׁוֹ *but he could not wholly drive them out* Judg. 1, 28 שִׁמְעוּ שָׁמוֹעַ וְאַל תָּבִינוּ וּרְאוּ רָאוֹ וְאַל תֵּדָעוּ *ye hear continually but ye understand not, ye see continually but ye perceive not* Jes. 6, 9; אֹמְרִים אָמוֹר לִמְנַאֲצַי *they say continually unto them that hate me* Jer. 23, 17.

When the infinitive stands after the *verbum finitum*, which frequently occurs with הָלוֹךְ, then another infinitive or participle, or even finite verb, of a different stem is frequently added; e. g. וַיֵּצֵא יָצוֹא וָשׁוֹב *and it went to and fro* Gen. 8, 7; וְנָגַף נָגֹף וְרָפוֹא *he shall smite and shall again heal* Jes. 19, 22; וַיֵּלֶךְ הָלוֹךְ וְגָדֵל *and*

§ 22. THE INFINITIVE.

he waxed continually greater Gen. 26, 13; יָצֹא וְגָדֵל יָצוֹא וּמָקֵל
and as he came out he cursed 2 Sam. 16, 5; הָלוֹךְ הֹלְכִים
וְתָקְעוּ *blowing with the trumpets as they went on* Jos. 6, 13.

Rem. 1 The infinitive, when it is connected in this manner with a *verbum finitum*, need not agree with it as to the conjugation (בִּנְיָן); e. g. טָרֹף טֹרַף יוֹסֵף *Joseph is without doubt torn into pieces* Gen. 37, 33; טָרֹף יִטָּרֵף *if it be indeed torn into pieces* Ex. 22, 12; וְהָפְדֵּה לֹא נִפְדָּתָה *and not at all redeemed* Lev. 19, 20; עֶרְיָה תֵעוֹר קַשְׁתֶּךָ *thy bow was made quite bare* Hab. 3, 9.

Rem. 2 In negative sentences the negation is placed between the infinitive and the finite verb; e. g. וְהָפְדֵּה לֹא נִפְדָּתָה Lev. 19, 20; וְהוֹרֵישׁ לֹא הוֹרִישׁוֹ Judg. 1, 28; 15, 13; 1 Kings 3, 27; but it very seldom precedes; e. g. לֹא מוֹת תְּמֻתוּן *ye shall not surely die* Gen. 3, 4; Ps. 49, 8; Amos 9, 8.

Rem. 3 We shall see later on (§ 32, 5) that, like the infinitive, nouns also are commonly connected as objects with a *verbum finitum* and that a noun sometimes takes the place of an infinitive; e. g. לֹא יוּכְלוּ נָקוֹן *shall they not be capable of escaping punishment* Hosea 8, 5.

5) On the other hand, the infinitive is not unfrequently used instead of a *verbum finitum*, both with or without a preceding *verbum finitum*.

A. after a preceding *verbum finitum*:

α after the עָבַר; e. g. הֲנִגְלֹה נִגְלֵיתִי .... וּבָחוֹר אֹתוֹ *did I reveal myself .... and choose him?* 1 Sam. 2, 28; נִכְתָּב וְנֶחְתָּם בְּטַבַּעַת הַמֶּלֶךְ וְנָשְׁלוֹחַ סְפָרִים *it was written, and it was sealed with the king's ring; and letters were sent* Esther 3, 13.

β after עָבַר with ו conversive; e. g. וְהָמֵר .... וְסָפְדוּ עָלָיו

עָלָיו *and they shall mourn for him, and bitterly weep for him* Zech. 12, 10.

γ after the עָתִיד; e. g. וְכִי תִמְכְּרוּ מִמְכָּר ..... אוֹ קָנֹה *if thou sell aught ..... or buy* Lev. 25, 14; מוֹת יוּמַת הָאִישׁ ..... רָגֹם אֹתוֹ *the man shall be surely put to death, all the congregation shall stone him.* Num. 15, 35.

δ after עָתִיד with ו conversive; e. g. וְנָתוֹן ..... וַיַּרְכֵּב אֹתוֹ אֹתוֹ *and he made him to ride ..... and he set him* Gen. 41, 43.

Rem. 4 Sometimes even after a participle; e. g. נִכְתָּב בְּשֵׁם הַמֶּלֶךְ וְנַחְתּוֹם *written in the king's name and sealed* Esther 8, 8.

B. without a preceding *verbum finitum*, and consequently, in the beginning of the sentence:

α instead of the עָבַר (more or less like the Latin *Infinitivus Historicus*); e. g. אָלֹה וְכַחֵשׁ וְרָצֹחַ וְגָנֹב וְנָאֹף *they swear, they lie, they kill, they steal, they commit adultery* Hos. 4, 2.

β instead of the עָתִיד; e. g. אָכוֹל וְהוֹתֵר *they shall eat and leave thereof* 2 Kings 4, 43.

γ frequently instead of the imperative; e. g. זָכוֹר אֶת הַיּוֹם הַזֶּה *remember this day* Ex. 13, 3; שָׁמוֹר אֶת יוֹם הַשַּׁבָּת *observe the sabbath day* Deut. 5, 12.

In all these instances the intention appears to be to add emphasis and force to the idea.

Rem. 5 When the infinitive takes the place of a *verbum finitum*, the subject may be added to it; e. g. הִמּוֹל לָכֶם כָּל זָכָר *every male among you shall be circumcised* Gen. 17, 10; הַקְרֵב אַתָּה בְּנֵי אַהֲרֹן *the sons* *of Aaron shall offer it* Lev. 6, 7; רָגֹם אֹתוֹ בָאֲבָנִים כָּל הָעֵדָה *all the congregation shall stone him with stones* Num. 15, 35; פָּגוֹשׁ דֹּב שַׁכּוּל בְּאִישׁ *let a bear robbed of her whelps meet a man* Prov. 17, 12.

§ 23. Use of the Participle.

1) Since the participle is a verbal adjective it is partly used as an adjective, partly as a verb, and follows the construction of both.

2) As for its signification, it may express as well the past and future, as an action which takes place the moment the writer speaks; e. g. אֲשֶׁר הָאֱלֹהִים עֹשֶׂה *what God will do* Gen. 41, 25; מֵת *dead*; נוֹלָד *born*; לְעַם נוֹלָד *to a people that shall be born* Ps. 22, 32; וְעַם נִבְרָא *a people which shall be created* Ps. 102, 19; אֲדֹנִי דֹּבֵר *my Lord speaketh* Num. 32, 27; אֲשֶׁר אַתֶּם גָּרִים שָׁם *the land wherein ye (now) sojourn* Jer. 35, 7. In like manner it generally signifies the present.

The בִּינוֹנִי פָּעוּל (part. passivum) of קַל however has almost exclusively the meaning of something past.

Rem. 1. The בֵּינוֹנִי פָּעוּל sometimes expresses an enduring quality, while the בֵּינוֹנִי פּוֹעֵל only denotes a momentary condition; e. c. בָּטוּחַ *confident (always)* בּוֹטֵחַ *to have confidence (under certain circumstances)*; שָׁכוּן *(permaneut) inhabitant* שׁוֹכֵן *a sojourner*; אֲחֻזֵי חֶרֶב *who are able to handle the sword* Cant. 3, 8 אֹחֲזֵי חֶרֶב would mean: *who have girded on the sword*. (conf. § 4, 2).

3) When the participle takes the place of a *verbum finitum*, with or without הָיָה, it has in most cases the signification of the present; e. g. כִּי יָרֵא אָנֹכִי אֹתוֹ

for I fear him Gen. 32, 12; אֲשֶׁר אַתָּה עֹשֶׂה *which thou doest* Ex. 18, 17; וְעַתָּה הִנֵּה יָבֵשׁ וְהָיָה נִקֻּדִים *and now behold it is dry and is become mouldy* Jos. 9, 12.

Not unfrequently however it stands instead of the future; e. g. כִּי לְיָמִים עוֹד שִׁבְעָה אָנֹכִי מַמְטִיר *for yet seven days and I will cause it to rain* Gen. 7, 4; יוֹרֵשׁ אֹתִי *will inherit from me* Gen. 15, 3 (conf. יִירָשְׁךָ v. 4); דָּן אָנֹכִי *I shall judge* Gen. 15, 14. Often also it occurs instead of the imperfect; e. g. וְהוּא יֹשֵׁב *as he sat* Gen. 18, 1; וּמֹשֶׁה הָיָה רֹעֶה *and Moses pastured the flock* Ex. 3, 1; or of the perfect; e. g. עֵינֵיכֶם הָרֹאֹת *your eyes have seen* Deut. 4, 3.

Rem. 2 When the participle has the signification of a verbum finitum whether in the present, perfect, or future, it is frequently preceded by הִנֵּה; e. g. הִנֵּה עֵשָׂו אָחִיךָ מִתְנַחֵם לְךָ לְהָרְגֶךָ *behold thy brother Esau thinks to kill thee* Gen. 27, 42; וְהִנֵּה עֹמֵד עַל הַיְאֹר *that he stood by the river* Gen. 41, 1; הִנְנִי מֵבִיא אֶת הַמַּבּוּל *and I will bring the flood of waters* Gen. 6, 17.

4) Sometimes a sentence commences with a participle having the signification of a *verbum finitum*, and is continued by a *verbum finitum* in עָבַר or עָתִיד with or without ו conversive or ו conjunctive.

(*a*) with a verbum in עָבַר; e. g. אֱלֹהִים מוֹשִׁיב יְחִידִים בַּיְתָה.... אַךְ סוֹרְרִים שָׁכְנוּ צְחִיחָה *God maketh the desolate to return home.... but the rebellious to dwell in a parched land* Ps. 68, 7.

(*b*) with a verb in עָבַר with ו conversive; e. g. אָנֹכִי מֵת וְהָיָה אֱלֹהִים *I am dying, but God shall be with you* Gen. 48, 21.

§ 23. USE OF THE PARTICIPLE, 63

(c) with a verb in עָבַר with ו conjunctive; e. g. שׁוֹפֵךְ בּוּז עַל נְדִיבִים וּמְזִיחַ אֲפִיקִים רִפָּה *he poureth contempt upon the princes and looseth the belt of the strong* Job. 12, 21.

(d) with a verb in עָתִיד; e. g. הַשָּׂם גְּבוּלֵךְ שָׁלוֹם חֵלֶב חִטִּים יַשְׂבִּיעֵךְ *he maketh thy border peace, he filleth thee with the fat of wheat* Ps. 147, 14 conf. v. 15.

(e) with a verb in עָתִיד with ו conversive; e. g. מִי אֵפוֹא הוּא הַצָּד צַיִד וַיָּבֵא לִי *who then is he that hath caught venison, and brought it to me* Gen. 27, 33.

(f) with a verb in עָתִיד with ו conjunctive; מוֹלִיךְ יוֹעֲצִים שׁוֹלָל וְשֹׁפְטִים יְהוֹלֵל *he leadeth counsellors away as spoil, and judges he maketh fools* Job. 12, 17 conf. vv. 19 ff.

Rem. 3. When the subject has not been named before, a personal pronoun is added to the participle as subject. Sometimes, however, this pronoun is omitted, and must be supplied from the context; e. g. with the 1st pers. כִּי פֹעַל פֹּעֵל בִּימֵיכֶם (supply אָנֹכִי from v. 6) *for I work a work in your days* Hab. 1, 5; with the 2d pers. וְחוֹטֵא נַפְשֶׁךָ *and thou hast sinned against thy soul* Hab. 2, 10; with the 3d pers. וְהִנֵּה עֹמֵד עַל הַגְּמַלִּים *and behold he stood by the camels.* Gen. 24, 30. Conf. Gen. 32, 7; 37, 15; 38, 24; 39, 22 (plur.); Jes. 26, 3; 33, 5.

5) A participle of the same stem as the verb to which it belongs is not unfrequently used to express the indefinite idea: *one, somebody*, e. g. וְכִי יָמוּת מֵת *if anyone die* Num. 6, 9; כִּי יִפֹּל הַנֹּפֵל *if anyone fall* Deut. 22, 8; וְשָׁמַע הַשֹּׁמֵעַ *whosoever heareth it* 2 Sam. 17, 9; לֹא יִדְרֹךְ הַדֹּרֵךְ *no one shall tread* Jes. 16, 10; יִרְאֶה הָרֹאֶה *anyone who seeth it* Jes. 28, 4; יַחֲרֹשׁ הַחֹרֵשׁ *doth anyone plough*

Jes. 28, 24; לֹא יָנוּס לָהֶם נָס וְלֹא יִמָּלֵט לָהֶם פָּלִיט *there shall not one of them flee away, there shall not one of them escape* Amos 9, 1.

6) As regards its construction also, the twofold character of the participle should be borne in mind. When used as an adjective it follows the rules of the adjectives (conf. § 4; gramm. §§ 66, 68, 69.), while with a verbal meaning it follows the construction of the verb, taking the verbal suffixes and not the nominal; e. g. חָפֵץ רֶשַׁע *who hath pleasure in wickedness* Ps. 5, 5; הָרֹדִים בָּעָם *who ruled over the people* 1 Kings 9, 23; יוֹרֵשׁ אֹתִי *shall inherit from me* Gen. 15, 3; עֹשֵׂנִי *who has created me* Job. 31, 15.

Rem. 4 A combination of both constructions is found in the expression מְשָׁרְתַי אֹתִי *who minister unto me* Jer. 33, 22.

Rem. 5 Owing to the st. constr. a somewhat free construction is often employed with the participle; e. g. שָׁבֵי פֶשַׁע *who turn (from) transgression* Jes. 59, 20; יוֹרְדֵי בוֹר *who go down (into) the abyss* Jes. 38, 18; שֹׁכְבֵי קֶבֶר *who lie in the grave* Ps. 88, 6. (conf. § 5, 4). The same construction is obtained by means of the nominal suffixes; the expressions קָמַי and קָמָיו, for instance, have the same meaning as קָמִים עָלַי and קָמִים עָלָיו *who stand up against me* or *against him*.

PART III.

THE PARTICLES.

CHAPTER VI. — ADVERBS AND ADVERBIAL EXPRESSIONS.

§ 24 Adverbs.

1) The adverbs not only serve to determine verbs, verbal expressions, and adjectives, but they occur also as the determination of a noun. (Compare ἡ χθὲς ἡμέρα). As such they stand:

(a) as opposition after the noun; e. g. תְּבוּנָה הַרְבֵּה מְאֹד *very much understanding* 1 Kings 5, 9; אֲנָשִׁים מְעַט *a few men* Neh. 2, 12.

(b) connected in st. constr. with the noun; e. g. דְּמֵי חִנָּם *innocent blood,* (*blood shed without cause*) 1 King 2, 31; עֵד חִנָּם *a false witness,* (*a witness without cause*) Prov. 24; 28; עֹלַת תָּמִיד *a continual burnt offering* Num. 28, 6; אֱלֹהֵי מִקָּרוֹב and אֱלֹהֵי מֵרָחוֹק *a God at hand, a God afar off* Jer. 23, 23.

Rem. 1 The adverb is in this case entirely considered as a noun, which is also evident from the fact that prepositions are prefixed to it; e. g. וְכֵן = וּבְכֵן *and thus* Esther 4, 16; אֱל־חִנָּם *in vain* Ez. 6, 10.

2) The repetition of an adverb expresses the enduring increase or the intensity of the determination; e. g. מַטָּה מַטָּה *lower and lower* Deut. 28, 43; מְעַט מְעַט *by little and little* Ex. 23, 30; מְאֹד מְאֹד *much* מְאֹד *very much* Gen. 7, 19.

3) Several of the particles do not exactly refer to the nearest following word, but to the nearest following sentence, sometimes even to the main sentence which follows after the subordinate sentence containing the particle; e. g. with אָז; אָז תִּקְרָא וַה' יַעֲנֶה *then the Eternal, when thou callest, will hear thee* Jes. 58, 9; אָז יִקְרָאֻנְנִי וְלֹא אֶעֱנֶה *then will I not answer when they call on me* Prov. 1, 28.

with גַּם; גַּם לְכֻלְּכֶם יִתֵּן בֶּן־יִשַׁי שָׂדוֹת וּכְרָמִים *the son of Jesse will certainly also give every one of you fields and vineyards* 1 Sam. 22, 7; גַּם ..... שִׁלַּחְתִּי אֲסִירַיִךְ מִבּוֹר *I also release thine prisoners out of the pit* Zech. 9, 11.

with רַק; רַק ..... אֵלָיו לֹא יַגִּיעוּ *him alone they shall not touch* Ps. 32, 6; רַק בְּזָדוֹן יִתֵּן מַצָּה *by insolence one produceth only contention.* Prov. 13, 10.

with interrogative particles See § 26, 8.

The same thing occurs with certain conjunctions; e. g. Deut. 8, 12, where פֶּן refers to v. 14; (Conf. Rashi on Ex. 23, 5) and with particles of negation, as לֹא e. g. Deut. 22, 1.

Rem. 2. Concerning the manner of expressing adverbial ideas by means of verbs, see § 21.

§ 25. Words expressing negation.

1) The principal adverbs of negation are:

לֹא (as noun in כְּתִיב Job 6, 21) *not;*

אַל (as noun Job 24, 25) *not so;*

אֵין (opposite of יֵשׁ) *it is not;*

טֶרֶם *not yet;*

§ 25. WORDS EXPRESSING NEGATION. 67

אֶ֫פֶס *no more*, (אַפְסִי) with the prolonged ending ־ִי is only found in the expression אֲנִי וְאַפְסִי עוֹד *I am, and there is none else beside me* Jes. 47, 8. 10; Zeph. 2, 15).

Almost exclusively poetic are בַּל, בְּלִי, בִּלְתִּי *not*.

Rem. 1. אַל is also used as a negative conjunction = פֶּן, לְבִלְתִּי, *that not, lest*. (Conf. § 28, 5 E γ) e. g. אַל יִמְשְׁלוּ בִי *lest they should have dominion over me* Ps. 19, 14.

2) Regarding the use of these adverbs the following points should be remarked.

A. as to לֹא.

α לֹא serves principally as an *objective* and *unconditional* negation, and hence it is usually connected with עָבַר or עָתִיד in the indicative. As to the עָתִיד with לֹא to express a prohibition see § 15, 4.

Rem. 2 לֹא seldom occurs in a nominal sentence instead of אֵין; e. g. וְלֹא שֵׁבֶט אֱלוֹהַּ עֲלֵיהֶם *and no rod of God is upon them* Job. 21, 9.

β לֹא connected with כָּל, when the latter is not followed by ה' הידיעה or by another determination (hence, used in a general and indefinite sense, § 3, 10, Rem. 3), means: *none, none at all (nullus, ne-personne, ne-rien)*; e. g. כָּל מְלָאכָה לֹא יֵעָשֶׂה *no work shall be done* Ex. 12, 16; כָּל דְּבָרָיו לֹא יַעֲנֶה *to none of his words he will answer* Job 33, 13; (or, as is more usual לֹא followed by כָּל) וְלֹא נוֹתַר כָּל יֶ֫רֶק *and no green thing was left* Ex. 10, 15; לֹא יְאֻנֶּה לַצַּדִּיק כָּל אָ֫וֶן *no mischief shall happen to the righteous* Prov. 12, 21; וְלֹא יָשׁוּב מִפְּנֵי כֹל *and turneth not away for any* Prov. 30, 30; כִּי לֹא יוּכַל כָּל אֱלוֹהַּ כָּל גּוֹי וּמַמְלָכָה

for no God of any nation or kingdom was able 2 Chr. 32, 15.

If however בָּל is determined, it has, when connected with לֹא, a different signification; e. g. וְכָלוֹ לֹא תִרְאֶה *but thou shalt not see the whole of it* Num. 23, 13.

Rem. 3. In like manner אֵין with בָּל; e. g. וְכָל רוּחַ אֵין בְּקִרְבּוֹ *and there is no breath at all in the midst of it* Hab. 2, 19; אֵין כָּל חָדָשׁ *there is nothing new* Ecc. 1, 9. On the same principle אִישׁ = ... לֹא *no one, nobody*; e. g. אִישׁ מִמֶּנּוּ .... לֹא יִכְלֶה *no one of us shall withhold* Gen. 23, 6.

γ לֹא is also used absolutely as a negative answer: *nay, no*; e. g. וַיֹּאמְרוּ לֹא *they said: no* Gen. 19, 2; לֹא אֲדֹנִי *nay, my lord* Gen. 42, 10; לֹא אַךְ הוּא יָשֶׂם בִּי *nay; he would only give heed unto me* Job 23, 6 (conf. § 26, 9).

δ לֹא is sometimes connected with a noun or adjective, with which it forms a sort of *compound*; e. g. לֹא־אֵל *a no-god*; לֹא־דָבָר *a nothing*; לֹא חָסִיד *an impious* Deut. 32, 21; Amos 6, 13; Ps. 43, 1.

Rem. 4. Concerning the place of לֹא in the sentence conf. § 40, 1 and Rem. 1.

B. As to אַל.

α אַל denotes a *subjective* and *conditional* negation and is, by preference, construed with the *jussive*; e. g. אַל יָבֹא *may he not come*, or, *let him not come*, (conf. § 17, 3 *b*).

β אַל (like לֹא see A *γ*) is sometimes used also in an

§ 25. WORDS EXPRESSING NEGATION. 69

absolute sense = *nay, not so* (conf. μή = μὴ γένηται) e. g, אַל־בְּנֹתַי *nay, my daughters,* Ruth 1, 33; אַל־נָא *not so* Gen. 19, 18; 33, 10 (Conf. § 26, 9).

Rem. 5. Places such as Joel 2, 13 וְקִרְעוּ לְבַבְכֶם וְאַל בִּגְדֵיכֶם *rend your hearts and not your garments;* Am. 5, 14 דִּרְשׁוּ טוֹב וְאַל רָע *seek good, and not evil,* should not be considered as belonging to rule β, for the verbs תִּקְרָעוּ and תִּדְרְשׁוּ are to be supplied after אַל. Similarly, 2 Sam. 1, 21 אַל טַל וְאַל מָטָר *let there be no dew, nor rain;* Jes. 62, 6; Ps. 83, 2 אַל דֳּמִי *let there be no silence* (or *rest*), do not belong to it, because אַל is elliptical for אַל יְהִי טַל, אַל יְהִי דֳמִי.

Rem. 6. Concerning the interrogative use of אַל, see § 26, Rem. 9.

C. As to אֵין.

α אֵין (st. constr. of אַיִן) is the negation of יֵשׁ, and implies the verb *to be* as to all its tenses; e. g. אֵין יוֹסֵף בַּבּוֹר *Joseph was not in the pit* Gen. 37, 29; אֵין ה' בְּקִרְבְּכֶם *the Eternal is not amongst you* Num. 14, 42. Hence the positive formulas with יֵשׁ are negatively expressed by אֵין; e. g. יֶשׁ לְאֵל יָדִי *I have it in my power* Gen. 31, 29; אֵין לְאֵל יָדֵנוּ *we have it not in our power* Neh. 5, 5.

β A further consequence of this is:

1. that a personal pronoun, which is subject of a sentence with אֵין, is joined to it as a suffix, as אֵינֶנִּי *I am not, I was not I shall not be;* אֵינֶנּוּ, אֵינָם etc.
2. that the verb, which is predicate of a sentence with אֵין always takes the form of a participle (because in אֵין the verb *to be* is already implied); e. g, אֵינֶנִּי נֹתֵן *I will not give* Ex. 5, 10; תֶּבֶן אֵין נִתָּן *no*

straw is given Ex. 5, 16; אֵינְךָ מְשַׁלֵּחַ *if thou wilt not let my people go* Ex. 8, 17; אֵינְכֶם מַאֲמִינִים *ye did not believe* Deut. 1, 32.

Rem. 7. Once, Jer. 38, 5, אֵין is found constructed with a *verbum finitum:* כִּי אֵין הַמֶּלֶךְ יוּכַל אֶתְכֶם דָּבָר *for the king cannot do any thing against you.*

γ Just as יֵשׁ signifies: *to exist, to be present, to be at hand*, so אֵין expresses the contrary; e. g. וְאֵינֶנּוּ *and he was no more* Gen. 5, 24; וְהָאֶחָד אֵינֶנּוּ *and one is not* Gen. 42, 13; וְאֵינָם *and they are not* Jer. 10, 20.

Rem. 8. אֵין is sometimes separated from the word to which it belongs by another word; e. g. from its participle אֵין בְּפִיהוּ נְכוֹנָה *there is no sincerity in his mouth* Ps. 5, 10; or from its noun (especially by the smaller words such as לוֹ, גַם or by a determination of place), אֵין לָהּ וָלָד *she had no child* Gen. 11, 30; אֵין לוֹ סְנַפִּיר *that have no fins* Lev. 11, 10. 12; אֵין בּוֹ מְתֹם *there is no soundness in it* Jes. 1, 6; אֵין גַּם אֶחָד *there is not one* Ps. 14, 3; אֵין בַּמָּוֶת זִכְרֶךָ *in death there is no remembrance of thee* Ps. 6, 6; וְאֵין בְּרוּחוֹ רְמִיָּה *and in whose spirit there is no guile* Ps. 32; 2. The same sometimes occurs with אַל; e. g. אַל בְּאַפְּךָ תוֹכִיחֵנִי *rebuke me not in thine anger* Ps. 6, 2.

It should be noticed also that the usual order of אֵין and its noun or participle is sometimes reversed; e. g. אֲשֶׁר מַיִם אֵין לָהּ *that has no water* Jes. 1, 30; וּפֹתֵר אֵין אֹתוֹ *and there is none to interpret it* Gen. 40, 8.

Rem. 9. In Neh. 4, 17 we find אֵין connected first with אֲנִי, then with other subjects, and finally all these comprised in אֵין אֲנַחְנוּ.

Rem. 10. In Job 35, 15 כִּי אַיִן פָּקַד אַפּוֹ *but now his anger is withheld* אַיִן stands before עָבַר to emphasise the negation. In like manner

§ 25. WORDS EXPRESSING NEGATION.

אַיִן emphasises the negation in אֵין זוּלָתִי Jes. 45, 21 and אֵין בִּלְתִּי Hos. 13, 4 *there is none beside me.*

δ Further אֵין is now and then connected with a noun for the purpose of expressing a negative adjective; e. g. אֵין אֹנִים *powerless* Jes. 40, 29; אֵין עֵינַיִם *blind* Jes. 59, 10; אֵין מִסְפָּר *innumerable* Joel 1, 6; אֵין אֱיָל *powerless* Ps. 88, 5; אֵין חֵקֶר *unsearchable* Prov. 25, 3.

Rem. 11. אִי (an abbreviation of אֵין 1 Sam. 21, 9 = אֵין, אַיִן) is sometimes connected in a similar manner אִי נָקִי *not innocent* Job 22, 30.

D. טֶרֶם *not yet*, (like the adverb אָן) is generally construed with the עָתִיד even when the verb expresses an *actio perfecta*. It is rarely construed with the עָבַר; e. g. טֶרֶם יָדַע *he did not yet know* 1 Sam. 3, 7.

E. The poetic negation בַּל *not*, is almost exclusively connected with a *verbum finitum*. The exceptions where it is found with the infinitive are very rare; e. g. בַּל קְרוֹב אֵלֶיךָ *they come not near unto thee.* Ps. 32, 9.

F. The equally poetic בְּלִי is (like לֹא see A δ) and אֵין C δ) sometimes connected with a noun to express the negation of the latter's idea; e. g. בְּלִי חֹק *beyond measure* Jes 5, 14.

3) The other particles of negation are mostly all exclusively used as conjunctions.

Concerning them the following particulars should be remarked.

(a) לְבִלְתִּי (st. constr. of בֶּלֶת *to disappear, to cease to exist*, from the stem בָּלָה, with the termination ־ִי

see gramm. § 60 D., and the letter preposition לְ is usually construed with the infinitive, to express the negation of an action; e. g. לְבִלְתִּי אֲכָל מִמֶּנּוּ *not to eat of it* Gen. 3, 11; rarely with a verbum finitum in the sense of: *that not, lest*; e. g. לְבִלְתִּי שָׁבוּ *that none doth return from his wickedness* Jer. 23, 14; or *without* (*quin*) וּלְבִלְתִּי רָאוּ *who follow their own spirit without seeing* Ez. 13, 3.

(*b*) פֶּן (litt. *removing, taking away* stem פָּנָה) *lest, that not*, stands at the beginning of a sentence, which expresses fear or anxiety, especially after the verbs: *to fear, to beware,* (*vereor ne*); e. g. הִשָּׁמֶר לְךָ פֶּן תָּשִׁיב *beware that thou bring not* Gen. 24, 6; כִּי יָרֵאתִי כִּי אָמַרְתִּי פֶּן תִּגְזֹל *because I was afraid, because I said: "Lest thou shouldest take"* Gen. 31. 31 חַפְּשׂוּ וּרְאוּ פֶּן יֵשׁ פֹּה עִמָּכֶם *search and look that there be not here with you* 2 Kings 10, 23.

Rem. 12. The verb expressing fear or anxiety is sometimes omitted, and is to be supplied from the context; e. g. וְעַתָּה פֶּן יִשְׁלַח יָדוֹ *and now (I fear) lest he put forth his hand* Gen. 3, 22.

Rem. 13. In Num. 20, 18. פֶּן is separated from its verb by the noun בַּחֶרֶב which the writer wished to emphasise: *lest I come out with the sword against thee* (Conf. Rem. 8).

4) Two negations in the same sentence do not destroy one another, but on the contrary strengthen the negation (conf. οὐκ οὐδείς, οὐκ οὐδαμῶς); e. g. הֲמִבְּלִי אֵין קְבָרִים *are there no graves in Egypt* Ex. 14, 11 conf. 2 Kings 1, 16; אֵין כֶּסֶף לֹא נֶחְשָׁב *silver was not accounted*

§ 26. INTERROGATIVE WORDS. 73

of 1 Kings 10, 21; (in the parallel place 2 Chr. 9, 20 לֹא is omitted); מֵאֵין יוֹשֵׁב *without a single inhabitant* Jes. 5, 9; בְּטֶרֶם לֹא יָבֹא *before the day of the Lord's anger come upon you* Zeph. 2, 2; מִבְּלִי אֲשֶׁר לֹא יִמְצָא *that man cannot find out* Eccl. 3, 11; אַל בְּאַפְּךָ פֶּן תַּמְעִטֵנִי *lest in thy anger thou bring me to nothing* Jer. 10, 24.

5) When one negative sentence follows another, often the first sentence alone, especially in poetic parallelism, takes the negation; e. g. אַל תַּרְבּוּ ..... יֵצֵא עָתָק *talk no more so exceeding proudly, let no arrogancy come out of your mouth* 1 Sam. 2, 3 לֹא גִדַּלְתִּי בַחוּרִים רוֹמַמְתִּי בְתוּלוֹת *I have not nourished young men, nor brought up virgins* Jes. 23, 4; לֹא יַעַרְכֶנָּה זָהָב וּזְכוֹכִית וּתְמוּרָתָהּ כְּלִי פָז *gold an crystal cannot equal it, neither shall the exchange thereof be jewels of fine gold.* Job 28, 17, (conf. § 27, 7.)

Rem. 14. Concerning the preposition מִן as negation See § 27, 6 C γ.

CHAPTER VII. — INTERROGATIVE PARTICLES.

§ 26. Interrogative words and sentences.

1) An interrogative sentence, is generally introduced by a conjunction or letter of interrogation.

To the interrogative conjunctions (besides אִם which will be spoken of later on) belong also the interrogative pronouns, and the words derived from them; e. g. בַּמָּה מַדּוּעַ, לָמָּה (these call for no particular comment), אֵי which transforms a pronoun or adverb into a question (as to which the lexicon should be consulted), and finally a few particles, such as אֵיפֹה, אֵפוֹא, אַיֵּה.

Rem. 1. The formula מִי יוֹדֵעַ אִם Esther 4, 14 has an affirmative signification *who knoweth whether* .... *not* (= *I believe that*, *nescio an*).

Rem. 2. In Jon. 1, 7. 8 שֶׁ- and אֲשֶׁר have owing to the subsequent לְמִי the signification of: *for whose cause?*

2) *Direct simple questions* are generally introduced by prefixing הֲ to the first word of the sentence; while *direct disjunctive questions* have הֲ in the first member and אִם in the second; e. g. הֲנֵלֵךְ .... אִם נֶחְדָּל *shall we go to battle, or shall we forbear*; 1 Kings 22, 15.

3) The ה interrogative is mostly used in questions, of which the answer is uncertain; e. g. הֲשַׂמְתָּ לִבְּךָ *hast thou considered?* Job 2, 3; occasionally also in questions to which a negative answer is expected; e. g. הֲשֹׁמֵר אָחִי אָנֹכִי *am I my brother's keeper?* Gen. 4, 9; הֲיִחְיֶה *shall he live?* Job. 14, 14. Sometimes הֲ is used for the simply purpose of emphasising the negation; e. g. הַאַתָּה תִבְנֶה *shalt thou build me a house?* 2 Sam. 7, 5. (the parallel place, 1 Chr. 17, 4, reads לֹא אַתָּה תִבְנֶה). On the contrary הֲ connected with לֹא (הֲלֹא) serves to express and to strengthen the affirmation, with the consequence that הֲלֹא (*nonne*) is almost equal to הִנֵּה; e. g. הֲלֹא דָוִד מִסְתַּתֵּר *doth not* (= *behold*) *David hide himself?* Ps. 54, 2; הֲלֹא הֵם כְּתוּבִים *are they not written?* 2 Kings 15, 21; 20, 20; Esther 10, 2 = הִנָּם כְּתוּבִים conf. 2 Chr. 27, 7; 32, 32. But even the simple הֲ without לֹא sometimes

§ 26. INTERROGATIVE WORDS. 75

differs but little from הֲלֹא; e. g. הֲנִגְלֹה נִגְלֵיתִי *did I not reveal myself?* 1 Sam. 2, 27; הֲיֹדְעְתֶּם *do ye not know?* 1 Kings 22, 3; הֲזֹאת יָדַעְתָּ *knowest thou not this.* Job 20, 4. (See Kimchi on 1 Sam. 2, 27).

Rem. 3. The few instances, where a simple question is introduced by אִם, are based upon the omission of the preceding member of a disjunctive question; e. g. אִם מֵאֵת אֲדֹנִי הַמֶּלֶךְ נִהְיָה הַדָּבָר הַזֶּה *is this thing done by my lord the king?* 1 Kings 1, 27; אִם כַּחֹמֶר הַיּוֹצֵר יֵחָשֵׁב *shall the potter be counted as clay?* Jes. 29, 16; אִם כֹּחַ אֲבָנִים כֹּחִי *is my strength the strength of stones?* Job 6, 12. (Conf. Lat. *an* and § 28, 5 A β.)

Rem. 4. Instead of הֲ .... אִם in a disjunctive question, we also find הֲ .... וְאִם; e. g. הֲהָיְתָה זֹּאת .... וְאִם בִּימֵי אֲבֹתֵיכֶם *has this been in your days or in the days of your fathers?* Joel 1, 2; .... הֶאָנֹכִי וְאִם *is my complaint of man, or why should I not be impatient?* Job 21, 4; sometimes with הֲ being repeated after וְאִם; e. g. .... הַלְּבֶן וְאִם שָׂרָה הֲבַת *shall a child be born unto him that is a hundred years old? or shall Sara, who is ninety years old, bear?* Gen. 17, 17; or with special emphasis on the first member of the question; e. g. הַאַף שׂוֹנֵא .... וְאִם צַדִּיק *shall even one that hateth right govern? or wilt thou condemn the just and mighty?* Job 34, 17; Conf. 40, 8, 9.

After a negative sentence וְאִם sometimes stands as if in the second member of a disjunctive question; e. g. כִּי לֹא לְעוֹלָם חֹסֶן וְאִם נֵזֶר לְדוֹר וָדוֹר *for riches are not for ever, or doth the crown endure for all generations?* Prov. 27, 24.

Rem. 5. In the second member אוֹ *or*, is occasionally found instead of אִם; e. g. הֲקֵץ לְדִבְרֵי רוּחַ אוֹ מַה יַּמְרִיצְךָ כִּי תַעֲנֶה *shall vain words have an end? or what provoketh thee that thou answerest?* Job 16, 3; Conf. Eccl. 2, 19.

4) Questions with הֲ .... אִם need not always express an opposition, for they frequently merely repeat the same question with different words; e. g. הֲמָלֹךְ תִּמְלֹךְ עָלֵינוּ אִם מָשׁוֹל תִּמְשֹׁל בָּנוּ *shalt thou indeed reign over us? or shalt thou indeed have dominion over us?* Gen. 37, 8. This especially occurs in poetic parallelisms; e. g. הֲיִתְפָּאֵר הַגַּרְזֶן .... אִם יִתְגַּדֵּל הַמַּשּׂוֹר *shall the axe boast itself against him that heweth therewith? or shall the saw magnify itself against him that shaketh it?* Jes. 10, 15; Conf. Jer. 5, 29; Job 4, 17; 6, 5. 6; 8, 3; 10, 4. 5; 11, 2. 7; 22, 3.

Rem. 6. In questions of this kind the second member is now and then introduced by וְ instead of by אִם or וְאִם; e. g. הַלְאֵל תְּדַבְּרוּ עַוְלָה וְלוֹ תְּדַבְּרוּ רְמִיָּה *will ye speak unrighteously for the Lord, or talk deceitfully for him?* Job 13, 7; הֲרִאישׁוֹן אָדָם תִּוָּלֵד וְלִפְנֵי גְבָעוֹת חוֹלָלְתָּ *art thou the first man that was born, or wast thou brought forth before the hills?* Job 15, 7. Sometimes וְ is even omitted; e. g. הֲיִגְאֶה גֹּמֶא בְּלֹא בִצָּה יִשְׂגֶּה אָחוּ בְלִי מָיִם *can the rush grow up without mire, or can the flag grow without water?* Job. 8, 11; הֲתֵדַע עַל־מִפְלְשֵׂי עָב .... תַּרְקִיעַ עִמּוֹ לִשְׁחָקִים *dost thou know the balancings of the clouds, ... or dost thou with him spread out the sky?* Job 37, 16. 18.

Rem. 7. The second member is rarely introduced by הֲ and then it really continues the question of the preceding member; e. g. הֲיַסְגִּרֻנִי בַעֲלֵי קְעִילָה בְיָדוֹ הֲיֵרֵד שָׁאוּל *will the men of Keilah deliver me up into his hand, and will Saul come down?* 1 Sam. 23, 11. Yet even in the case of an opposition הֲ is found in the second member; e. g. הַלְיָרְשֵׁנוּ קְרָאתֶם לָנוּ הֲלֹא *have ye called us to take our possessions, or not?* Judges 14, 15.

Rem. 8. Once, Job 6, 12, we find אִם both in the first and in the

§ 26. INTERROGATIVE WORDS. 77

second member, while the third member (v. 13) is introduced by הַאִם:

אִם כֹּחַ אֲבָנִים כֹּחִי אִם בְּשָׂרִי נָחוּשׁ ׃ הַאִם אֵין עֶזְרָתִי בִי וְתֻשִׁיָּה נִדְּחָה מִמֶּֽנִּי *is my strength the strength of stones, or my flesh of brass, or is it not that there is no help for me, and that sound counsel is driven away from me?*

5) A question may further be expressed by the tone of speech (gathered from the context) without either word or letter of interrogation; e. g. שָׁאוּל יִמְלֹךְ עָלֵינוּ *shall Saul reign over us?* 1 Sam. 11, 12; שָׁלוֹם לַנַּעַר *is it well with the boy?* 2 Sam. 18, 29; and especially before gutturals הֲ is omitted; e. g. אַתָּה זֶה Gen. 27, 24 (although v. 21 we read הַאַתָּה זֶה); הַיּוֹם הַחִלֹּתִי *have I to-day begun?* 1 Sam. 22, 15; הוּא יוֹרֶה *shall this teach?* Hab. 2, 19; עֹדְךָ מַחֲזִיק *dost thou still hold fast?* Job 2, 9.

This manner of asking a question more frequently occurs, when such question is connected with a preceding sentence by וְ; e. g. וְאַתָּה תִירָשֶׁנּוּ *and shouldest thou possess them?* Judges 11, 23; וְאַתָּה תִנָּצֵל *and shalt thou be delivered?* Jes. 37, 11; וַאֲנִי לֹא אָחוּם *and should not I have pity?* Jonas 4, 11; or by גַם; e. g. גַּם בְּעֵינַי יִפָּלֵא *should it also be marvellous in my eyes?* Zech. 8, 6.

Negative sentences are now and then pronounced in an interrogative manner. They are then introduced by לֹא or וְלֹא, and cause an affirmative answer to be expected; e. g. מִפִּי עֶלְיוֹן לֹא תֵצֵא *out of the mouth of the most High cometh there not evil and good?* Lam 3, 38; וְלֹא יִסְקְלֻנוּ *and will they not stone us?* Ex. 8, 22.

Rem. 9 Once, however, we find such a negative question introduced by אַל; אַל פְּשַׁטְתֶּם הַיּוֹם *did ye not make a raid today?* 1 Sam. 27, 10 (conf. however LXX which suggests the reading אֶל־מִי) *Translator.*

6) Indirect simple questions (after verbs of *inquiring, doubting, observing*) are introduced as well by הֲ; e. g. לִרְאוֹת הֲקַלּוּ הַמַּיִם *to see if the waters were abated* Gen. 8, 8; as by אִם; e. g. נִרְאֶה אִם פָּרְחָה *let us see whether the vine has budded* Cant. 7, 13; דִּרְשׁוּ .... אִם אֶחְיֶה *inquire whether I shall recover* 2 Kings 1, 2.

Indirect disjunctive questions are introduced by הֲ .... אִם; e. g. לָדַעַת הַהִצְלִיחַ ה' דַּרְכּוֹ אִם לֹא *to know whether the Lord has made his journey prosperous or not* Gen. 24, 21; אֲנַסֶּנּוּ הֲיֵלֵךְ בְּתוֹרָתִי אִם־לֹא *that I may prove them whether they will walk in my law or not* Ex. 16, 4; sometimes by הֲ .... הֲ; e. g. וּרְאִיתֶם .... הֶחָזָק הוּא הֲרָפֶה *and see whether they be strong or weak* Num. 13, 18.

7) To intensify the question the words זֶה and זֹאת (conf. § 11, 3 c) and אֵפוֹא (not to be confounded with אֵיפֹה *where?*) *then, now* are added; e. g. מַה לָּךְ אֵפוֹא *what aileth thee now?* Jes. 22, 1; אַיֵּה אֵפוֹא *where is then my hope?* Job 17, 15.

Rem. 10 אֵפוֹא is sometimes placed after the real question is finished; e. g. וּבַמֶּה יִוָּדַע אֵפוֹא *for wherein now shall it be known* Ex. 33, 16; sometimes also after a word on which the emphasis falls, and consequently before the real question; e. g. מִי אֵפוֹא הוּא הַצָּד צַיִד *who then is he that hath taken venison* Gen. 27, 33.

8) The particles of interrogation like the other particles (conf. § 24, 3) sometimes refer not to that part of the sentence in which they stand, but to that which

§ 25. INTERROGATIVE WORDS.

follows; e. g. מַדּוּעַ בָּאתִי וְאֵין אִישׁ *wherefore was there no one when I came?* Jes. 50, 2; הֲנִסָּה דָבָר אֵלֶיךָ תִּלְאֶה *if one assay to commune with thee, wilt thou be grieved?* Job 4, 2.

9) An affirmative answer is expressed by repetition of the main word in the question (changing of course the 2ᵈ person into the 1ˢᵗ, if necessary); e. g. הֲתֵלְכִי .... אֵלֵךְ *wilt thou go .... and she said, I will go* Gen. 24, 58; אַתָּה .... אָנִי *is it thou .... aud he said: it is I.* Gen. 27, 24; Judg. 13, 11; הַיְדַעְתֶּם .... יָדָעְנוּ *know ye .... and they said: we do know* Gen. 29, 5; הֲשָׁלוֹם .... שָׁלוֹם *is it well with him .... and they said: it is well*; ibid. v. 6; הַכְּתֹנֶת בִּנְךָ .... כְּתֹנֶת בְּנִי *is it thy son's coat .... and he said: it is my son's coat.* Gen. 37, 33 ! הֲיֵרֵד .... יֵרֵד *will Saul come down .... and the Lord said: he will come down* 1 Sam. 23, 11.

A negative answer is expressed by repetition of the main word with לֹא; e. g. אֶת־מִי עָשַׁקְתִּי אֶת־מִי רַצּוֹתִי וּמִיַּד־מִי לָקַחְתִּי כֹפֶר .... וַיֹּאמְרוּ לֹא עֲשַׁקְתָּנוּ וְלֹא רַצּוֹתָנוּ וְלֹא לָקַחְתָּ מִיַּד־אִישׁ מְאוּמָה *whom have I defrauded? whom have I oppressed? of whose hand have I taken a bribe? .... and they said: thou hast not defrauded us, nor oppressed us, neither hast thou taken aught of any man's hand* 1 Sam. 12, 4. 5; הַאַכֶּה .... וַיֹּאמֶר לֹא תַכֶּה *shall I smite them? and he said thou shalt not smite them* 2 Kings 6, 21. 22; or by לֹא (or אַל) alone. (Gonf. § 25, 2 A γ, B β).

CHAPTER VIII. — THE REMAINING PARTICLES.

§ 27. The Prepositions.

1) Most of the simple prepositions had originally only a local meaning, but subsequently came also to be used to express ideas of *time, causality*, etc.

The prepositions express either *rest* in a place, or *motion to* or *from* a place.

2) The principal prepositions of place are:

(a) of *rest*: בְּ *at, in, on*; עַל *upon, over*; תַּחַת *under, in the place of*; אַחַר, אַחֲרֵי *behind, after*; לִפְנֵי *before*; נֹכַח, נֶגֶד, מוּל *over against, before*; אֵצֶל *at the side of, by*; אֵת *near, by, with*; בְּעַד (lit. *in distance from*) *behind, round about* (ἀμφί); בֵּין *between*, עֵבֶר *at the side of*.

(b) of *motion*: מִן *from*; אֶל and לְ *to, towards*; עַד *to, unto, as far as, towards*.

3) Many of the above mentioned prepositions express also ideas of *time*; e. g. בְּ *within, in*; אֶל, מִן, עַד etc.

4) The other relations are expressed by כְּ *as* (כְּדֵי *as often as*; כְּפִי *according to*); עִם *with, together with*; זוּלַת, בִּלְעֲדֵי *without, besides*; לְמַעַן, יַעַן *because of*; עֵקֶב, חֵלֶף (*in reward of, in consequence of*) *for*.

5) The Hebrew language is, owing to the *compounding* of prepositions exceedingly well fitted to express various grammatical relations with the greatest accuracy. Thus the prepositions of *motion* are often prefixed to other prepositions of place in order to denote the local state which existed before the action, or that which

§ 27. PREPOSITIONS.

will exist after the action is completed. (conf. *de chez*, *d'auprès*). When Moses, for instance, says to Aaron, Num. 17, 11 *"Take thy censer and put fire therein* מֵעַל הַמִּזְבֵּחַ *from off the altar"* he expresses most accurately that the fire is to be found on the altar.

Thus we find the following compounds:

(a) with מִן (מֵ or מִ); מֵאַחַר usually מֵאַחֲרֵי *from behind*; מִבֵּין or מִבֵּינוֹת *from between*; מֵעַל *from upon, from above*; מֵעִם or מֵאֵת *from, from with, from at*; מִתַּחַת *from under*.

(b) with אֶל, בֵּינוֹת .... אֶל *between, into between*; אֶל מִבֵּית לְ (and לְמִבֵּית לְ Num. 18, 7) *forth within* (lit. *to the place which is within*) 2 Kings 11, 15; אֶל ···· מִן (lit. *to out from*) *even out from* Job 5, 5; אֶל מִחוּץ לְ *forth without* (lit. *to the place which is without*) Num. 5, 3; אֶל מִתַּחַת *beneath, underneath* (lit. *to the place underneath*).

Rem. 1 I Kings 8, 6 is instructive as to this use of prepositions.

(c) with לְ (more rarely with מִן) following; owing to which adverbs composed of prepositions return again into prepositions; e. g. מֵעַל *above* (adv.) מֵעַל לְ *over* (prep.); מִתַּחַת *below* (adv.) מִתַּחַת לְ *under* (prep.); מִחוּץ *without, outside* (adv.) מִחוּץ לְ *outside* (prep.); לְבַד *separately*, לְבַד מִן *besides*.

Rem. 2 מִן also stands before adverbs; e. g. מִלְּבַד (= לְבַד מִן) *besides*; מִבַּלְעֲדֵי (= בִּלְעֲדֵי מִן) *besides, without, except*.

Rem. 3 It seldom occurs that the preposition is omitted; e. g. מִתַּחַת מַיִם Job. 26, 5 (= מִתַּחַת לְמַיִם) *below the waters*.

6) The following remarks may serve as a compendium of the main significations of the more frequently recurring prepositions, as also of their construction with verbs, and of their principal idioms.

A. בְּ denotes:

α originally *to be in a place* בַּבַּיִת; then reference to *time* בְּרֵאשִׁית, to a state or condition בְּשָׁלוֹם, or to a multitude (= *amongst*) בַּגּוֹיִם; בַּנֹּקְדִים *among the herdmen* Amos 1, 1 בְּמִשְׁמַנֵּיהֶם *amongst their noble ones.* Ps. 78, 31.

It further serves to enumerate the component parts of a genus or collective idea; e. g. כָּל בָּשָׂר בָּעוֹף וּבַבְּהֵמָה וּבַחַיָּה וּבְכָל הַשֶּׁרֶץ *and all flesh died both fowl, and cattle, and beast, and every creeping thing.* Gen. 7, 21 conf. 8, 17; 9, 10.

With reference to enclosing boundaries it means *within*; e. g. בַּשְּׁעָרִים *within the gates*; בְּעֵינֵי *in the eyes of, within the reach of the eyes;* בְּאָזְנֵי *in the ears of, within hearing.*

Connected with things of high stature it is = *on*, as בַּסּוּסִים *on the horses.*

β It should be noticed also that the Hebrews say *to drink in* or *at a cup* (because the lips of one drinking are placed at the brim of the cup); e. g. אֲשֶׁר יִשְׁתֶּה אֲדֹנִי בּוֹ *out of which* (lit. *in which*) *my lord drinketh* Gen. 44, 5; הַשֹּׁתִים בְּמִזְרְקֵי יַיִן *that drink out of bowls of wine* Amos 6, 6. (In like manner in Aramaic Dan. 5, 2. conf. ἐν ποτηρίῳ πίνειν; in ossibus bibere; boire dans une tasse).

§ 27. PREPOSITIONS.

γ *in the manner* = *after the manner*; e. g. כִּדְבַר *according to the command*; כַּעֲצַת *according to the counsel of*; כְּצַלְמֵנוּ *after our image* Gen. 1, 26; כִּדְמוּתוֹ *after his likeness* Gen. 5, 3; כְּיִצְחָק *after Isaac* Gen. 21, 12; כְּכֶסֶף *like silver* Jes. 48, 10; כְּעָשָׁן *like smoke* Ps. 37, 20; 102, 4; כְּצֶלֶם *like an image* (*shadow*) Ps. 39, 7.

With this is closely connected:

δ *as, in the quality of* (lat. *tamquam*, french *en*) the so called כְּ *essentiae*; e. g. בְּאֵל שַׁדַּי *as God Almighty* Ex. 6, 3; בְּחָזָק *as a strong one* Jes. 40, 10; בְּרַבִּים *as a mulitude* Ps. 55, 19; בְּיָהּ שְׁמוֹ *Jah is his name* Ps. 68, 5; Conf. Jes. 26, 4; בְכִסְלֶךָ *the Lord shall be thy confidence* Prov. 3, 26; וְהוּא בְאֶחָד *but He is one* = *He remains the same* Job 23, 13; בְּכֹהֲנָיו *like his priests* Ps. 99, 6.

ε *through, with* (בְּ *instrumentalis*); e. g. בְּשֵׁבֶט *with a rod* Micha 4, 14. Also with persons as *auctores*; e. g. בְּךָ *by, through thee* Ps. 18, 30 (conf. Ps. 44, 6 where בְּשִׁמְךָ is parallel to it); בְּקֶשֶׁת וּבְחֶרֶב וּבְמִלְחָמָה *by sword by bow, or by battle* Hos. 1, 7; and with עָבַד in the sense of *to make one work* אֲשֶׁר עָבְדוּ בָהֶם *wherein they made them to work* Ex. 1, 14; in passive אֲשֶׁר עֻבַּד בָּךְ *wherein thou wast made to work* Jes 14, 3 (Conf. § 34, 2).

Hence it is also used in the sense of *propter*, e. g. בַּחֲמִשָּׁה *because of five* Gen. 18, 28; and as בְּ *pretii*, because the price is considered as a *means* of transaction; e. g. בַּחֲמִשָּׁה עָשָׂר כָּסֶף *for fifteen silver pieces* Hos. 3, 2.

ζ *to be on a spot*; e. g, בִּנְהַר כְּבָר *on the river Kebar* Ez. 10, 15; more frequently *near, unto a spot* (whereas אֶל means *towards*, without deciding whether the end is reached, and עַד *unto* denotes the end to be reached); e. g. ראשׁוֹ בַשָּׁמַיִם *whose top (may reach) unto heaven* Gen. 11, 4. It signifies therefore a sort of *being joined to, to touch at*. Hence with transitive verbs it is frequently used to introduce their object (Lat. *ad* and *in*); e. g. שָׁאַל בְּ *to ask at, to consult*; אָחַז בְּ *to take hold of*; נָגַע בְּ *to touch*; קָרָא בְּ *to call upon*; נִשְׁבַּע בְּ *to swear by*; רָאָה בְּ *to look upon*; שָׁמַע בְּ *to listen to*. When used with the two last verbs and others of the same kind, בְּ frequently implies the idea of sharing in joy, sorrow or pain; e. g. אַל אֶרְאֶה בְּמוֹת הַיָּלֶד *I will not behold the death of the child* Gen. 21, 16.

The same fundamental idea of *being joined to* shows itself in the construction of the *verba cordis* with בְּ; e. g. בָּטַח בְּ *to trust in*; הֶאֱמִין בְּ *to believe in*; שָׂמַח בְּ *to rejoice in*.

To this signification belongs also the partitive use of בְּ, as in נָשָׂא בְּ *to take part in bearing a thing (mit daran tragen)*; e. g. וְנָשְׂאוּ אִתְּךָ בְּמַשָּׂא הָעָם *and they shall bear the burden of the people with thee* Num. 11, 17; Ex. 18, 20. Job. 7, 13. אָכַל בְּ *to take part in eating anything (mit essen)*; e. g. לֹא יֹאכַל בּוֹ *no alien shall eat thereof* Ex. 12, 43; Lev. 22, 11;

§ 27. PREPOSITIONS. 85

Judges 13, 16; Job 21, 25. חָלַק בְּ *to impart (antheil geben an)*; e. g. וְלֹא חָלַק לָהּ בַּבִּינָה *neither has he imparted to her understanding* Job. 39, 17; בָּנָה בְּ *to assist in building anything (an etwas mitbauen)*; e. g. לֹא נוּכַל לִבְנוֹת בַּחוֹמָה *we are not able to build the wall* Neh. 4, 4.

Rem. 4 concerning בְּ *objecti* and its signification see § 35, 6.

η *with*, implying an *accompaniment*, which idea is affiliated to that of *vicinity*; e. g. בְּנַפְשׁוֹ *but flesh with the life thereof* Gen. 9, 4; בִּרְכֻשׁ גָּדוֹל *with great possessions* Gen. 15, 14; בְּמַקְלִי *with my staff* Gen. 32, 11. In connection with this it should be noticed that verbs of *coming* and *going* with בְּ express the idea of *coming with something*, hence of *bringing*; e. g. לֹא קִדְּמוּ בַּלֶּחֶם וּבַמַּיִם *because they met you not with bread and with water* = *because they brought not* Deut. 23, 5; וַיִּפְקֹד .... בִּגְדִי עִזִּים *and Samson brought his wife a kid* Judges 15, 1.

B. עַל signifies:

α *upon, over*; frequently implying an idea of motion, *upwards, towards*. (German *hinauf, hinüber*). In the sense of *down upon* (Germ. *herab auf*) it is governed by the verbs *to press, to be heavy, to be burdensome* (lit. *to lay heavily upon*); e. g. הָיוּ עָלַי לָטֹרַח *they are burdensome to me* Jes. 1, 14; וָאֶהְיֶה עָלַי לְמַשָּׂא *so that I am a burden to myself* Job 7, 20; יָדִי כָבְדָה עַל אַנְחָתִי *mine hand* (LXX יָדוֹ *his hand*) *layeth heavily upon mine groaning* Job 23, 2. Hence it is used with the verbs *to appoint*, *to command* פָּקַד עַל, because the *command* or *duty* is laid upon (conf. 2 Sam. 18, 11 וְעָלַי *it would have been incumbent on me to give*), and with the verbs *to pity*, *to have compassion* חָס עַל, חָמַל עַל, also in the sense *to spare*.

β *in addition to*, *besides*; a sense closely allied to the preceding (the *addition* being considered as *laying upon*); e. g. עַל נָשָׁיו *besides the wives whom he had* Gen. 28, 9; עַל בְּנוֹתַי *besides my daughters* Gen. 31, 50; אֵם עַל בָּנִים *mother with children* Gen. 32, 12; Deut. 22, 6; Hos. 10, 14.

according to, *in consequence of* (the consequence being considered an addition to the *utterance* or *action*) עַל צִבְאוֹתָם *according to their hosts* Ex. 12, 51; עַל שְׁמוֹת בְּנֵי יִשְׂרָאֵל *according to the names of the children of Israel* Ex. 28, 11; עַל פִּי ה' *according to (on) the command of the Lord*.

because of, *concerning* אַל יֵרַע בְּעֵינֶיךָ עַל הַנַּעַר *be not anxious concerning the boy* Gen. 21, 12; עַל חַטֹּאות יָרָבְעָם *because of the sins of Jeroboam* 1 King 15, 30. (as to the signification *although*, see § 28, 5, G β.)

γ *over*, used frequendly with the verbs *to cover*, *to protect* כִּסָּה עַל, גָּנַן עַל (lit. to make a *covering* or *protection upon* or *over* anything), *to propitiate* כִּפֶּר עַל (which also really means *to cover* conf. בַּפֹּרֶת *cover* and כַּסֵּה עַל עָוֹן *forgive not* (lit. *cover not*) *their iniquity* Neh. 3, 37); and with other affiliated verbs, as נִלְחַם עַל Judges 9, 17 *to fight for anyone (in order to protect him)*.

§ 27. PREPOSITIONS.

δ *at*, (*by*) *before*, *at the side of*, chiefly when the position of a person or object implies an elevation above other persons or objects, such as the position of a person standing being higher than that of one sitting; e. g. לְהִתְיַצֵּב עַל ה' *to present themselves* (lit. *to take a stand*) *before the Lord* Job 1, 6; עֹמֵד עַל הַיְאֹר *standing by the river* Gen. 41, 1; שָׁתוּל עַל פַּלְגֵי מָיִם *planted by streams of water* Ps. 1, 3. Later also with the signification of אֶל *at*, *to*; e. g. וַתִּתְפַּלֵּל עַל ה' *and she prayed to the Lord* 1 Sam. 1, 10; and even with the meaning of *towards*; e. g. עַל הַשָּׁמַיִם *towards heaven* Ex. 9, 22; עַל יְדֵי, עַל יַד *at the side of* Job 1, 14.

ε *down upon*, *forth upon* when considered as implying a motion; and *against*, chiefly in a hostile sense.

C. מִן signifies:

α a *motion*, *removal away from*. The principal signification is that of *separation from a whole* (because מִן probably is the *st. constr.* of a *nomen* signifying *part of*). Thus it means *some*, *something of* (more rarely *somebody of*), and is placed before the whole from which a part is separated; e. g. מִן הַבְּהֵמָה Lev. 1, 2 מֵהַבְּהֵמָה *of the cattle* 1 Kings 18, 5; מִשָּׂרֵי יִשְׂרָאֵל *of the princes of Israel* 2 Chr. 21, 4; מִדַּם הַפָּר *of the blood of the bullock* Ex. 29, 12; מִיָּמָיו *during a part of his days* = *ever in his life* 1 Kings 1, 6; מִיָּמַי *as long as I live* Job 27, 6; מִיָּמֶיךָ *ever in thy life* Job 38, 12; and is used with *singularia* not having the force of *collectiva*; e. g. מִמְּךָ *out of thee* Micha

5, 1; מִנֵּצֶר *out of a shoot*, Dan. 11, 7. Hence, *place of origin, descent*; as, מִתְּקֹעַ *from Thecoa* Am. 1, 1; and *from amongst (e numero)*; e. g. מִמֶּנּוּ Gen. 3, 22; מִכָּל־הָעַמִּים *from among all nations* Ex. 19, 5; מִנָּשִׁים *among women* Judges 5, 24; and thus with verbs of *choosing*; e. g. וּבָחֹר אֹתוֹ מִכָּל־שִׁבְטֵ *and choose him out of all the tribes* 1 Sam. 2, 28.

N.B. From this subordination of the idea which is connected with מִן may be fitly explained the use of מִן to express the comparative and superlative. (Conf. § 8.)

β the same signification, more absolutely considered, becomes, *removed from, empty of, without*; e. g. מִקֶּשֶׁת *without bow* Jes. 22, 3; מִמּוּם *without defect* Job 11, 15; וּמִבְּשָׂרִי *empty, destitute of my flesh I shall behold God* Job 19, 26; מִפַּחַד *without fear* Job 21, 9.

γ as the opposite of אֶל and עַד, it is found not only with such verbs as, *to go away, to flee from*, but also with the kindred verbs *to fear, to hide, to beware* (conf. *custodire ab, cavere ab*, καλύπτω ἀπό); e. g. הֲיִפָּלֵא מֵה׳ דָּבָר *is anything too wonderful for the Lord* Gen. 18, 14; נֹעֵר כַּפָּיו מִתְּמֹךְ *who shaketh his hands from holding of bribes* Jes. 33, 15. Hence, it frequently has the pregnant sense, *to be concealed from, so that not* (ut non), *that not* (ne); e. g. מִלֶּדֶת *that (I) should not bear* Gen. 16, 2; מִקְּבֹר *so that (thou) art not able to bury thy dead* Gen. 23, 6; מֵעֵינֵי הָעֵדָה *hidden from the sight of the congregation* Num. 15, 24; מִבּוֹא *so that no one can come in* Jes. 24, 10; מֵעֲבֹר *that the waters should no more go over*

§ 27. PREPOSITIONS. 89

Jes. 54, 9. With the same meaning also before nouns; e. g. מִמְּלֹךְ (= מִהְיוֹת מֶלֶךְ) *from being king* 1 Sam. 15, 23 conf. v. 26; מֵעָם *that it be no longer a people* Jes. 7, 8; מֵעִיר *from being a city* Jes. 17, 1; מִבַּיִת *so that there is no house* Jes. 23, 1; מִפְּדוֹת *that I cannot redeem* Jes. 50, 2; מֵרְעֶה *from being a shepherd* Jer 17, 16; מִגּוֹי *from being a nation* Jer. 48, 2; Ps. 83, 5 (Conf. § 28, 5 E towards the end.)

Rem. 5 With the same signification it is often pleonastically prefixed to אֵין; e. g. מֵאֵין אָדָם מֵאֵין יוֹשֵׁב *without man without inhabitant* Jes. 6, 11 (conf. § 25, 4).

Sometimes even without a negation מִן is used pleonastically, as מֵאַחַת מֵהֵנָּה *anyone of them* Lev. 4, 2; מֵאַחַד מֵאֵלֶּה *anyone of these things* (conf. § 13, 8).

δ used with reference to time מִן signifies either *from*, when reckoning is made from the beginning of a period (conf. *de nocte*, ἀπὸ νυκτός), or *immediately after*, reckoning being made from the end of a period (conf. *ab itinere*, ἐξ ἀρίστου); e. g. מֵהָקִיץ *as a dream when one awaketh* Ps. 73, 20; מִשְּׁלֹשׁ חֳדָשִׁים *after about three months* Gen. 38, 24; מִיּוֹמָיִם *after two days* Hos. 6, 2. Of frequent occurence are the expressions מִקֵּץ *from the end = after*; מִקְצֵה *towards the end*.

ε upon the idea *to go out from* is based the frequent *causative* signification *because of*, *in consequence of*; e. g. מֵרֹב *because of the multitude* Gen. 32, 13; 1 Kings 3, 8 (Conf. A ε).

Rem. 6 Concerning the use of מִן for expressing the idea of rest *at the side of* an object, with which *a removal away from* the object is not lost sight of (conf. *prope abesse ab, stare ab, pendere ab*) see n° 5 *a*, *b* and *c*.

D. אֶל (poetic אֱלֵי lit. *region, direction*) denotes:

α *motion, direction towards,* (also in a moral sense = *with regard to, concerning*; e. g. וַיֹּאמֶר אַבְרָהָם אֶל שָׂרָה *and Abraham said concerning Sara* Gen. 20, 2); sometimes implying that the *terminus* or *finis* of the action has been reached hence = עַד e. g. אֶל פִּיהוּ *unto his mouth* Job 40, 23; sometimes denoting *entering into*, hence = אֶל תּוֹךְ; e. g. בֹּא אֶל הַתֵּיבָה *come into the ark* Gen. 7, 1. Generally however it is used without implying the *terminus* to have been reached.

β *by, at, in,* rare and pregnant, because instead of the *terminus* the *motion* towards it is present to the mind, hence = *rest in a place reached*; e. g. אֶל הַמָּקוֹם ..... תִּזְבַּח *at the place which .... thou shalt sacrifice* Deut. 16, 6; אֶל מְקוֹם שִׁבְתְּךָ אֶל הַשָּׁמַיִם *in thy dwelling place, in heaven* 1 Kings 8, 30; אֶל מַיִם רַבִּים *by the great waters* Jer. 41, 12; אֶל־הָהָר מִזֶּה *on the mountain* 1 Sam. 17, 3. (Conf. the analogous use of *zu* in Germ. e. g. *zu Hause*).

E. לְ is an abbreviation from אֶל, but is distinguished from it.

α לְ generally expresses only *a direction* (not *a motion*) *towards*, and is more frequently used in figurative language.

§ 27. PREPOSITIONS.

β from the idea *direction towards, turning to* may be explained the use of לְ as *dative* and as a qualification of the *possessor* or *auctor* (conf. § 7, 2) with the meaning: *respective of, with regard to*; e. g. לְעֹשֶׁר וּלְחָכְמָה *as regards riches and wisdom* 1 Kings 10, 23; לָרֶכֶב וּלְפָרָשִׁים *as for chariots and horsemen* Jes 36, 9; לֶאֱמוּנָה *but not what regards faithfulness* Jer. 9, 2; לִלְשֹׁנֵנוּ *as regards our tongue we will prevail* Ps. 12, 5; לְאִשָּׁה *unto (for) a wife.* Hence the so called לְ *inscriptionis* = *for, in behalf of*; e. g. לַמְנַצֵּחַ *for the chief musician.* (Conf. § 41 Rem. 1).

From the fundamental idea *direction towards* may perhaps also be explained the use of לְ with the infinitive, as in the frequently occurring לֵאמֹר lit. *ad loquendum*, hence *for the purpose of saying* = *namely, to wit*; Conf. לִרְאוֹת עֻזְּךָ (*namely*) *gazing upon thy power and majesty* Ps. 63, 3; לַמְרוֹת עֶלְיוֹן (*namely*) *rebelling against the most High* Ps. 78, 17; 101, 8; Jer. 44, 7. 8.

γ לְ also expresses the *dativus commodi* (rarely the *dativus incommodi*; e. g. נִגְזַרְנוּ לָנוּ *we are entirely cut off* Ez. 37, 11), in which sense it stands with many verbs, especially with the imperative, pleonastically; e. g. לֶךְ לְךָ *go*; בְּרַח לְךָ *flee (to save thyself)*; עֲלִי לָךְ *go up* Jes. 40, 9; וַתִּבְטַח לָךְ *and thou trusted* Jes. 36, 9; חִדְלוּ לָכֶם *cease ye* Jes. 2, 22; דְּמֵה לְךָ *and be thou like* Cant. 2, 17; הִשָּׁמֶר לְךָ *beware.*

δ *rest* in a place; e. g. לִימִינֶךָ *at thy right hand* Ps.

45, 10; and with reference to time *towards* לָעֶ֫רֶב *towards the evening*.

ε to the solecisms of later Hebrew belongs the introduction of the object by לְ (which is common in Aramaic); e. g. שָׁלַח לְשָׂרָיו *he sent his princes* 2 Chr. 17, 7; Conf. Ezra 8, 16; כְּהַעֲלוֹת הַיָּם לְגַלָּיו *as the sea causeth its waves to come up* Ez. 26, 3; יָדַ֫עְתָּ לְאִוַּלְתִּי *thou knowest my foolishness* Ps. 69, 6; פִּתַּ֫חְתָּ לְמוֹסֵרָי *thou hast loosed my bonds* Ps. 116, 16; וַיַּהֲרֹג .... לְסִיחוֹן וּלְעוֹג *and he slew Sihon and Og* Ps. 136, 19. 20; Conf. Job 5, 2; סוֹמֵךְ ה' לְכָל הַנֹּפְלִים *the Lord upholdeth all that fall* Ps. 145, 14; וַיַּעֲמֵד .... לַכֹּהֲנִים וְלַלְוִיִּם (where other objects with אֶת precede) *and he appointed both the priests and the Levites* 2 Chr. 31, 2.

Rem. 7 As to the use of לְ with passive verbs and ideas see § 34, 2*

F. כְּ (as adverb *almost, about, circiter*) used as preposition signifies:

α *as* (used in a comparison conf. § 35, 4). When doubled כְּ .... כְּ (or כְּ .... וּכְ); e. g. כְּכֹחִי אָז וּכְכֹחִי עָ֫תָּה *as my strength was then, so is my strength now* Jos. 14, 11) it means *as .... so*; e. g. כָּעָם כַּכֹּהֵן *as with the people so with the priest* Jes. 24, 2; but also *so .... as*; e. g. כַּצַּדִּיק כָּרָשָׁע *that so the righteous should be as the wicked* Gen. 18, 25; כִּי כָמ֫וֹךָ כְּפַרְעֹה *for thou art as Pharaoh* Gen. 44, 18. (Conf. Abn-Ezra on Hosea 4, 9). We find also כַּאֲשֶׁר .... כְּ; e. g. כַּאֲשֶׁר שֵׁ֫מַע .... כְּשֵׁ֫מַע צֹר *as the report concerning Egypt so the report of Tyre* Jes. 23, 5 (Conf. § 28, 5 H).

β *after, according to, in proportion as*. With reference

§ 27. PREPOSITIONS. 93

to time *about* (lit. *at*); e. g. כָּעֵת חַיָּה *about the same time* (lit. *at the time as it is reviving* or *returning*) Gen. 18, 10; כָּעֵת מָחָר *to morrow about this time* (lit. *as the time to morrow*) 1 Sam. 9, 16.

Confer בְּ as a conjunction prefixed to an infinitive with reference to time (*when*); e. g. כְּבוֹא אַבְרָם *when Abram was come* Gen. 12, 14; כִּשְׁמֹעַ עֵשָׂו *when Esau heard* Gen. 27, 34.

γ the use of the so called בְּ *veritatis* should also be noticed; e. g. כִּי הוּא כְאִישׁ אֱמֶת *for he is like a true man* (the meaning is: *he behaves as a true man, and he truly is such*) Neh. 7, 2; וַיְהִי כְּמַחֲרִישׁ *and he held is peace* 1 Sam. 10, 27; כִּמְעַט *very small* Jes. 1, 9; Ps. 105, 12 (otherwise כִּמְעַט = *nearly, almost*); כְּרָשָׁע *as the wicked* Job 27, 7. In like manner כְּמַהְפֵּכַת זָרִים Jes. 1, 7 after זָרִים אֹכְלִים אֹתָהּ *strangers devour it, and it is as overthrown by strangers*.

7) In poetic parallelisms the influence of a preposition in the first member not unfrequently extends itself to the corresponding part of the second member; e. g. (בְּכַשְׂדִּים =) יַעֲשֶׂה חֶפְצוֹ בְּבָבֶל וּזְרֹעוֹ כַּשְׂדִּים (בְּ) *the Lord shall perform his pleasure on Babylon and his strength on the Chaldeans* Jes. 48, 14; conf. Job 15, 3; (כְּ) ... כְּיוֹם אֶתְמוֹל (= וּכְאַשְׁמוּרָה) ... וְאַשְׁמוּרָה *are but as yesterday ..... and as a watch in the night* Ps. 90, 4; (לְ) ... וַיְשִׂימֵנִי לְאָב לְפַרְעֹה (= וּלְמֹשֵׁל) ... וּמֹשֵׁל *and he has made me a father to Pharaoh ..... and a ruler over all the land* Gen. 45, 8; conf. Jes. 28, 6; Job 34, 10; (עַד) עַד אֶגְלַיִם יִלְלָתָהּ וּבְאֵר אֵילִים (= וְעַד בְּאֵר אֵילִים) יִלְלָתָהּ *the howling thereof unto Eglaim*

and the howling thereof unto Beer-elim Jes. 15, 8; (לְמַעַן וּלְמַעַן תְּהִלָּתִי =) לְמַעַן שְׁמִי אַאֲרִיךְ אַפִּי וּתְהִלָּתִי אֶחֱטָם־לָךְ *for mine name's sake will I defer mine anger, and for my praise will I refrain from thee* Jes. 48, 9; תַּחַת בָּשְׁתְּכֶם (תַּחַת וְתַחַת כְּלִמָּה =) מִשְׁנֶה וּכְלִמָּה יָרֹנּוּ חֶלְקָם *instead of your shame (ye shall have) double, and instead of confusion they shall rejoice in their portion* Jes. 61, 7. Conf. § 25, 5.

§ 28. Conjunctions.

1) Conjunctions may be formed of prepositions by connecting them with אֲשֶׁר, כִּי or אִם; e. g. עַד אֲשֶׁר, עַד אִם. עַד כִּי *until*, כַּאֲשֶׁר *as*, מִפְּנֵי אֲשֶׁר *because* etc. (Conf. Grammar § 85, 4). Yet the means at hand for accurately expressing the connection between sentences are not always used. (Conf. § 19, 1). The Hebrew writers more than once content themselves with imperfect means of connecting two sentences. Hence, some frequently occurring conjunctions, chiefly כִּי, וְ and אֲשֶׁר, have a great number of significations.

2) The conjunction more frequently used than any other is וְ or וּ (conf. Gramm. § 85 B).

It's use is as follows:

    A. properly as *copulative* = *and*, connecting both words and sentences. A few instances וְ·····וְ *and* . . . . *and*; e. g. וְרֶכֶב וָסוּס *both chariot and horse* Ps. 76, 7; וְקֹדֶשׁ וְצָבָא *both the sanctuary and the host* Dan. 8, 13; sometimes also וְ·····וְ *without emphasis*; e. g. וְאַיָּה וַעֲנָה *and Ajah and Anah* Gen. 36, 24. When three

§ 28. CONJUNCTIONS.

or more words are connected it may be prefixed to each one of them; e. g. אֶת הַקֵּינִי וְאֶת הַקְּנִזִּי וְאֶת הַקַּדְמֹנִי וְאֶת הַחִתִּי וְאֶת הַפְּרִזִּי *the Kenite aud the Kenizzite and the Kadmonite and the Hittite and the Perizzite* Gen. 15, 19; or to some of them, or to the second word only; e. g. מוֹר וַאֲהָלוֹת קְצִיעוֹת *myrrh, and aloes, and cassia* Ps. 45, 9; or to the last word only; e. g. רְאוּבֵן שִׁמְעוֹן לֵוִי וִיהוּדָה *Reuben, and Simeon, and Levi, and Judah* Ex. 1, 2. 3. (Conf. Abn-Ezra on this place).

Further in the sense of *or*; e. g. וּמַכֵּה אָבִיו וְאִמּוֹ *and he that smiteth his father or his mother* Ex. 21, 15 (conf. below 5 B α.)

Rem. 1 וְ is omitted in certain idiomatic expressions; e. g. תְּמוֹל שִׁלְשׁוֹם *the day before yesterday (heretofore)* Ex. 5, 8; and also in vivid descriptions to express greater emphasis *(Constructio asyndeta)*; e. g. כָּרַע נָפַל שָׁכָב *he bowed, he fell, he lay* Judges 5, 27; חָלַף עָזַב דַּלִּים *he has oppressed and forsaken the poor* Job 20, 19; וְדוֹדִי חָמַק עָבַר *but my beloved had withdrawn himself and was gone* Cant. 5, 6; הַגֶּשֶׁם חָלַף הָלַךְ לוֹ *the rain is over and gone* Cant. 2, 11.

B. it is *explicative* (= *isque, et quidem* וְ *explicativum*) = *namely, to wit*; e. g. אֶל הֶבֶל וְאֶל מִנְחָתוֹ *and the Lord had respect unto Abel and to his sacrifice* Gen. 4, 4; בְרָמָה וּבְעִירוֹ *in Ramah, namely, in his own city* I Sam. 28, 3; הָאֲרִי וְאֶת הַדּוֹב *and when there came a lion, even with a bear* 1 Sam. 17, 34; וּמִזֶּרַע הַמְּלוּכָה וּמִן הַפַּרְתְּמִים *of the seed royal, namely, of the nobles* Dan. 1, 3; occasionally also emphasising the idea;

e. g. מִכַּף כָּל אֹיְבָיו וּמִכַּף שָׁאוּל *from the hand of his enemies and (especially) from the hand of Saul* 2 Sam. 22, 1; עַל יְהוּדָה וִירוּשָׁלָיִם *concerning Judah and (chiefly) Jerusalem* Jos. 1, 1; 2, 1.

Two ideas are sometimes so connected by ו that they form one idea (ἓν διὰ δυοῖν); e. g. עִצְּבוֹנֵךְ וְהֵרֹנֵךְ *the sorrow of thy conception* Gen. 3, 16; חֲלִפוֹת וְצָבָא עִמִּי *thou multiplieth changes of hosts (host after host) against me* Job 10, 17; בְּשָׂמִים וָמִינִים *spices of different sorts* 2 Chr. 16, 14.

C. it is used for effecting a climax, both with words and sentences (= *and even*), for the purpose of strengthening an idea already expressed; e. g. וּבְשֶׁבַע לֹא יִגַּע *he shall deliver thee in six troubles; yea, in seven no evil shall touch thee* Job 5, 19; frequently with numbers; e. g. עַל שְׁלֹשָׁה פִּשְׁעֵי דַמֶּשֶׂק וְעַל אַרְבָּעָה לֹא אֲשִׁיבֶנּוּ *for three transgressions of Damascus, yea, for four I will not turn away the punishment thereof* Amos 1, 3. 6; conf. Prov. 6, 16; 30, 18; וְכִי יִדְרֹךְ בְּאַרְמְנֹתֵינוּ *even when he shall tread in our palaces* Micha 5, 4; וְשַׁאֲלִי לוֹ *ask rather (at once) for him the kingdom* 1 Kings 2, 22.

D. it is also used in comparisons, chiefly in proverbial language, when facts of the moral order are compared with those of the physical order, and then often is equivalent to *even as, so*; e. g. וּבְנֵי רֶשֶׁף יַגְבִּיהוּ עוּף *just as the sparks (by their nature) fly upwards* Job 5, 7; וְחֵךְ אֹכֶל יִטְעַם לוֹ *even as the palate tasteth its meat?* Job 12, 11; conf. 34, 3; וּבֹחֵן לִבּוֹת יְהוָֹה *so*

§ 28. CONJUNCTIONS.

the Lord trieth the hearts Prov. 17, 3; וּשְׁמוּעָה טוֹבָה *so is good news from a far country* Prov. 25, 25. (The transition to this signification may be easily found in Prov. 25, 3 שָׁמַיִם לָרוּם וָאָרֶץ לָעֹמֶק וְלֵב מְלָכִים אֵין חֵקֶר *the heaven as regards height, and the earth as regards depth, and the heart of kings is unsearchable = just as the height of heaven and the depth of the earth, so is the heart of kings unsearchable.*)

Rem. 2 Sometimes such sentences are found together without a proper conjunction or even without וְ; e. g. מוֹכִיחַ חָכָם עַל אֹזֶן שֹׁמָעַת *so is a wise reprover upon a listening ear* Pr. 25, 12 conf. v. 26.

E. most frequently of all it stands for the purpose of introducing the *apodosis*; e. g. וְהִיא עָלָתָה *and before they were laid down, she came up* Jos. 2, 8; וְעֵשָׂו אָחִיו בָּא *when Jacob was gone, Esau his brother came in from his hunting* Gen. 27, 30. This is chiefly the case after determinations of time; e. g. כִּי בְּיוֹם... וְנִפְקְחוּ עֵינֵיכֶם *that on the day ye eat thereof, then shall your eyes be opened* Gen. 3, 5; בַּיּוֹם הַשְּׁלִישִׁי וַיִּשָּׂא *on the third day, when Abraham lifted up his eyes* Gen. 22, 4; עוֹדֶנּוּ מְדַבֵּר עִמָּם וְרָחֵל בָּאָה *while he yet spoke with them, Rachel came* Gen. 29, 9; אַחַר וּבָנִיתָ בֵיתֶךָ *and afterwards build thine house* Prov. 24, 27; or after other determinations; e. g. בַּחֲלוֹמִי וְהִנֵּה *in my dream, behold a vine was before me* Gen. 40, 9; or also after a conditional sentence; e. g. אִם הַשְּׂמֹאל וְאֵימִנָה *if (thou wilt take) the left hand, then I will go the right* Gen. 13, 9 (conf. § 41, 3).

F. it introduces the subject of a sentence (generally a *nominal sentence*), denoting a simultaneous condition; e. g. וְלוֹט יֹשֵׁב *and the two angels came to Sodom at even, while Lot sat in the gate of Sodom* Gen. 19, 1; וְהוּא שֹׁכֵב *when they came into the house, while he lay on his bed* 2 Sam. 4, 7; also when such a sentence at the same time expresses a contrast (= *whereas, and yet, while yet*); e. g. וְאָנֹכִי הוֹלֵךְ עֲרִירִי *O Lord what wilt thou give me, while yet I go childless* Gen. 15, 2; וְהִוא בְּעֻלַת בָּעַל *because of the woman thou hast taken, seeing that she is a man's wife* Gen. 20, 3; וְלִבְּךָ אֵין אִתִּי *how canst thou see I love thee, whereas (while yet) thine heart is not with me* Judges 16, 15; וַאֲנִי לֹא שְׁלַחְתִּים *and yet I did not send them* Jer. 14, 15.

Rem. 3 Such a וְ, when following a negation, is equivalent to כִּי אִם *on the contrary*; e. g. וַעֲבָדֶיךָ בָּאוּ לִשְׁבָּר *and they said unto him: nay my lord, but to buy food are thy servants come* Gen. 42, 11.

G. it also introduces a *causal sentence* (= *because*); e. g. וְשָׁוְא תְּשׁוּעַת אָדָם *for vain is the help of man* Ps. 60, 13; וְלֹא חָשַׂכְתָּ *because thou hast not withheld thy son* Gen. 22, 12; וְאַתֶּם יְדַעְתֶּם *for ye know* Ex. 23, 9; וּבֹחֵן לִבּוֹת *for the righteous God trieth the hearts and reins* Ps. 7, 10, וּרְאֵה רֹאשׁ כּוֹכָבִים *for behold the head of the stars* (i. e. *the highest stars*) Job. 22, 12.

H. in inferential sentences (= *then, so then, therefore*); e. g. וְהָשִׁיבוּ וִחְיוּ *wherefore be converted, and live* Ez.

§ 28. CONJUNCTIONS.

18, 32. Sometimes with the same signification even at the beginning of a sentence; e. g. וְקָחוּ *but he said: bring therefore meal* 2 Kings 4, 41; וְיִקְחוּ *let them therefore take five of the horses* 2 Kings 7, 13; וּדְעוּ *know ye then that the Lord* Ps. 4, 4. (In all these instances וְעַתָּה is usually employed).

I. it is likewise found at the beginning of a sentence, uttered under the impulse of grief, or connected with a protasis which through haste was suppressed, and which therefore has to be supplied; e. g. וְאָבִיהָ יָרֹק יָרַק בְּפָנֶיהָ *and the Lord said unto Moses: if her father had but spit in her face* Num. 12, 14; וְאַהֲרֹן מַה הוּא *and Aaron, what then is he that ye murmur against him* Num. 16, 11; וְלָמָּה תִּשְׁאָלֵנִי *wherefore then doest thou ask of me* 1 Sam. 28, 16; וְאַתֶּם בְּעַרְתֶּם *Ah ye, ye have destroyed* Jes. 3, 14; וַאֲנִי נָסַכְתִּי *know ye, I my self have annointed my king* Ps. 2, 6.

K. finally, it very frequently introduces a *final sentence* (= *that*), and is then construed as ו *consecutivum* with the *cohortative* or *jussive*; e. g. וְאִבָּנֶה *that I also may be builded* (i. e. *obtain children*) *by her* Gen. 30, 3; וְיוֹכִיחוּ בֵּין שְׁנֵינוּ *that they may judge betwixt us two* Gen. 31, 37; וְתִשָּׂרֵף *that she may be burnt* Gen. 38, 24; וְיַעֲלוּ *that they come up out of Jordan* Jos. 4, 16; וְנִדְרְשָׁה מֵאוֹתוֹ *that we may inquire from him* 1 Kings 22, 7; וְיַעַל וְיִפֹּל *that he may go up and fall* 1 Kings 22, 20.

Rem. 4 The ו is sometimes found pleonastically at the beginning of the main sentence to emphasise the idea; e. g. וְיוֹסֵף ה' *may the Lord add* 1 Sam. 24, 3; וְלָכֵן הִנֵּה *now therefore behold* Jes. 8, 7.

Rem. 5 Concerning וְ conversive see § 16.

3) The *relativa* אֲשֶׁר and כִּי *that, because* are of an almost equally extensive use, and parallel in their signification, except that אֲשֶׁר also serves as *nota relationis*, and as a *relative pronoun*, whereas כִּי, as a conjunction, is used more frequently and in a more general manner.

Both stand at the beginning of sentences, which as *accusative objecti* are governed by a preceding *verbum activum* (conf. Lat. *quod*). אֲשֶׁר in these cases is sometimes even preceded by אֵת as *nota objecti*; e. g. כִּי שָׁמַעְנוּ אֵת אֲשֶׁר הוֹבִישׁ *for we have heard how the Lord dried up* Jos. 2, 10; רָאוּ עֵינֶיךָ אֵת אֲשֶׁר נְתָנְךָ *thine eyes have seen how the Lord has delivered thee into my hands* 1 Sam. 24, 11; וְאַתָּה הִגַּדְתָּ הַיּוֹם אֵת אֲשֶׁר עָשִׂיתָ אִתִּי *and thou hast declared this day how that thou hast dealt well with me* 1 Sam. 24, 19.

4) With regard to the use of אֲשֶׁר and כִּי the following points should be noted. כִּי stands:

(*a*) as an introduction of the *oratio recta* (ὅτι); e. g. כִּי אָמְרָה כִּי רָאָה ה' בְּעָנְיִי *for she said: the Lord has looked upon my affliction* Gen. 29, 32.

In a few instances also אֲשֶׁר; e. g. וַיֹּאמֶר שָׁאוּל ... אֲשֶׁר שָׁמַעְתִּי *and Saul said unto Samuel: I have listened to the voice* 1 Sam. 15, 20.

(*b*) as a *temporal conjunction* (conf. ὅτε properly, *at the time that, when*) *when, further, supposing that, in*

§ 28. CONJUNCTIONS

case that, not of course in the same sense as the conditional אִם *if*.¹)

seldom אֲשֶׁר (= *when*) אֲשֶׁר תָּבֹאןָ הַצֹּאן *when the flocks came to drink* Gen. 30, 38; אֲשֶׁר יֶחֶטְאוּ לָךְ *in case that they have sinned against thee* 1 Kings 8, 33.

Rem. 6 Now and then, however, כִּי occurs with the signification of אִם; e. g. כִּי תֵדַע *if thou knowest* Job 38, 5 conf. v. 4 and 18. Sometimes also אֲשֶׁר; e. g. אֲשֶׁר נָשִׂיא יֶחֱטָא *when (if) a ruler sinneth*, Lev. 4, 22; אֲשֶׁר יִשְׁמְעוּ *if ye shall hearken* Deut. 11, 27.

(c) as a *causal* conjunction = *because* (Lat. *eo quod*), fully יַעַן כִּי; frequently to be rendered by *for*, in which sense it is sometimes also used as a particle of affirmation: *yes, indeed* (= *it is certain that*), chiefly after other particles of the same kind; e. g. כִּי רַבָּה....כִּי כָבְדָה מְאֹד *and the Lord said: verily the cry of Sodom is great; verily their sin is very grievous.* Gen. 18, 20.

Also אֲשֶׁר sometimes has a *causal* meaning; e. g. אֲשֶׁר מִי אֵל *for what God is there* Deut. 3, 24; אֲנִי קָצַפְתִּי מְעָט *for I was but a little angry* Zech. 1, 15.

(d) כִּי (never אֲשֶׁר) when following a negation, has an *adversative* meaning *but* (properly *on the contrary because*); e. g. לֹא כִּי צָחָקְתְּ *nay; but thou didst laugh* (prop. *nay it is not so, because thou* etc.) Gen. 18, 15; לֹא כִּי בָרְחוֹב נָלִין *nay; but we will abide the night*

---

1) For the better understanding of this distinction Ex. ch. 21 will be found to be very instructive.

in the street (prop. *no, we refuse, because we will* etc.) Gen. 19, 2.

In like manner, when the negation is not clearly expressed, but virtually implied; for instance after a question which is equivalent to a negation; e. g. מֶה עָשִׂיתִי לְךָ ..... כִּי הֶעֱלִיתִיךָ *what have I done unto thee* (i. e. *I have done nothing against thee*) .... *nay* (= *on the contrary*), *I brought thee up out of Egypt* etc. Micha 6, 3. 4; כִּי מִנְּעוּרַי גְּדֵלַנִי כְאָב *nay,* (*the orphan can say*), *from my youth he brought me up as a father* Job 31; 18. In this sence, therefore כִּי is equivalent to כִּי אִם conf. below 5, I β.

Rem. 7 כִּי sometimes has a *concessive* sense = *although*; e. g. וַיּוֹאֶל לָלֶכֶת כִּי לֹא נִסָּה *and he would go, although he was not accustomed to it* (prop. *he wanted just to try to walk with the arms, for he had never yet carried such arms*) 1 Sam. 17, 39. (Conf. Pr. Driver's "notes on the Hebrew text" on this place); וְלֹא נָחָם אֱלֹהִים .... כִּי קָרוֹב הוּא *God led them not by the way of the land of the Philistines, although that was near* (prop. *God did not lead them* etc. *although this might have been expected, for it was the shorter way*) Ex. 13, 17.

It follows, therefore, that כִּי in such cases retains its value as a *causative* conjunction; only the reason stated does not refer to the entire preceding clause, but merely to a part of it.

(*e*) אֲשֶׁר (never כִּי) serves as a *final* conjunction in the sense of *that* (= לְמַעַן אֲשֶׁר see below 5, E α); e. g. אֲשֶׁר לֹא יִשְׁמָעוּ *that they may not understand* Gen. 11, 7; אֲשֶׁר יִיטַב לָךְ *that he may do good unto thee* Deut. 6, 3; אֲשֶׁר יֵדְעוּן *that they may know* Jos. 3, 7.

(*f*) אֲשֶׁר occasionally also possesses the meaning of

§ 28. CONJUNCTIONS. 103

כַּאֲשֶׁר; e. g. אֲשֶׁר לֹא יִסָּפֵר צְבָא הַשָּׁמַיִם *as the host of heaven cannot be numbered* (the main sentence commences with כֵּן) Jer. 33, 22.

Rem. 8 With אֲשֶׁר as *nota relationis* the demonstrative word is sometimes omitted, so that the relative particle is expressed by אֲשֶׁר alone; e. g. אֲשֶׁר שָׁם = אֲשֶׁר רָבוּ *where the children of Israel strove with the Lord* Num. 20, 13; אֲשֶׁר הִלְלוּךָ אֲבוֹתֵינוּ *where our fathers praised thee* Jes. 64, 10.

5) Subjoined is a short compendium of the different classes of conjunctions with remarks as to what is of importance concerning the use of some of them.

What remains beyond this more properly belongs to the sphere of the Lexicon.

A. as *copulative*, besides וְ, we find גַּם *also*, and the intensive or progressive אַף (*in addition to*) *yet more, even*.

α. גַּם often serves to reduce two or more persons or objects to one head or group; e. g. גַּם שְׁנֵיכֶם *why should I be bereaved of both of you* Gen. 27, 45; גַּם כָּל *all together*.

It is further used simply to emphasise the words following; e. g. גַּם אֶת רָחֵל מִלֵּאָה *and he loved Rachel even more than Lea* Gen. 29, 30 (conf. in Lat. the comparative with *etiam*); רְאֵה גַם רְאֵה *see, yea, see* 1 Sam. 24, 12.

גַּם .... גַּם (or גַּם .... וְגַם Gen. 24, 44 גַּם אַתָּה שְׁתֵה וְגַם לִגְמַלֶּיךָ אֶשְׁאָב *both drink thou, and I will also draw for thy camels*) means *as well ...... as*, *both* ..... *and*. Sometimes we find גַם in this sense thrice repeated; e. g. גַם תֶּבֶן גַם מִסְפּוֹא גַם מָקוֹם *we have both straw and provender enough and room to lodge in* Gen. 24, 25; Conf. 32, 20. Also וְ ..... וְ is used in the same sense; e. g. וַיָּבֹאוּ אֶל־גְּדַלְיָה הַמִּצְפָּתָה וְיִשְׁמָעֵאל וְיוֹחָנָן וְיוֹנָתָן *then came to Gedaliah to Mizpah, both Ismael, and Johanan and Jonathan* Jer. 40, 8; מָה אֲדַבֵּר וְאָמַר לִי וְהוּא עָשָׂה *what shall I say? he hath both spoken unto me and himself has done it* Jer. 38, 15.

β אַף כִּי (prop. *add to this that, not to mention that*) = *surely then*, and according to the context *quanto magis* or *tanto minus*; *how much more, how much less*. In a question, as exclamation it means *perhaps, perchance, mayhap*; e. g. אַף כִּי אָמַר אֱלֹהִים *hath God perchance said, ye shall not* Gen. 3, 1.

Once we find אַף גַם together Lev. 26. 44 וְאַף גַם זֹאת בִּהְיוֹתָם בְּאֶרֶץ אֹיְבֵיהֶם *and yet for all that, when they be in the land of their enemies, I will not reject them*.

B. The *disjunctive* conjunctions are:

α principally אוֹ *or* (prop. *from free choice*, just as the Latin conjunction *vel*). It occurs however also with an exclusive meaning (like the Lat. *aut*); e. g. בְּאַחַד הֶהָרִים אוֹ בְּאַחַת הַגֵּאָיוֹת *upon some mountain, or into some valley* 2 Kings 2, 16.

אוֹ sometimes stands elliptically, and is equivalent to אוֹ כִּי *or (if it should be) that*; e. g. אוֹ יַחֲזֵק בְּמָעֻזִּי *or else let him take hold of my strength* Jes. 27, 5. Hence the transition to the conditional meaning *if*,

§ 28. CONJUNCTIONS.

if however; e. g. אוֹ נוֹדַע כִּי *if, however, it were known* Ex. 21, 36. With the same signification we once find אוּלַי Hosea 8, 7 אוּלַי יַעֲשֶׂה *if however it yield, strangers shall swallow it up*.

Now and then the signification of אוֹ coincides with that of וְ *copulative*; e. g. אוֹ לָאַיִל *and as for a ram, thou shalt prepare* etc. Num. 15, 6.

β the *disjunctive: whether ..... or* (Lat. *sive ... sive* is expressed by אִם...אִם, וְאִם...אִם, אוֹ...אוֹ, מִן...עַד, מִן...וְעַד.

C. *Temporal conjunctions are:*

α אֲשֶׁר and כִּי (see above 4 B), כַּאֲשֶׁר = *when* (Lat. *quum*). Of rarer occurrence the conditional אִם (*if*) = *when*; e. g. אִם רָחַץ *when the Lord shall have washed away* Jes. 4, 4; אִם כָּלָה בָצִיר *when the vintage is done* Jes. 24, 13. Once we find כְּמוֹ in this sense Gen. 19, 15 וּכְמוֹ הַשַּׁחַר עָלָה *and when the morning arose*.

β עַד כִּי, עַד אֲשֶׁר, and עַד alone *until*, sometimes עַד אִם, עַד אֲשֶׁר אִם.

γ עַד *while, as long as*; בְּ with the infinitive *while*.

δ אַחַר אֲשֶׁר, אַחֲרֵי אֲשֶׁר *after* (אַחַר אֲשֶׁר) אַחַר הֻכְּתָה הָעִיר Ez. 40, 1 *after the city was smitten*; אַחַר Job 40, 2 וַיְהִי אַחַר דְּבֶר ה' *and it came to pass after the Lord had spoken these words*); and אַחֲרֵי כַּאֲשֶׁר e. g. אַחֲרֵי כַּאֲשֶׁר יָצְאוּ *and after they were gone* Jos. 2, 7; and אַחֲרֵי alone; e. g. אַחֲרֵי הוֹדִיעַ אֱלֹהִים *after God has shewed thee all this* Gen. 41, 39; אַחֲרֵי נִמְכָּר *after he is sold* Lev. 25, 48. מֵאָז (= מֵאָז אֲשֶׁר) *since*, בְּטֶרֶם, טֶרֶם *before, not yet* (בְּטֶרֶם לֹא) בְּטֶרֶם לֹא יָבוֹא עֲלֵיכֶם Zephania 2, 2 *before* the fierce anger of the Lord come upon you), also e. g. שֶׁקַּדְמַת שָׁלַף יָבֵשׁ (קַדְמַת אֲשֶׁר=קַדְמַת) which withereth before it groweth up Ps. 129, 6.

ε כְּ when, as; generally with the infinitive, sometimes with a participle; e. g. כְּמֵשִׁיב as he drew back his hand Gen. 38, 29; וְהוּא כְפֹרַחַת and as it budded Gen. 40, 19.

D. *Causal:*

אֲשֶׁר and כִּי (conf. above 4 C); עַל כֵּן אֲשֶׁר *propterea quod* (lit. *therefore because*) *because*; עַל דְּבַר אֲשֶׁר and עַל אוֹדוֹת אֲשֶׁר (prop. *for this cause that*) *because*; more emphatic עַל כָּל אוֹדוֹת אֲשֶׁר Jer. 3, 8 *for this very cause that, simply because*; בַּעֲבוּר אֲשֶׁר and יַעַן אֲשֶׁר *because*; תַּחַת כִּי and תַּחַת אֲשֶׁר (prop. *therefore that*) *because*; עֵקֶב אֲשֶׁר and עֵקֶב כִּי (prop. *as reward that; as consequence that*) *because*.

Rem. 9 אֲשֶׁר עַל כֵּן Job 34, 27, and more frequently כִּי עַל כֵּן everywhere means *because*, עַל כֵּן having been changed into a *relativum* by the *nota relationis* אֲשֶׁר and כִּי.

Rem. 10 Very remarkable is the use of עַל in Jer. 30, 14 עַל רֹב עֲוֹנֵךְ עָצְמוּ חַטֹּאתָיִךְ, for first it stands as the preposition *propter* עַל רֹב עֲוֹנֵךְ *on account of the greatness of thine iniquity*, and then it exercises its force as a causal conjunction עַל אֲשֶׁר עָצְמוּ ח׳ *because thy sins were increased*.

E. *final:*

α לְמַעַן אֲשֶׁר and לְמַעַן alone (*with the intention that*) *that, to the end that*; לְבַעֲבוּר, בַּעֲבוּר *that, in order that*. These are also construed with the infinitive,

§ 28. CONJUNCTIONS.

in which case however they really are prepositions.

Once we find בַּעֲבוּר לַחְקֹר *in order to search* 1 Chr. 19, 3; but the parallel place 2 Sam. 10, 3 reads בַּעֲבוּר חֲקֹר.

β) וְ *to the end that* (see above 2 K); perhaps also לְ in לְתֵת שָׁם *to place there the ark of the covenant* 1 Kings 6, 19.

γ as to the negation אַל conf. § 25 Rem. 1; פֶּן *lest, that not* § 25, 3 B; לְבִלְתִּי § 25, 3 A.

Once we find מִן prefixed to the imperfect with the *final* meaning *that not* Deut. 33, 11 מִן יְקוּמוּן *that they prevail not*.

F. *Conditional*:

α אִם, לוּ (rarely אִלּוּ = לוּ אִם Esther 7, 4) *if*; but with difference of use.

אִם leaves uncertain whether anything takes place, has taken place, will take place, or not (but rather the former alternative); it therefore denotes the pure and simple hypothesis (= *if I do so; if I did so; if I shall do so*).

לוּ on the contrary implies that what is supposed does not take place, has not taken place, or will not take place; or at least that such would be improbable, (= *if I did so, had done so, should do so*). Hence לוּ is used to express a wish; e. g. לוּ יִשְׁמָעֵאל יִחְיֶה *O that Ismael might live before thee* Gen. 17, 18; לוּ מָתְנוּ *would that we had died* Num. 14, 2; and even with the imperative (conf. § 17, 4 *b* and § 18, 2 *b*). Yet also אִם is used for stating a wish (conf. § 17, 4 b); and sometimes even in hypothetical sentences of which the condition is known not to be fulfilled; e. g. אִם אֶרְעַב *if I were hungry* Ps. 50, 12; אִם אֶסַּק שָׁמַיִם *if I ascend up unto heaven* Ps. 139, 8; אִם יְגַדְּלוּ אֶת בְּנֵיהֶם *if they bring up their children* Hos. 9, 12.

לוּ on the contrary can not be used when the possibility exists that the condition will be realised.

β אִם is always used in expressions of grief, and in conditional curses; e. g. אִם עָשִׂיתִי זֹאת *if I have done this* Ps. 7, 4—6; אִם שָׁכַחְנוּ *if we forget the name of our Lord* Ps. 44, 21; אִם אָמַרְתִּי *if I had said* Ps. 73, 15; אִם אֶשְׁכָּחֵךְ *if I forget thee* Ps. 137, 5.

Rem. 11 The apodosis is sometimes omitted after a protasis with אִם; e. g. וַתֹּאמֶר אִם תִּתֵּן עֵרָבוֹן עַד שָׁלְחֶךָ *and she said if thou wilt give me a pledge, till thou send it* Gen. 38, 17; chiefly with threatening sayings; e. g. אִם עַנֵּה תְעַנֶּה אֹתוֹ *if in any way thou afflict him* Ex. 22, 22.

γ What has been said concerning אִם and לוּ applies also to their compounds אִם לֹא, לוּלֵא, לוּלֵי.

δ After formulas used in swearing אִם has a negative sense; e. g. חֵי פַרְעֹה אִם תֵּצְאוּ מִזֶּה *by the life of Pharao, ye shall not go forth hence* Gen. 42, 15; and (consequently) אִם לֹא an affirmative sense. To understand this it must be borne in mind that such formulas contain an ellipsis of what will happen or would happen, were the condition to be fulfilled or to remain unfulfilled. This is evident from 1 Sam. 25, 22; כֹּה יַעֲשֶׂה אֱלֹהִים לְאֹיְבֵי דָוִד וְכֹה יֹסִיף אִם אַשְׁאִיר מִכָּל

§ 28. CONJUNCTIONS.

אֲשֶׁר לוֹ עַד אוֹר הַבֹּקֶר מַשְׁתִּין בְּקִיר *may God do so unto the enemies of David, and more also, if I leave of all that pertain to him by the morning light so much as one man child* 1 Sam. 25, 22.

Rem. 12. Once 2 Sam. 3, 35 כִּי אִם is found with a conditional sentence after an oath formula; כֹּה יַעֲשֶׂה לִי אֱלֹהִים כִּי אִם לִפְנֵי בוֹא הַשֶּׁמֶשׁ אֶטְעַם לֶחֶם *May God do so to me and more also if I taste bread till the sun go down.*

ε אִם and אִם לֹא not only possess this sense after formulas and verbs used in swearing, but also when they are used absolutely; אִם then denotes a strong negation; e. g. מָגֵן אִם יֵרָאֶה *not a shield was seen* Judges 5, 8; אִם יְכֻפַּר הֶעָוֹן *surely this iniquity shall not be purged from you* Jes. 22, 14; also when connected with a particle of interrogation; e. g. הַאִם תַּמְנוּ לִגְוֹעַ *is there no end to our dying* (= *shall we all perish*) Num. 17, 28; and אִם לֹא expresses an equally strong affirmation (= *truly, really*), e. g. אִם לֹא נִכְחַד קִימָנוּ *surely they that did rise up against us are cut off* Job 22, 20.

Rem. 13. Concerning the conditional signification of אֲשֶׁר, אוֹ, and כִּי conf. above n° 5 Bα and n° 4 Rem. 6.

G. *Concessive*:

α אִם *even if, though*, with the perfect; e. g. אִם צָדַקְתִּי *though I were righteous*; and the imperfect; e. g. אִם יִהְיוּ חֲטָאֵיכֶם *though your sins be as scarlet* Jes. 1, 18; אִם יִהְיֶה עַמְּךָ *though thy people be as the sand of the sea* Jes. 10, 22.

β עַל = עַל אֲשֶׁר (prop. *add to this that*) *although*; e. g. עַל לֹא חָמָס עָשָׂה *although he had done no violence* Jes. 53, 9; עַל לֹא חָמָס בְּכַפִּי *although there is no violence in my hands* Job 16, 17; also with the infinitive; e. g. עַל דַּעְתְּךָ *although thou knowest* Job 10, 7.

Concerning the concessive meaning of כִּי conf. above Rem. 7.

H. *Comparative*:

α כַּאֲשֶׁר *as*, *just as*, *such as*, often followed by the corresponding כֵּן in the *apodosis*; e. g. וְכַאֲשֶׁר יְעַנּוּ אֹתוֹ כֵּן יִרְבֶּה וְכֵן יִפְרֹץ *but the more they afflicted them*, *the more they multiplied and the more they spread* Ex. 1, 12. (Conf. § 27, 6 F).

כַּאֲשֶׁר, however, is sometimes omitted in the protasis; e. g. גָבְהוּ שָׁמַיִם מֵאָרֶץ כֵּן גָּבְהוּ *for as the heavens are higher than the earth*, *so are my ways higher than your ways* Jes. 55, 9; הֵמָּה רָאוּ כֵּן תָּמָהוּ *when they saw it*, *they were amazed* Ps. 48, 6; and in like manner also כֵּן in the apodosis; e. g. כִּי כַּאֲשֶׁר שְׁתִיתֶם עַל הַר קָדְשִׁי יִשְׁתּוּ כָל הַגּוֹיִם תָּמִיד *for as ye have drunk upon my holy mountain so shall all the nations drink continually* Obadja 16.

β כָּל עֻמַּת שֶׁ... כֵּן *in all points as .... so*, denotes an extremely precise comparison; e. g. כָּל עֻמַּת שֶׁבָּא כֵּן יֵלֵךְ *in all points as he came, so shall he go* Eccl. 5, 15.

Rem. 14. In sentences such as Ps. 42, 2 כְּאַיָּל תַּעֲרֹג .... כֵּן נַפְשִׁי *as the hart panteth after the waterbrooks, so panteth my soul after thee*, certain authors wish to explain כְּ by considering it = כַּאֲשֶׁר

with a comparative sense. Such sentences may however be easily explained by admitting an ellipsis of אֲשֶׁר as relativum; e. g. כְּאַיָּל אֲשֶׁר תַּעֲרֹג *like the hart that panteth.* Conf. Deut. 32, 11; Ps. 125, 1.

I. *Adversative*:

α אָפֵס כִּי (*only that*) = *but, however, nevertheless.*

β כִּי אִם (*but if*) = *before, except when* governing the Perfect, and following a negation in the Imperfect; e. g. לֹא אֶחֱשֶׁה כִּי אִם שִׁלַּמְתִּי *I will not keep silence before I have given recompense* Jes. 65, 6. In this case כִּי אִם stand together as one conjunction = *but if, except that, unless*, and follow after a negation or the equivalent of a negation. Conf. above 4 (*d*).

Yet כִּי אִם are also used in such a manner that כִּי belongs to the the main sentence and אִם to the conditional sentence; e. g. כִּי אִם תְּכַבְּסִי בַּנֶּתֶר *for even if thou wash thee with lye, thine iniquity is marked before me* Jer. 2, 22.

The adversative כִּי אִם before a noun means *besides* e. g. כִּי אִם לֶחֶם קֹדֶשׁ *there is no common bread under mine hand, besides the holy bread* 1 Sam. 21, 5.

Rem. 15. The main sentence to which the adversative כִּי אִם belongs has sometimes to be supplied from the context; e. g. כִּי אִם זְכַרְתַּנִי (*I desire nothing) except that thou remember me* Gen. 40, 14; כִּי אִם פָּנָיו אֶשָּׂא *for him will I respect* (prop. *for it cannot be otherwise than that I should respect him)* Job 42, 8.

K. Finally there is the conjunction וְעַתָּה which in most cases only serves to introduce the apodosis after a preceding subordinate sentence. Sometimes however, it implies also a causative sense; e. g. וְעַתָּה בְּרַח לְךָ אֶל מְקוֹמֶךָ *therefore now flee to thy place* Num. 24, 11; or a concessive sense; e. g. וְעַתָּה שְׁבוּ נָא בָזֶה גַּם אַתֶּם הַלָּיְלָה *However, I pray you, tarry ye also here this night* Num. 22, 19. (See Essay on the signification of עַתָּה reprinted from the "Israel. Letterbode" 1884).

6) Of two particles, of which the compound forms a conjunction, frequently only one or the other of them is used. This already appears from what has been said before. Thus, instead of the complete יַעַן אֲשֶׁר *on account of, because* we find either אֲשֶׁר alone, or יַעַן; instead of בַּאֲשֶׁר *as*, either כְּ (see Rem. 14) or אֲשֶׁר; e. g. כִּי אֲשֶׁר רְאִיתֶם אֶת מִצְרַיִם הַיּוֹם *for as ye have seen the Egyptians today, ye shall see them again no more* Ex. 14, 13; אֲשֶׁר שָׁמַרְתָּ לְעַבְדְּךָ דָוִד אָבִי אֵת אֲשֶׁר דִּבַּרְתָּ לּוֹ *as thou hast kept with thy servant David my father that which thou didst promise him* 1 Kings 8, 24.

On the other hand a certain tendency to be prolix sometimes shows itself; e. g. מִן....עַד = מִן....וְעַד; רַק אַךְ - רַק (conf. above 5 A β). The repetition, no doubt, of the same particle points to greater emphasis; e. g. מְאֹד מְאֹד, בִּמְאֹד מְאֹד, as וַיַּעַצְמוּ בִּמְאֹד מְאֹד *waxed exceeding mighty* Ex. 1, 7,; יַעַן וּבְיַעַן בְּמִשְׁפָּטַי מָאָסוּ *because, even because they rejected my judgments* Lev. 26, 43; which now and then also occurs with nomina; e. g. צֶדֶק צֶדֶק תִּרְדֹּף *that which is altogether just shalt thou follow* Deut. 16, 20; conf. Jes. 6, 3; Jer. 22, 29; Ez. 21, 32 (conf. § 22, 4).

7) The *consecutio temporum* in Hebrew not unfre-

§ 28. CONJUNCTIONS.

quently allows the expression of the relation between two sentences by simply placing them one after the other without any conjunction at all. This occurs:

α with *conditional* sentences; e. g. וּדְפָקוּם יוֹם אֶחָד וָמֵתוּ כָּל הַצֹּאן *and if they overdrive them one day, all the flock will die* Gen. 33, 13; חָטָאתִי מָה אֶפְעַל לָךְ (prop. *well! I have sinned) if I have sinned, what (harm) do I unto thee* Job 7, 20; בְּמוֹתִי וּקְבַרְתֶּם אֹתִי (*at my death*) *when I die* etc. 1 Kings 13, 31; עוֹד מְעַט וּסְקָלוּנִי *if* (*this last*) *a little longer, they will stone me*, or, *they be almost ready to stone me* Ex. 17, 4; מָצָא אִשָּׁה מָצָא טוֹב *whoso findeth a wife findeth a good thing* Pr. 18, 22.

Such sentences are sometimes introduced by another word, generally by הִנֵּה; e. g. עַתָּה יָבֹא דְבָרֶיךָ מַה יִּהְיֶה *now when thy words come to pass, what shall be the ordering of the child* Judges 13, 12; כִּי הִנֵּה הָלְכוּ מִשֹּׁד *for when they escape destruction, Egypt shall gather them up* Hosea 9, 6.

β with *comparisons*, e. g. אֹכְלֵי עַמִּי אָכְלוּ לֶחֶם *they devour my people, as if they eat bread* (lit. *devouring my people, they eat bread*) Ps. 14, 4; קֹרֵא דָגַר וְלֹא יָלָד עֹשֶׂה עֹשֶׁר *as the partridge sitteth on eggs which she hath not laid, so is he that getteth riches* Jer. 17, 11; צִיָּה גַם חֹם יִגְזְלוּ מֵימֵי שֶׁלֶג שְׁאוֹל חָטָאוּ *as drought and heat consume (steal) the snowwater, so doth sheol those that have sinned* Job 24, 19.

γ with sentences, which otherwise would have been introduced by a relative conjunction (*oratio obliqua*);

e. g. כִּי אֲחֹתִי אָתְּ = אֲחֹתִי אָתְּ say, *I pray, thou art my sister* Gen. 12, 13; כִּי תִשְׁמַע = תִשְׁמַע *that when thou hearest a dream* Gen. 41, 15; וְיֵדְעוּ גוֹיִם אֱנוֹשׁ הֵמָּה *that the nations may know, that they are but men* Ps. 9, 21; Ps. 50, 21; מָה רְאִיתֶם עָשִׂיתִי *what ye have seen me do* (prop. *what ye have seen that I did*) Judges 9, 48. כִּי יָדַעְתִּי בָּגוֹד תִּבְגּוֹד *for I knew that thou didst deal very treacherously* Jes. 48, 8.

N.B. In English such a sentence is always an *object sentence*, but according to Hebrew ideas it is to be considered as a direct and independent sentence.

§ 29. Interjections.

1) The Interjections which signify *ah, alas, woe*, (אֲהָהּ, הוֹי, אוֹי) are either connected with the object of the threatening or lamentation by means of the particles אֶל, לְ or עַל, or they stand absolutely, so that the object of lament remains without a particle.

The first named construction is the more usual with denunciations, (conf. the Latin *vae tibi*), the latter with expressions of grief (conf. Latin *vae te* in Plautus); e. g. אוֹי לָנוּ *woe us!* Sam. 5, 16; הוֹי גּוֹי חֹטֵא *Ah, sinful nation!* Jes. 1, 4; הוֹי אָחִי *Alas, my brother!* 1 Kings 13, 30.

2) With אַשְׁרֵי *O happy!* the noun, expressing the object praised, is sometimes omitted; e. g. אַשְׁרֵי שֶׁיְשַׁלֶּם לָךְ ..... אַשְׁרֵי שֶׁיֹּאחֵז *happy shall he be that rewardeth thee as thou hast served us, happy shall he be that taketh* etc. Ps. 137, 8. 9; and in Ps. 65, 5 even the nota relationis אֲשֶׁר = שֶׁ; אַשְׁרֵי תִבְחַר *happy the man whom thou choosest.*

אַשְׁרֵי moreover, like הִנֵּה, is not unfrequently connected with suffixes; e. g. אַשְׁרֶיךָ, אַשְׁרֵיךְ *happy thou!* אַשְׁרֵיכֶם *happy you!* אַשְׁרָיו or אַשְׁרֵהוּ *happy he.*

PART IV

CONSTRUCTION OF THE SENTENCE

CHAPTER IX — NOMINAL SENTENCES

§ 30. Subject and Predicate.

1) Nominal sentences are sentences which only express a state of *existence* or *being*, and of which the predicate is a *nomen*.

2) The predicate of a nominal sentence is either a noun, adjective, participle or pronoun; e. g. ה' מַלְכֵּנוּ *the Lord is our king* Jes. 33, 22; וְאַנְשֵׁי סְדֹם רָעִים וְחַטָּאִים *and the men of Sedôm were wicked and sinners* Gen. 13, 13; וְנָהָר יֹצֵא מֵעֵדֶן *and a river went out* (prop. *is going out) of Eden* Gen. 2, 10; זֶה הַדָּבָר *this is the case.*

Rem. 1. The subject may also be a pronoun; e. g. זֹאת הַפַּעַם עֶצֶם מֵעֲצָמַי *this is now bone of my bones* Gen. 2, 23; וְהוּא כֹהֵן *and he was priest* Gen. 14, 18.

3) A remarkable class of nominal sentences are those, of which the predicate itself forms a nominal sentence; e. g. חֲסִידָה בְּרוֹשִׁים בֵּיתָהּ *as for the stork ..... the fir trees are her nest* (= בְּרוֹשִׁים בַּיִת לַחֲסִידָה conf. v. 18) Ps. 104, 17; הָאֵל תָּמִים דַּרְכּוֹ *God ..... perfect is his way* Ps. 18, 31;

אֲנִי הִנֵּה בְרִיתִי אִתָּךְ *as for me, behold my covenant is with thee* Gen. 17, 4.

In these sentences the subject is sometimes introduced by the (so called) וְ *apodosis*; e. g. וַאֲנִי הִנְנִי מֵקִים *and I ..... behold I establish my covenant* [1]) Gen. 9, 9.

Rem. 2 It is evident that by such sentences the Hebrews intend to emphasise the position of the true subject of the sentence. In English we should say *the fir trees are the stork's nest*, both when it is desired to indicate what the nest of the stork is made of, and when it is intended to convey where the stork (in contrast with other birds) builds herself a nest. Now, in the last named alternative something is said concerning *the choice of the stork*, and it is, therefore, quite correct when the Hebrews both place the *stork* as subject in the beginning of the sentence, and mention her again in the predicate by means of a suffix. Sometimes, however, the subject is not again mentioned in the predicate, and is then to be supplied from the context; e. g. וְנֶפֶשׁ רְעֵבָה כָּל מַר מָתוֹק *as for a hungry stomach, every thing bitter is sweet (to it)* Prov. 27, 7.

Rem. 3 Certain exclamations also, in which the reader is left to supply a nominal or verbal predicate, are to be considered as nominal sentences; e. g. פַּחַז כַּמַּיִם *a rashness (as quick) as water* Gen. 49, 4; הֲמוֹנִים הֲמוֹנִים בְּעֵמֶק הֶחָרוּץ *multitudes after multitudes (are seen) in the valley of Haruti* Joel 4, 14.

4) The use of a noun as predicate of a nominal sentence chiefly occurs when the equivalent adjective is wanting; e. g. וְקִירֹתָיו עֵץ *and the walls thereof were of wood* Ez. 41, 21 (conf. § 4, 7 and Rem. 1). The harshness of such

---

1) This kind of nominal sentence is called by certain Grammarians a *compound nominal* sentence.

§ 30. SUBJECT AND PREDICATE.

an expression is occasionally softened by repeating the subject nomen and connecting it in st. constr. with the predicate; e. g. אִם כֹּחַ אֲבָנִים כֹּחִי *is then my strength (the strength) of stone?* Job 6, 12; שֵׁבֶט מִישֹׁר שֵׁבֶט מַלְכוּתֶךָ *a sceptre of equity is the sceptre of thy kingdom* Ps. 45, 7.

This repetition of the subject nomen is the more usual construction when a comparison is intended; e. g. וְהָיָה אוֹר הַלְּבָנָה כְּאוֹר הַחַמָּה *and the light of the moon shall be as the light of the sun* Jes. 30, 26; or when the predicate cannot be expressed by an adjective; e. g. מַלְכוּתְךָ מַלְכוּת כָּל־עֹלָמִים *thy kingdom is a kingdom of all eternity* Ps. 145, 13. (No adjective can be formed to express כָּל־עֹלָמִים *of all eternity*, for the adjective formed from עֹלָם would mean *eternal*). הַקֹּל קוֹל יַעֲקֹב וְהַיָּדַיִם יְדֵי עֵשָׂו *the voice is Jacob's voice, but the hands are the hands of Esau* Gen. 27, 22.

The construction in the two last named cases becomes very bold, when the subject nomen is not repeated in the predicate; e. g. וְצֶאֱצָאֵי מֵעֶיךָ כִּמְעֹתָיו *thy seed also had been as the sand, and the offspring of thy bowels as (the offspring) of its bowels* Jes. 48, 19; וּבְגָדַיִךְ כְּבִגְדֵי דֹרֵךְ בְּגַת = וּבְגָדֶיךָ כְּדֹרֵךְ בְּגַת *and thy garments are like (the garments) of him that treadeth in the winefat* Jes. 63, 2; חִצָּיו כְּגִבּוֹר = חִצָּיו כְּחִצֵּי גִבּוֹר נָבוֹר *their arrows shall be like (the arrows of) a skilled mighty man* Jer. 50, 9; הָעֵת גְּשָׁמִים = הָעֵת עֵת גְּשָׁמִים *and it is a time of much rain* Ezra 10, 13; and this construction becomes still bolder when the כ *comparationis* is omitted; e. g. כִּסְאֲךָ אֱלֹהִים = כְּסַאֲךָ כְּכִסֵּא אֱלֹהִים *thy throne is (like the throne of) God*

Ps. 45, 7; עֵינַיִךְ בְּעֵינֵי יוֹנִים = עֵינַיִךְ יוֹנִים *thine eyes are (like the eyes of) doves* Cant. 1, 15 (conf. § 3 Rem. 2).

5) When the subject of a nominal sentence is an infinitive, it is by preference introduced by לְ; e. g. טוֹב לָשֶׁבֶת *it is better to dwell in the corner of the housetop* Prov. 21, 9 (in v. 19 לְ is omitted טוֹב שֶׁבֶת בְּאֶרֶץ מִדְבָּר *it is better to dwell in a desert land*); לֹא לְךָ עֻזִּיָּהוּ לְהַקְטִיר *it is not thine office, Uzia, to sacrifice* 2 Chr. 26, 18; seldom by בְּ; e. g. אַל יִקְשֶׁה בְעֵינֶךָ בְּשַׁלֵּחֲךָ אֹתוֹ *let it not seem hard unto thee to let him go free* Deut. 15, 18; but never when the infinitive stands in the *st. constr.*; e. g. לֹא טוֹב הֱיוֹת הָאָדָם לְבַדּוֹ *it is not good that the man should be alone* Gen. 2, 18; שְׂאֵת פְּנֵי רָשָׁע לֹא טוֹב *to accept the person of the wicked is not good* Prov. 18, 5.

Rem. 4 Now and then an adverb is found as predicate; e. g. כִּי כִי בְרַע הוּא תְּמוֹל אֲנַחְנוּ *for we are but of yesterday* Job. 8, 9; כִּי בְרַע הוּא *that they are set on evil* Ex. 32, 22; [2]) but more rarely as subject; e. g. וְגַם הַרְבֵּה נָפַל מִן הָעָם *and many of the people also are fallen* 2 Sam. 1, 4; כָּמֹהוּ לֹא נִהְיָתָה מִן הָעוֹלָם *there has not ever been the like* Joel 2, 2. Concerning הֲלוֹא כָמֹהוּ כְּאַיִן בְּעֵינֵיכֶם *is it not as nothing in your eyes?* Haggai 2, 3. Conf. § 27, 6 F α.

6) The infinitive also as predicate is sometimes found with לְ and sometimes without לְ; e. g. ה' לְהוֹשִׁיעֵנִי *the Lord is ready to save me* Jes. 38, 20; דִּבְרֵי רְשָׁעִים אֱרָב דָּם *the words of the wicked are a lying in wait for blood*

---

[2]) The Samaritan text reads כִּי פָרֻעַ הוּא *that they were broken loose;* conf. v. 25.

Prov. 12, 6; וְתוֹעֲבַת כְּסִילִים סוּר מֵרָע *it is an abomination to fools to depart from evil* Prov. 13, 19.

§ 31. Expression of the copula in nominal sentences.

1) The subject and predicate of a nominal sentence are generally placed next to one another without any copula; e. g. וּזְהַב הָאָרֶץ הַהִוא טוֹב *and the gold of that land (is) good* Gen. 2, 12; עֶשֶׂר אַמּוֹת אֹרֶךְ הַקֶּרֶשׁ *ten cubits (shall be) the length of a board* Ex. 26, 16; גַּם הוּא חָכָם *he also (is) wise* Jes. 31, 2; נִצָּב מֶלֶךְ *a deputy (was) king* 1 Kings 22, 48.

2) The personal pronoun of the 3d person is but seldom used as copula; e. g. חֲלוֹם אֶחָד הוּא *the dream is one* Gen. 41, 26; זֹה מַתַּת אֱלֹהִים הִיא *this is the gift of God* Eccl. 5, 18; בָּנִים סְכָלִים הֵמָּה *they are sottish children* Jer. 4, 22; שֶׁבַע פָּרֹת הַטֹּבֹת שֶׁבַע שָׁנִים הֵנָּה *the seven good kine are seven years* Gen. 41, 26.

This chiefly occurs when the relative pronoun אֲשֶׁר is the subject; e. g. כָּל רֶמֶשׂ אֲשֶׁר הוּא חַי *every moving thing that liveth* Gen. 9, 3; and especially in negative sentences; e. g. וּמִן הַבְּהֵמָה אֲשֶׁר לֹא טְהֹרָה הִוא *and of the beasts that are not clean* Gen. 7, 2; אֲשֶׁר לֹא מֵעָרֵי הַגּוֹיִם הָאֵלֶּה הֵנָּה *which are not of the cities of these nations* Deut. 20, 15.

The same pronoun is sometimes used as copula even when the subject is a pronoun of the 1st or 2d person; e. g. כִּי אֲנִי אֲנִי הוּא *see now: it is I, even I* Deut. 32, 39; אַתָּה הוּא מַלְכִּי *thou art my king* Ps. 44, 5; גַּם אַתֶּם כּוּשִׁים חַלְלֵי חַרְבִּי הֵמָּה *ye Ethiopians also, are victims of my sword* Zephania 2, 12.

3) Still more rarely the forms of הָיָה are used as copula; e. g. וְהָאָרֶץ הָיְתָה תֹהוּ וָבֹהוּ *and the earth was waste and void* Gen. 1, 2. וְהַנָּחָשׁ הָיָה עָרוּם *now the serpent was more subtil* Gen. 3, 1; וְכֹל לֶחֶם צֵידָם יָבֵשׁ הָיָה נִקֻּדִים *and all the bread of their provision was dry and mouldy* Jos. 9, 5; שִׁבְעִים מְלָכִים....הָיוּ מְלַקְּטִים *threescore and ten kings were gathering (their meat) under my table* Judges 1, 7.

4) If the subject should be a personal pronoun, and the predicate is expressed by a participle, the subject is then sometimes, as suffix, joined to יֵשׁ or אֵין (which are properly substantiva), according as the sentence is affirmative or negative; e. g. אִם יֶשְׁךָ מוֹשִׁיעַ *if thou savest* Judges 6, 36; וְאִם אֵינְךָ מְשַׁלֵּחַ *and if thou wilt not send him* Gen. 43, 5.

CHAPTER X — VERBAL SENTENCES.

§ 32. Object of the verb.

1) Verbal sentences are sentences of which the predicate is a *verbum finitum* and which express an action.

A verbum finitum, by its indication of persons, independently of all further determinations, may form a complete sentence; e. g. וַיֹּאכַל וַיֵּשְׁתְּ וַיָּקָם וַיֵּלַךְ *and he ate, and drunk, and rose up, and went his way.* Gen. 25, 34.

A single verb therefore is found more than once to suffice when intransitive, but when transitive an object generally follows as an important factor of the sentence.

2) The most simple manner of connecting a noun

§ 32. OBJECT OF THE VERB.

as object with a verb, is by adding it to the verb without preformative, afformative, or particle indicative of its relation as object; e. g. יֹאכַל לֶחֶם *he eats bread*, or (when definite) יֹאכַל הַלֶּחֶם *he eats the bread*. לֶחֶם or הַלֶּחֶם in this case is called the object.

The object however is frequently connected with the preposition אֵת (אֶת־), chiefly when it is determined by ה׳ הַיְדִיעָה, a st. constr., a pronominal suffix, or in any other way; e. g. בָּרָא אֵת הַשָּׁמַיִם *God created the heaven* Gen. 1, 1; וַיַּגֵּשׁ אֵת פַּר הַחַטָּאת *and he brought the bullock of the sin offering*. Lev. 8, 14; וּמָלַק אֶת רֹאשׁוֹ *and wring off its head* Lev. 1, 15; הוֹלִיד אֶת לוֹט *and Haran begat Lot* Gen. 11, 27; לֹא יָבִין אֶת־זֹאת *neither doth a fool understand this* Ps. 92, 7; אֶת־מִי אֶשְׁלַח *whom shall I send* Jes. 6, 8.

Rem. 1 אֵת seldom stands before an *indefinite* noun; e. g. וְכִי יִגַּח שׁוֹר אֶת־אִישׁ אוֹ אֶת־אִשָּׁה *and when an ox gore a man or woman* Ex. 21, 28; generally only in poetical style; e. g. וְאֶת־צַדִּיקִים יְשַׁלֶּם טוֹב *but the righteous shall be recompensed with good* Prov. 13, 21.

3) The use of the object without preposition is more frequent in Hebrew than in English. For almost all ideas which are in any way related to the action of the verb, may be expressed as object of the verb. We have already seen something similar with regard to the st. constr. See § 5, 4.

4) Thus it is that many verbs may be used both with an object (transitive), and without an object (intransitive); e. g. בָּכָה means as well *to weep*, as *to de-*

plore (conf. Lat. *flere*); יָשַׁב and שָׁכַן *to dwell* and *to inhabit*) הָלַךְ *to go* and *to go through*; as וַנֵּלֶךְ אֵת כָּל הַמִּדְבָּר *and we went through all the wilderness* Deut. 1, 19.

5) Even verbs, the action of which can really only be conceived as intransitive, often have as object a noun of the same stem; e. g. פָּחַד *to fear*, פָּחֲדוּ פָחַד *they were in great fear* Ps. 14, 5; חָטָא *to sin* חָטְאָה חָטָא *Jerusalem has grievously sinned* Sam. 1, 8.

This chiefly occurs with *verba denominativa*; e. g. תַּדְשֵׁא דֶּשֶׁא *let the earth put forth grass* Gen. 1, 11; בְּעַנְנִי עָנָן *when I bring a cloud* Gen. 9, 14; נִלְבְּנָה לְבֵנִים *let us make brick* Gen. 11, 3; מְאַלְּמִים אֲלֻמִּים *binding sheaves* Gen. 37, 7; הַמַּבְעִר אֶת־הַבְּעֵרָה *he that kindled the fire* Ex. 22, 5.

Especially when the action of the verb is determined by an adverbial expression, such determinations are generally in the form of an adjective, or in any other form, added to a noun of the same stem as the verb; e. g. נֶגַע נְגָעִים גְּדֹלִים *to plague severely* Gen. 12, 17; חָרַד חֲרָדָה גְדֹלָה *to fear greatly* Gen. 27, 33; חָטָא חֲטָאָה גְדֹלָה *to sin grievously* Ex. 32, 31; צָעַק צְעָקָה גְדֹלָה וּמָרָה *to cry loudly and bitterly* Est. 4, 1; שָׂנֵא שִׂנְאָה גְדֹלָה *to hate keenly* 2 Sam. 13, 15; חָלָה אֶת־חָלָיו אֲשֶׁר יָמוּת בּוֹ *to be deathly sick* 2 Kings 13, 14; הִכָּה מַכַּת בִּלְתִּי סָרָה *to smite irresistibly* Jes. 14, 6; הִקְשִׁיב קֶשֶׁב רַב־קָשֶׁב *to answer much* Jes. 21, 7; וְאֻסְּפוּ אֲסֵפָה אַסִּיר עַל־בּוֹר *to be gathered as prisoners* Jes. 24, 22; נוֹשַׁע תְּשׁוּעַת עוֹלָמִים *to save for ever* Jes. 45, 17; שׂוֹשׂ מְשׂוֹשׂ חָתָן עַל כַּלָּה *to rejoice thoroughly* Jes. 62, 5; קִנֵּא קִנְאָה גְדֹלָה שָׂמַח שִׂמְחָה גְדֹלָה Jon. 4, 6; 1 Chr. 29, 9;

§ 32. OBJECT OF THE VERB.   123

to be very jealous, to strive jealously Zech. 1, 14; קָצַף קֶצֶף גָּדֹל *to be very wroth* Zech. 1, 15 (conf. also n°. 11).

In all these instances the noun adds nothing to the meaning already expressed by the verb.

6) The same connection of the object without preposition or prefix also occurs with determinations of *place* of the most general kind, in answer to the questions: *where, whither, unto what, whence* e. g. נֵצֵא הַשָּׂדֶה *let us go forth into the field* Cant. 7, 12; יָצְאוּ אֶת הָעִיר *they were gone out of the city* (conf. Lat. *egredi urbem*) Gen. 44, 4; וְשָׁפַכְתָּ הַיַּבָּשָׁה *and thou shalt pour it upon the dry land* Ex. 4, 9; וִיבֹאֻנִי חֲסָדֶךָ *may thy favours come unto me* Ps. 119, 41.

Rem. 2 Suchlike expressions, however, may also be expresssd in a different manner. See § 35, 2.

7) With the verbs signifying *to flow, to stream* etc., that which flows, or better that with which overflows anything, stands in poetry as object; e. g. עֵינִי יָרְדָה מַּיִם *mine eye overflows with water* (= *tears*) Lam. 1, 16 conf. 3, 48 Jer. 9, 17; 13, 17; יִטְּפוּ הֶהָרִים עָסִיס וְהַגְּבָעוֹת תֵּלַבְנָה חָלָב וְכָל אֲפִיקֵי יְהוּדָה יֵלְכוּ מָיִם *the mountains shall drop new wine, the hills shall flow with milk, and all the brooks of Judah shall flow with waters.* Joel 4, 18. conf. Amos 9, 13; שׁוֹטֵף צְדָקָה *overflowing with righteousness* Jes. 10, 22. In like manner also expressions such as וְהִנֵּה עָלָה כֻלּוֹ קִמְּשׂוֹנִים *and, lo, it all* (= *the field*) *is gone up in thorns* Prov. 24, 31; conf. Jes. 5, 6; 34, 13.

8) Further large classes of verbs are to be found

which are construed with an accusative of object; namely:

a) all verbs signifying *a putting on* or *putting off one's garments, covering, enveloping, adorning*, and suchlike, as לָבַשׁ, פָּשַׁט, עָדָה, עָטָה, also when used in metaphorical language; e. g. לָבְשׁוּ כָרִים הַצֹּאן *the pastures are clothed with flocks* Ps. 65, 14; עֹטֶה אוֹר *who envelops himself with light* Ps. 104, 2; יִלְבְּשׁוּ שׂוֹטְנַי כְּלִמָּה וְיַעֲטוּ כַמְעִיל בָּשְׁתָּם *may mine adversaries be clothed with dishonour, and may they cover themselves with their shame as with a mantle* Ps. 109, 29. (Conf. § 35, 3).

b) verbs signifying: *to be full, to lack*, as מָלֵא *to be full*; שָׁרַץ *to swarm, to abound* Gen. 1, 20; שָׂבַע *to be satisfied*; פָּרַץ *to increase, to overflow* (conf. n°. 7) Prov. 3, 10; חָסֵר *to want* (that which is wanting being object, and the person or thing to which anything is wanting subject); e. g. אוּלַי יַחְסְרוּן חֲמִשִּׁים הַצַּדִּיקִם חֲמִשָּׁה *peradventure there shall lack five of the fifty righteous* Gen. 18, 28; שָׁכַל *to be bereaved* Gen. 27, 45.

c) several verbs of *dwelling*, and not only *near or in a place*, as שָׁכַן Jes. 33, 16, יָשַׁב Gen. 4, 20, גּוּר Judges 5, 17, but also *with somebody, with a people*; e. g. לֹא יְגֻרְךָ רָע *the evil man shall not dwell with thee* Ps. 5, 5. Conf. Ps. 120, 5.

9) The same construction without preposition or prefix is also used to express the adverbial relations, as *after the manner of, in proportion to, what regards, as for, according to*, etc.; e. g. מֵתִים אֲבָל לֹא הַמַּעֲשֶׂה *as for the*

§ 32. OBJECT OF THE VERB.

dead thou shalt make no mourning Ez. 24, 17; וְהֶעֱלָה עֹלוֹת מִסְפַּר כֻּלָּם *and he offered burnt offerings according to the number of them all* Job 1, 5; רַק הַכִּסֵּא אֶגְדַּל מִמֶּךָּ *only as regards the throne will I be greater than thou* Gen. 41, 40; סָגוּר חוֹתָם צָר *shut up as with a close seal* Job 41, 7; לְהִלָּחֵם פֶּה אֶחָד *to fight (as with the decision of) one mouth = with one consent* Zeph. 3, 9.

It further expresses all sorts of adverbial determinations; e. g. שֶׁקֶר רְדָפוּנִי *they persecute me wrongfully* Ps. 119, 86; וְאֵיךְ תְּנַחֲמוּנִי הָבֶל *and how will ye foolishly comfort me?* Job 21, 34; אֹהֲבֵם נְדָבָה *I love them freely* Hosea 14, 5; הִכְעִיס אֶפְרַיִם תַּמְרוּרִים *Ephraim has bitterly grieved* Hosea 12, 15; וַתֵּרֶד פְּלָאִים *she is come down astonishingly* Lam. 1, 9; very frequently with the verb הָלַךְ; e. g. הָלְכוּ שְׁבִי *they are gone unto captivity* Lam. 1, 5; וְאִם תֵּלְכוּ עִמִּי קֶרִי *and if ye resist me* Lev. 26, 21; וַיֵּלֶךְ מֵעֲרָנוֹת *and he came joyfully* 1 Sam. 15, 32; וְהָלְכוּ אֵלַיִךְ שְׁחוֹחַ *they shall come bending unto thee* Jes. 60, 14; וְלֹא תֵלְכוּ רוֹמָה *neither shall ye walk straight = haughtily* Mich 2, 3.

Rem. 3 These kinds of determination are often also expressed in a different manner. See § 35, 4.

10) The determination of *time* also is frequently expressed as object to the verb, namely in answer:

a) to the question *how long?* e. g. שְׁתֵּים עֶשְׂרֵה שָׁנָה עֲבָדוּ *they served twelve years* Gen. 14, 4; conf. Deut. 1, 46; 9, 25.

b) to the question *when?* עֶרֶב וָבֹקֶר וְצָהֳרַיִם אָשִׂיחָה *at morning, at evening, at noonday I pray* Ps. 55, 18.

11) With verbs signifying *to speak*, *to cry*, *to work*, *to save* etc. the organ with which the action is performed frequently stands as object, and the adverbial determination as determination of the organ (conf. n°. 5); e g. וָאֶזְעַק קוֹל גָּדוֹל *and I cried with a loud voice* Ez. 11, 13; conf. 2 Sam. 15, 23; רָאשׁ עֹשֶׂה כַף רְמִיָּה *the poor worketh with a slack hand* Prov. 10, 4 (conf. our expressions such as *to play football*); frequently also without determination; e. g. קוֹלִי אֶקְרָא *I cry unto the Lord with my voice* Ps. 3, 5; conf. 27, 7; 142, 2; Jes. 10, 30; פִּימוֹ דִבְּרוּ *they speak with their mouth* Ps. 17, 10 conf. 66, 17; פַּלְּטָה נַפְשִׁי מֵרָשָׁע חַרְבֶּךָ *deliver me from the wicked by the sword* Ps. 17, 13; הוֹשִׁיעָה יְמִינְךָ *save with thy right hand* Ps. 60, 7; 108, 7; conf. 44, 3. (In 1 Sam. 25, 26. 33 however יָד is subject).

This construction is known by the name of *accusativus instrumenti*.

Rem. 4 Other constructions of course are also possible. See § 34, 2 and 35, 6.

12) The *verba sentiendi*, chiefly רָאָה, sometimes govern as object a nomen which is really the subject of a subordinate clause (*antiptosis*); e. g. וַיַּרְא אֱלֹהִים אֶת־הָאוֹר כִּי טוֹב *and God saw that the light was good* Gen. 1, 4 conf. Gen. 6, 2; 12, 14; 49, 15; Ex. 2, 2; Ps. 25, 19; with יָדַע e. g. יָדַעְתָּ אֶת־הָעָם כִּי בְרָע הוּא *thou knowest that the people are set on evil* Ex. 32, 22, conf. 2 Sam. 3, 25; 17, 8; 1 Kings 5, 17.

13) The Hebrews, moreover, in the case of many verbs, consider as object the person who in the English

§ 32. OBJECT OF THE VERB.

language is but one interested in the action; e. g. with בִּשֵּׂר *to bring a message*; עָנָה *to answer*; עָבַד *to serve* (e. g. Gen. 15, 13); עָרַב *to stand security*; צִוָּה *to command*; רָב *to take up the quarrel, dispute*.

15) Many intransitive verbs, even passive and reflexive verbs (in נִפְעַל, הָפְעַל and הִתְפַּעֵל) may with a certain modification of meaning be connected with an object; e. g. חָפֵץ (*to be favourably inclined*, generally with בְּ) *to desire, to will* וְדַם פָּרִים לֹא חָפָצְתִּי *I desire not the blood of bullocks* Jes. 1, 11; נִבָּא (*to be moved to speak*) *to prophesy* אֲשֶׁר נִבָּא יִרְמְיָהוּ *which Jeremia hath prophesied* Jer. 25, 13; נָסַב (*to place oneself round anything*) *to surround* נָסַבּוּ אֶת־הַבַּיִת *they surrounded the house* Judges 19, 22; וַיִּלָּחֲמוּנִי *they fight against me* Ps. 109, 3; הִתְנַחֵל *to appropriate* Lev. 25, 46; Jes. 14, 2; וַיִּתְנַכְּלוּ אֹתוֹ *to make one the object of intrigue, to conspire against one* Gen. 37, 18; הִתְבּוֹנֵן *to consider* Job 37, 14; נִרְאָה אֶת־פְּנֵי ה׳ *to appear before the Lord* 1 Sam. 1, 22 (conf. n°. 4).

Rem. 5 The object is sometimes omitted in expressions which are frequently used; e. g. נָשָׂא פָנִים = נָשָׂא *to receive favourably* Gen. 4, 7; 18, 24. 26; or נָשָׂא עָוֹן = *to bear punishment* Jes. 2, 9; or כָּרַת בְּרִית = כָּרַת = נָשָׂא קוֹל *to raise the voice, to cry loudly* Jes. 3, 7; *to make a covenant* 1 Sam. 20, 16; שָׁלַח יָד = שָׁלַח *to put forth one's hand* 2 Sam. 6, 6 perhaps also Ps. 18, 17 יִשְׁלַח מִמָּרוֹם *He put forth his hand from on high;* נָטַר אַף = (שָׁמַר =) נָטַר *to remain angry* Jer. 3, 5; Ps. 103, 9.

Rem. 6 Concerning the use of לְ with the object see § 27, 6 E *s*.

§ 33. Verbs with a twofold object.

1) The causative forms (פָּעֵל and הִפְעִיל) of verbs which already in קַל have an object, often govern a twofold object; e. g. וַיַּפְשִׁיטוּ אֶת־יוֹסֵף אֶת־כֻּתָּנְתּוֹ *and they strip Joseph of his coat* Gen. 37, 23; הִלְבִּישׁ *to clothe* Gen. 41, 42; מִלֵּא *to fill* Ex. 28, 3; הֶאֱכִיל *to feed* Deut. 8, 16; עִטֵּר and חִסֵּר *to crown* and *to make any one to be wanting in a thing* Ps. 8, 6; אִזֵּר *to gird* Ps. 18, 33.

2) Many verbs also govern in קַל a twofold object; e. g. סָעַד *to strengthen* סְעָד לִבְּךָ פַּת־לֶחֶם *strengthen thine heart with a morsel of bread* Judges 19, 5; גָּמַל *to repay* 1 Sam. 24, 18; טָח *to spread over* Ez. 13, 10; עָטַר *to crown* Ps. 5, 13; [1]) מָשַׁח *to anoint* Ps. 45, 8; סָמַךְ *to uphold, to aid* Ps. 51, 14; *to bestow upon* Gen. 27, 37; קָבַע *to despoil* Prov. 22, 23; also expressions of *sowing* and *planting*; e. g. וַיִּזְרָעֶהָ מֶלַח *and sowed it with salt* Judges 9, 45; conf. Jes. 5, 2; 17, 10; 30, 23.

3) The Hebrews generally express the thing produced or obtained by any action, as object along with the object denoting the material of which it has been produced; e. g. קִנִּים תַּעֲשֶׂה אֶת הַתֵּבָה *with partitions shalt thou make the ark* Gen. 6, 13; כִּי אַב־הֲמוֹן גּוֹיִם נְתַתִּיךָ *for a father of a multitude of nations have I made thee* Gen. 17, 5 (conf. Lat. *reddere*); וְאֶעֱשֶׂה אֹתָם מַטְעַמִּים *and I will make them savoury meat for thy father* Gen. 27, 9; וַיָּשֶׂם אֹתָהּ מַצֵּבָה

---

1) תַּעַטְרֶנּוּ however may also be a form of הִפְעִיל, in which the חִירִק of the הַפְעַל ע has fallen away, like וַיַּדְרְכוּ Jer. 9, 2; conf. author's gramm. § 18, 4. Rem. 1.

§ 33. VERBS WITH A TWOFOLD OBJECT.

וַיָּ֫שֶׂם אֹתוֹ *and he set it up for a pillar* Gen. 28, 18; שֶׁ֫מֶן מִשְׁחַת קֹ֫דֶשׁ *and thou shalt make of it an holy anointing oil* Ex. 30, 25 ; וְאָפִיתָ אֹתָהּ שְׁתֵּים עֶשְׂרֵה חַלּוֹת *and thou shalt bake twelve cakes thereof* Lev. 24, 5; וַיִּ֫בֶן אֶת־הָאֲבָנִים מִזְבֵּחַ *and he built an altar with the stones* I Kings 18, 32.

This construction becomes remarkable when the object of the material stands last; e. g. כָּל־כֵּלָיו עָשָׂה נְחֹ֫שֶׁת *he made all its vessels of brass* Ex. 38, 3; וַיִּ֫יצֶר... אֶת־הָאָדָם עָפָר *he formed the man of dust* Gen. 2, 7.

4) When the speaker or writer wishes to indicate what part of the object is more especially affected by the action, then this part also takes the place of object; e. g. הוּא יְשׁוּפְךָ רֹאשׁ *he will wound thee in the head* Gen. 3, 15; לֹא נַכֶּ֫נּוּ נָ֫פֶשׁ *let us not take his life* Gen. 37, 21 (prop. *to smite him what regards his life* Conf. Deut. 19, 6; 22, 26); מָחַץ מָתְנַ֫יִם קָמָיו *smite his adversaries in the loins* Deut. 33, 11; וַיַּכֵּ֫הוּ שָׁם הַחֹ֫מֶשׁ *he smote him there in the belly* 2 Sam. 3, 27; הִכִּ֫יתָ אֶת־כָּל־אֹיְבַי לֶ֫חִי *thou hast smitten all mine enemies on the cheek* Ps. 3, 8.

The same construction also occurs with the intransitive verbs; e. g. חָלָה אֶת־רַגְלָיו *he was diseased in his feet* 1 Kings 15, 23. The parallel place 2 Chron. 16, 12 reads: בְּרַגְלָיו.

Concerning the construction of these verbs when used in the passive, see § 34.

Rem. 7 § 35, 7 will show that here also other constructions are possible.

9

§ 34. Construction of the Passive.

1) A passive expression in Hebrew is frequently connected with an object; namely:

a) when a causative verb (פִּעֵל and הִפְעִיל) governs a double object (§ 33, 1), then in the passive that object alone which is directly affected by the action, changes into the subject, while the other object remains object, and this irrespective of whether the subject is a nomen or pronomen, or is implied in the *verbum finitum*; e. g. אֲשֶׁר הָרְאֵיתָ *which has been shewed thee* Ex. 26, 30; אֲשֶׁר אַתָּה מָרְאֶה Ex. 25, 40; פֻּקַּדְתִּי יֶתֶר שְׁנוֹתָי *I shall be deprived of mine remaining years* Jes. 38, 10; כָּסּוּ הָרִים צִלָּהּ *the mountains were covered with the shadow of it.* Ps. 80, 11; הָנְחַלְתִּי לִי יַרְחֵי שָׁוְא *so am I made to possess months of vanity* Job 7, 3.

b) with regard to the construction explained in § 33, 4, the person alone who undergoes the action, becomes subject, while the further determination remains object; e. g. וּנְמַלְתֶּם אֵת בְּשַׂר עָרְלַתְכֶם *and ye shall be circumcised in the flesh of your foreskin.* Gen. 17, 11. 14. 24. 25. [1])

c) a transitive verb with its object, is not unfrequently changed into passive in such a manner that the verb alone changes its gender, while the object re-

---

1) This construction of the passive is very similar to that of various intransitive verbs mentioned in § 32, 9.

§ 34. CONSTRUCTION OF THE PASSIVE.

tains its place as object; e. g. וַיִּוָּלֵד לַחֲנוֹךְ אֶת עִירָד *and unto Henoch was born Irad.* Gen. 4, 18 conf. 21, 5; 40, 20; וַיֻּגַּד לְרִבְקָה אֶת דִּבְרֵי עֵשָׂו *and the words of Esau were told to Rebeka* Gen. 27, 42 conf. 2 Sam. 21, 11; 1 Kings 18, 13; וְלֹא יִקָּרֵא עוֹד אֶת שִׁמְךָ *neither shall thy name any more be called* Gen. 17, 5; וַתִּמָּלֵא הָאָרֶץ אֹתָם *and the land was filled with them* Ex. 1, 6; וַיּוּשַׁב אֶת מֹשֶׁה וְאֶת אַהֲרֹן *and Moses and Aaron were brought again unto Pharaoh* Ex. 10, 8; יֻתַּן אֶת הָאָרֶץ *let this land be given* Num. 32, 5; conf. 1 Kings 2, 21; וְשִׁאִיָּה יֻכַּת שָׁעַר *and the gate is smitten with destruction* Jes. 24, 12. The same construction occurs with the participle; e. g. וְהַנּוֹתָר אֶת הֶהָמוֹן הַזֶּה *and this great store is left* 2 Chron. 31, 10. [2])

2) The *operating cause* in the passive is generally expressed by לְ; e. g. בָּרוּךְ אַבְרָם לְאֵל *blessed be Abram of* (= *by*) *God* Gen. 14, 19; וַיֵּעָתֶר לוֹ *and the Lord was intreated by him* Gen. 25, 21; גַּם לְרֵעֵהוּ יִשָּׂנֵא רָשׁ *the poor is hated even of his friend* Prov. 14, 20.

---

[2]) In many of these instances the passive may be changed into the active with an indefinite subject *(one)*. By this it becomes clearer to our western way of understanding, that the object may remain in the passive, and that it does not agree in number and gender with the verb, even when it precedes, seeing that it is not *subject* but *object*; e. g. הָעֲבוֹדָה הַקָּשָׁה אֲשֶׁר עֻבַּד בָּךְ *the hard service wherein thou wast made to serve* = *wherein they made thee to serve* Jes. 14, 3; חָזוּת קָשָׁה הֻגַּד לִי *a grievous vision is declared unto me* Jes. 21, 2; וּזְרֹעוֹת יְתֹמִים יְדֻכָּא *and the arms of the fatherless have been broken* Job 22, 9; שָׁבֻעִים שִׁבְעִים נֶחְתַּךְ *seventy weeks are decreed upon* Dan. 9, 24.

More rarely by מִן (or מִ־) e. g. וְלֹא יִכָּרֵת כָּל בָּשָׂר עוֹד מִמֵּי הַמַּבּוּל *neither shall all flesh be cut off any more by the waters* Gen. 9, 11; מֵה' מִצְעֲדֵי גֶבֶר כּוֹנָנוּ *a man's steps are directed by the Lord* Ps. 37, 23; or by מִפְּנֵי; e. g. מָלְאָה הָאָרֶץ חָמָס מִפְּנֵיהֶם *the earth is filled with violence through them* Gen. 6, 13; or by בְּ e. g. בָּאָדָם דָּמוֹ יִשָּׁפֵךְ *by man shall his blood be shed* Gen. 9, 6; וַאדֹנִי צֻוָּה בַה' *and my lord was commanded by the Lord.* Num. 36, 2; בְּךָ יְרֻחַם *for in thee the fatherless findeth mercy.* Hosea 14, 4; finally also as object; e. g. חֶרֶב תְּאֻכְּלוּ *ye shall be devoured by the sword.* Jes. 1, 20 Conf. § 32, 11.

Rem. 8 Many intransitive verbs sometimes supply the place of passive verbs; e. g. עָלָה *to be brought up, to be offered* Lev. 2, 12; *to be booked, to be entered in* עָלָה הַמִּסְפָּר בְּמִסְפָּר *neither was the number entered into the account* 1 Chron. 27, 24; יָצָא *to be brought forth* Deut. 14, 22.

§ 35. Connection of the noun with the verb through the addition of letters or words.

1) In most of the cases, mentioned in § 32, letter or word prepositions are not unfrequently used. Even the passive object is sometimes connected with לְ; e. g. הָרְגוּ לְאַבְנֵר *they slew Abner* 2 Sam. 3, 30 conf. § 27, 6 E *ε*.

2) The answer to the question *whither?* (§ 32, 6) is frequently expressed by לְ or אֶל e. g. וַיֵּצְאוּ אֶל מִדְבַּר שׁוּר *and they went to the wilderness of Shur.* Ex. 15, 22; לְכוּ לְסִבְלֹתֵיכֶם *get you unto your burdens* Ex. 5, 4.

This is the only construction when a person is the

§ 35. CONNECTION OF THE NOUN WITH THE VERB.

terminus of the action, except in the case of those verbs with which a person may also stand as object (see § 32, 6). If however the terminus of the action is not a person הָ‍־ appended to the noun (*locative* ה) is also frequently used, sometimes even in answer to the question *where?* e. g. לָלֶכֶת אַרְצָה כְּנַעַן וַיָּבֹאוּ אַרְצָה כְּנָעַן *to go into the land of Canaan, and they came into the land of Canaan* Gen. 12, 5. Generally, however, *the place where* any thing occurs is indicated by the prefix בְּ; e. g. לָמָה תַעֲמֹד בַּחוּץ *wherefore standest thou without?* Gen. 24, 31.

3) Also with the verbs, named in § 32, 8, other constructions than those which have been there set forth not unfrequently occur; e. g. וְעַל שָׂפָם יַעְטֶה *and he shall cover his beard* Lev. 13, 45; כְּבוֹדִי מֵעָלַי הִפְשִׁיט *he hath stripped me of my glory* Job 19, 9.

4) The *manner* in which anything takes place is usually expressed by בְּ (כְּמוֹ); e. g. בִּמְצוֹלֹת כְּמוֹ אָבֶן *they went down into the depths like a stone* Ex. 15, 5; שִׂימֵנִי כַחוֹתָם *set me as a seal* Cant. 8, 6 (conf. § 32, 9).

The other conjunctive words or letters are in this case usually omitted; e. g. כִּנְעוּרֶיהָ *as in her youth* Lev. 22, 13; כְּדָבְרָם *as in their stable* Jes. 5, 17; כְּאֶבֶן מַיִם יִתְחַבָּאוּ *the waters are frozen as into a stone* Job 38. 30; וַיִּחֲלוּ כַמָּטָר לִי *and they waited for me as for rain* Job 29, 23; הַתְשַׂחֶק־בּוֹ כַּצִּפּוֹר *canst thou play with him as with a bird?* Job 40, 29.

Rem. 1 Other prepositions are rarely added; e. g. כְּבַחֲצִי מַעֲנָה *within as it were half a furrow* 1 Sam. 14, 14; כְּבַתְּחִלָּה and כְּבָרִאשׁוֹנָה

as in the beginning Jes. 1, 26; כְּמִפְּנֵי חֶרֶב *as it were before the sword* Lev. 26, 36; כְּעַל־כָּל־הוֹן *as much as in all riches* Ps. 119, 14.

5) Determinations of *time* in answer to the question *when* (Conf. § 32, 10 *b*) are usually expressed by בְּ; e. g. וַיַּשְׁכֵּם בַּבֹּקֶר *and he rose early in the morning* Gen. 22, 3; וּבְכָל יוֹם וָיוֹם מִתְהַלֵּךְ *he went every day* Est. 2, 11.

6) The organ also through which an action is performed (§ 32, 11), is usually expressed by בְּ (כְּמוֹ); e. g. אוֹדִיעַ בְּפִי *with my mouth will I make known* Ps. 89, 2; אוֹדֶה בְּפִי *with my mouth I wilt give thanks* Ps. 109, 30; בְּמוֹ פִי אֶתְחַנֶּן לוֹ *I intreat him with my mouth* Job 19, 16; וְאָנִיעָה עֲלֵיכֶם בְּמוֹ רֹאשִׁי *and I could shake mine head at you* Job 16, 4 (conf. יָנִיעוּ רֹאשׁ Ps. 22, 8); וְיָנִיד בְּרֹאשׁוֹ *and he shall shake his head* Jer. 18, 16. Conf. also Ps. 35, 16 and Lam. 2, 16 with Job 16, 9.

The בְּ *instrumentalis* is not unfrequently used in Hebrew even where we in English have the simple object; e. g. וַיָּרֶם בַּמַּטֶּה *and he lifted up the rod* Ex. 7, 20; נָתְנָה עֲלַי בְּקוֹלָהּ (conf. נָתַן קוֹלוֹ) *to raise one's voice* Jer. 12, 8; יַפְטִירוּ בְשָׂפָה *they open the mouth* Ps. 22, 8; וְתֶכֶס עָלֵינוּ בְצַלְמָוֶת *thou hast covered us with the shadow of death* Ps. 44, 20; פָּעֲרוּ עָלַי בְּפִיהֶם *they opened their mouth at me* Job 16, 10 with which conf. וּפָעֲרָה פִיהָ Jes. 5, 14; וְיַמְטֵר עָלֵימוֹ בִּלְחוּמוֹ *she shall rain his food upon him* Job 20, 23 with which conf. מַמְטִיר לֶחֶם Ex. 16, 4; פֵּרְשָׂה צִיּוֹן בְּיָדֶיהָ *Zion wrung her hands* Lam. 1, 17.

(For the rest, consult the Lexicon).

7) Prepositions are also occasionally used to express

a second object which is added to determine the first object more accurately; e. g. וַיַּכֵּהוּ אֶל הַחֹמֶשׁ *he smote him in the belly* 2 Sam. 2, 23; יַכּוּ עַל הַלְּחִי *they shall smite the judge upon the cheek* Michah 4, 14. Conf. Deut. 28, 35.

CHAPTER XI. — THE INFLUENCE OF THE SUBJECT UPON THE PREDICATE AS REGARDS GENDER AND NUMBER.

§ 36. Constructio ad Synesin.

1) The general rule that the predicate agrees in gender and number with the subject also exists in Hebrew. It is, however, frequently not observed, because the attention is directed more to the idea and signification of the subject than to its grammatical form. (Constructio ad synesin).

2) Hence singularia which express a collective idea, as עַם, גּוֹי *people*, בַּיִת *family*, צֹאן *flock*, or which in certain cases have acquired a collective signification (Conf. § 2, 1 c), are by preference construed in the plural; e. g. תָּבֹאןָ הַצֹּאן *the flock came* Gen. 30, 38; וַיַּעֲלוּ בֵית יוֹסֵף *and the house of Joseph went up* Judges 1, 22; וַיִּרְאוּ אִישׁ יִשְׂרָאֵל *and the men of Israel saw* Judges 9, 55; וַיָּנֻסוּ אֲרָם *and Aram fled* 1 Kings 20, 20; וְיָדְעוּ הָעָם *the people shall know* Jes. 9, 8; תַּמּוּ רֹמֵם *the oppressors are consumed* Jes. 16, 4; תְּשָׁבַּרְנָה (refers to עִיר v. 10) *it shall be broken up* Jes. 27, 11; וְגָלוּ עַם אֲרָם *and the people of Aram shall go into captivity.* Amos 1, 5; נָסוּ וְאֵין רֹדֵף רָשָׁע *the wicked flee when no man pursueth* Prov. 28, 1.

The predicate agrees with the signification of a collective noun not only in number but also in gender; e. g. וְכָל־הָאָרֶץ בֹּכִים *and all the country wept* 2 Sam. 15, 23 conf. 1 Sam. 17, 46, 1 Kings 10, 24; וּמוֹלַדְתְּךָ....לְךָ יִהְיוּ *and thy issue.....shall be thine* Gen. 48, 6; וְכָל־מַרְבִּית בֵּיתְךָ יָמוּתוּ *and all the increase of thine house shall die* 1 Sam. 2, 33; וְכָל־עֲדַת יִשְׂרָאֵל הַנּוֹעָדִים *and all the congregation of Israel that were assembled* 1 Kings 8, 5; וְאָבְדוּ שְׁאֵרִית פְּלִשְׁתִּים *and the remnant of the Philistines shall perish* Amos 1, 8; הַבָּקָר הָיוּ חֹרְשׁוֹת *the cows were plowing* Job 1, 14.

Rem. 1. The predicate seldom stands in the singular when the subject is a collectivum; e. g. לֹא יִשָּׂא גוֹי *nation shall not lift up sword against nation* Jes. 2, 4 (conf. however, the parallel place Michah 4, 3.

Rem. 2. Constructions such as Gen. 34, 30 are very peculiar; וַאֲנִי מְתֵי מִסְפָּר *while I (and those with me) are few in number.*

Rem. 3. The construction sometimes commences in the singular (chiefly when the verb precedes the subject) and changes, after the collectivum has been named, into the plural; e. g. וַיִּשְׁמַע הָעָם....וַיִּתְאַבָּלוּ וְלֹא שָׁתוּ *and when the people heard....they mourned, and no one put on* etc. Ex. 33, 4.

5) On the other hand, pluralia with a singular signification, chiefly the so called pluralia excellentiae, (§ 2, 2 *e*), are often construed in the singular; e. g. אִם־אֲדֹנָיו יִתֶּן־לוֹ אִשָּׁה *if his master give him a wife* Ex. 21, 4; וְגַם בְּעָלָיו יוּמָת *and his owner also shall be put to death* Ex. 21, 29. The same construction however also occurs with other nouns; e. g. רְנָנִים *the ostrich* Job 39, 13

§ 36. CONSTRUCTIO AD SYNESIN.

and ff. (conf. Talm. Babyl. Menach. 66 *b*); פָּנִים *face, front* 2 Sam. 10, 9; שְׁדֵמוֹת (= שָׂדֶה) *field* Hab. 3, 17.

When the subject is a feminine noun with a masculine signification the predicate is, for the same reason, construed masculine; e. g. הָיָה קֹהֶלֶת חָכָם *the preacher was wise* Eccl. 12, 9.

4) Pluralia which signify animals or material objects, whether of the masc. or fem. gender, are by preference construed with the fem. sing. (conf. § 1, 3 *b*); e. g. וְעָלְתָה אַרְמְנֹתֶיהָ סִירִים.....וְהָיְתָה נְוֵה תַנִּים *and thorns shall come up in her palaces ..... and it shall be an habitation of jackals* Jes. 34, 13 וַחֲבָלִים אֲחָזַתָה *sorrows have taken hold of her* Jer. 49, 24; לֹא סָר מִמֶּנָּה (the suffix refers to חַטֹּאת) *he departed not therefrom* (i. e. *the sins of Jeroboam*) 2 Kings 3, 3; תְּזוּרֶהָ.....תְּדוּשֶׁהָ (refers to בֵּיצֶיהָ) *that the foot may crush them that the wild beast may trample them* (i. e. *her eggs*) Job 39, 15.

5) Plural nouns also of persons are sometimes construed with the singular; namely when the attention is more directed to the individuals of the subject (conf. כֹּל = *omnis* and *omnes*); e. g. בָּנוֹת צָעֲדָה *his branches creep over the wall* Gen. 49, 22; יְבִיאֶנּוּ (referring to רְשָׁעִים) *when he* (i. e. *the wicked*) *bringeth it* Prov. 21, 27; וְצַדִּיקִים כִּכְפִיר יִבְטָח *but the righteous are bold as a lion* Prov. 28, 1; chiefly when the subject is a participle; e. g. אֹרֲרֶיךָ אָרוּר וּמְבָרֲכֶיךָ בָּרוּךְ *cursed be every one that curseth thee, and blessed be every one that blesseth thee* Gen. 27, 29; מְחַלְלֶיהָ מוֹת יוּמָת *every one that profaneth it shall surely be put to death* Ex. 31, 14; עַמִּי נְגָשָׂיו מְעוֹלֵל

as for my people, children are their oppressors Jes. 3, 12; וְתֹמְכֶ֫יהָ מְאֻשָּׁר֑ · *and happy is every one that retaineth her* Prov. 3, 18.

6) With duals the predicate stands in the plur., because no dualform exists of verbs, adjectives and pronouns; e. g. וְעֵינֵי לֵאָה רַכּוֹת *and Lea's eyes were tender* Gen. 29, 17; שְׂפָתֶ֫יהָ נָּעוֹת *her lips were moving* 1 Sam. 1, 13; יְדֵיכֶם דָּמִים מָלֵ֫אוּ *your hands are full of blood* Jes. 1, 15; גַּם הֵם אֵין אִתִּי (referring to עֵינַ֫יִם) *it* (i. e. *the light of mine eyes*) *also is gone from me* Ps. 38, 11; sometimes, however, it is found in the sing. (conf. n°. 4); e. g. וְעֵינָיו קָ֫מָה *and his eyes were set* 1 Sam. 4, 15; וְתַ֫חַז בְּצִיּוֹן עֵינֵ֫ינוּ *and let our eyes gaze upon Zion* Michah 4, 11.

§ 37. The construction of sentences in which the predicate precedes the subject.

1) The predicate frequently differs in gender and number from its subject because of its position in the sentence; for the speaker or writer, (as if not yet quite certain about the right grammatical construction), often begins with the most simple form, namely that of the masc. sing., although a fem. or plur. noun will follow; e. g.

a) with the verb as predicate; יְהִי מְאֹרֹת *let there be lights* Gen. 1, 14; וְשַׁח גַּבְהוּת הָאָדָם *and the loftiness of man shall be bowed down* Jes. 2, 17; לֹא יָסֻב כְּלִמּוֹת *reproaches shall not depart* Michah 2, 6; נִמְצָא נָשִׁים *no women were found* Job 42, 15.

This construction is more rare when the subject

§ 37. PREDICATE PRECEDING ITS SUBJECT. 139

is fem. plur., for then the predicate is construed at least in the plur. masc. יָצְאוּ בְנוֹת שִׁלוֹ *the daughters of Shiloh come out* Judges 21, 21; יִתְנַגְּפוּ רַגְלֵיכֶם *before your feet stumble* Jer. 13, 16; יֵלְכוּ יוֹנְקֹתָיו *his branches shall spread* Hosea 14, 7.

b) with an adj. as predicate; e. g. יָשָׁר מִשְׁפָּטֶיךָ *upright are thy judgments* Ps. 119, 37; רָחוֹק מֵרְשָׁעִים יְשׁוּעָה *salvation is far from the wicked* Ps. 119, 155.

c) with a participle as predicate; רֹעֵה צֹאן עֲבָדֶיךָ *thy servants are shepherds* Gen. 47. 3.

d) with the copula הָיָה or הוּא; וַיְהִי כָּל־יְמֵי חֲנוֹךְ *and all the days of Enoch were* Gen. 5, 23; וּבֹסֶר גֹּמֵל יִהְיֶה נִצָּה *and the flower becometh a ripening grape* Jes. 18, 5; אִשֵּׁי ה׳ ...... הוּא נַחֲלָתוֹ *the offerings of the Lord made by fire are his inheritance* Jos. 13, 14; חֻקּוֹת הָעַמִּים הֶבֶל הוּא *for the customs of the nations are vanity* Jer. 10, 3.

2) If, however, in such cases the sentence is continued after the subject, the subsequent predicates agree with the subject in gender and number; e. g. יְהִי מְאֹרֹת ... וְהָיוּ ... *let there be lights and let them be* Gen. 1, 14; וַיֶּחֱמוּ הַצֹּאן ...... וַתֵּלַדְןָ *and the flocks conceived and brought forth* Gen. 30, 39; וַיָּבֹא אֵלַי אֲנָשִׁים ...... וַיֵּשְׁבוּ לְפָנָי *and the elders of Israel came unto me and sat before me* Ez. 14, 1 (conf. § 38, 3).

Rem. 1. In general it is noticeable that the feminine forms are sparingly used, for, not unfrequently, only that particular predicate which stands nearest to the subject is construed fem. (Conf. § 4, 11); e. g. שְׁאוֹל מִתַּחַת רָגְזָה ...... עוֹרֵר לְךָ *sheol from beneath is moved* ...

... *it stirreth up the shades for thee* Jes. 14, 9; אָבַל אֻמְלְלָה אָרֶץ *the land mourneth and languisheth* Jes. 33, 9. The same thing may also be noticed as regards adjectives, suffixes, participles, and other words; viz. the feminine is only expressed once, and that by the word which is nearest to the subject; e. g. .... יִהְיֶה .... וְהָאֶבֶן הַזֹּאת *and this stone shall be God's house* Gen. 28, 22; הַמַּחֲנֶה הָאַחַת וְהִכָּהוּ *if he come to the one company and smite it* Gen. 32, 9; רוּחַ גְּדוֹלָה וְחָזָק *a great and strong wind* 1 Kings 19, 11; יָד שְׁלוּחָה אֵלַי וְהִנֵּה בוֹ *a hand put forth unto me, and, lo, therein a roll of a book* Ez. 1, 9.

In like manner, in a series of successive forms of the second pers. sing. imperf., it will more than once be found that the first form alone possesses the fem. termination ־י; e. g. וַתַּעֲלִי ..... וַתִּכְרָת *thou art gone up* ..... *and made thee a covenant* Jes. 57, 8; וַתַּקְרִיבִי יָמַיִךְ וַתָּבוֹא *thou hast caused thy days to draw near, and thou art come* Ez. 22, 4; תִּשְׁתִּי ..... תִּהְיֶה לִצְחֹק *thou shalt drink ..... thou shalt be laughed to scorn* Ez. 23, 32.

Finally, the masc. instead of the fem. is sometimes found in a subordinate sentence; e. g. אֵשׁ לֹא נֻפָּח *fire that is not blown* Job 20, 26.[1])

Rem. 2. The change of gender in Nah. 3, 15 is very irregular הִתְכַּבֵּד כַּיֶּלֶק הִתְכַּבְּדִי כָּאַרְבֶּה *make thyself many as the cankerworm, make thyself many as the locust.*

3) The instances in which a suffix, referring to something plural, is used with a distributive sense in the sing., are numerous; e. g. עַל אֹיְבֶיךָ ..... וְשָׁבִיתָ שִׁבְיוֹ *against thine enemies ..... and thou carriest them away captive* Deut. 21, 10; conf. 28, 48; שְׁנֵי כְרוּבִים ..... קוֹמָתוֹ

---

1) Instances such as Lev. 2, 1; 5, 1 are of a different kind, for the fem. noun נֶפֶשׁ as referring to a person of the male sex, is in the continuation of the sentence construed as masc.

§ 38. COMPOUND SUBJECTS.   141

two cherubim . . . . . each ten cubits high 1 Kings 6, 23; וְשָׁרַק לוֹ . . . . . לַגּוֹיִם *to the nations . . . . . and he will hiss for them* Jes. 5, 26; בְּעָרָיו . . . . . וְאָכְלָה אַרְמְנוֹתֶיהָ *upon his cities and it will devour the castles thereof* Hosea 8, 14 (See Abn-Ezra on this place); הֲתֹצִיא מַזָּרוֹת בְּעִתּוֹ *canst thou lead forth the Mazzaroth in their season?* Job 38, 32.

Rem. 3. The instances where the predicate, even when following its subject, differs from it in gender and number are to be explained on the one hand by the tendency to use the third pers. plur. masc. of עָתִיד instead of the third pers. plur. fem.; e. g. וְאֶת אִשְׁתּוֹ וְאַמְהֹתָיו וַיֵּלֵדוּ *and God healed his wife and maid servants, and they bore children* Gen. 20, 17; וּמְסִלֹּתַי יְרֻמוּן *and my high ways shall be exalted* Jes. 49, 11; וְהָרִיּוֹתָיו יְבֻקָּעוּ *and their women with child shall be ripped up* Hosea 14, 1; בָּנוֹת וַיְאַשְּׁרוּהָ מְלָכוֹת וּפִילַגְשִׁים וַיְהַלְלוּהָ *the daughters saw her and called her blessed, yea the queens and the concubines, and they praised her* Cant. 6, 9 (Conf. § 18, 3 Rem.); and on the other hand by the circumstance that the predicate is often a participle which should be considered as a noun; e. g. לַפֶּתַח חַטָּאת רֹבֵץ *sin coucheth at the door* Gen. 4, 7.

The same irregularity also occurs a few times with the verb הָיָה; e. g. וַעֲלָטָה הָיָה *and it was dark* Gen. 15, 17; וְאַרְבַּע הַיָּדוֹת יִהְיֶה *and four parts shall be your own* Gen. 47, 24; תּוֹרָה אַחַת יִהְיֶה לָאֶזְרָח *one law shall be to him that is homeborn* Ex. 12, 49; בְּנֵי בַיִת הָיָה לִי *I had servants born in my house* Eccl. 2, 7. In the last example הָיָה לִי may also be considered as a new sentence and may be translated *and homeborn slaves, also these were given to me*.

§ 38. The construction of subjects consisting of more than one word. (Compound subjects).

1) When the subject consists of a noun in *st. constr.*

connected with another noun, the predicate agrees in gender and number with the *nomen regens*. Sometimes, however, it agrees with the *nomen rectum*, chiefly when this contains the main idea of both nouns; e. g. קוֹל דְּמֵי אָחִיךָ צֹעֲקִים *the voice of thy brother's blood crieth* Gen. 4, 10; ¹) conf. Jes. 52, 8; Jer. 10, 22; Job 29, 10; וּמִבְחַר שָׁלִשָׁיו טֻבְּעוּ *and his chosen captains are sunk* Ex. 15, 4; נֶגַע צָרַעַת כִּי תִהְיֶה *when the plague of leprosy is in a man* Lev. 13, 9; כִּי הָיְתָה אֵלָיו פְּנֵי הַמִּלְחָמָה *that the battle was set against him* 2 Sam. 10, 9; (in this instance the verb agrees with the *nom. rectum*, although it precedes); וּשְׁאָר מִסְפַּר קֶשֶׁת גִּבּוֹרֵי בְנֵי קֵדָר יִמְעָטוּ *and the residue of the number of the archers, the mighty men of the children of Kedar, shall be few* Jes. 21, 17; וּמִסְפַּר חֳדָשָׁיו חֻצָּצוּ *and the number of his months is cut off* Job 21, 21; רֹב שָׁנִים יוֹדִיעוּ חָכְמָה *and multitude of years should teach wisdom* Job 32, 7.

For the same reason also the predicate generally stands in the plur. with the noun כֹּל; e. g. וַיִּהְיוּ כָּל יְמֵי אָדָם *and all the days of Adam were* Gen. 5, 5; נָמֹגוּ כֹּל יֹשְׁבֵי כְנָעַן *all the inhabitants of Canaan are melted away* Ex. 15, 15; with the cardinal numbers from *three* to *ten*, and with מֵאָה and אֶלֶף.

Rem. 1. With כֹּל however the predicate not unfrequently stands in the sing.; e. g. וַיִּהְי כָּל יְמֵי נֹחַ *and all the days of Noah were* Gen. 9, 29; וְכָל מַחֲמַדֵּינוּ הָיָה לְחָרְבָּה *and all our pleasant things are laid*

---

1) קוֹל is by some considered as an exclamation; e. g. *the voice of thy brother's blood, that crieth* or *lo, thy brother's blood crieth!*

§ 38. COMPOUND SUBJECTS. 143

waste Jes. 64, 10; כָּל־דַּרְכֵי־אִישׁ זַךְ בְּעֵינָיו *all the ways of a man are clean in his own eyes* Prov. 16, 2.

Rem. 2. The predicate occasionally agrees with the *nom. rectum* for no other reason than that it is nearest to it; e. g. קֶשֶׁת גִּבֹּרִים חַתִּים *the bows of the mighty men are broken* 1 Sam. 2, 4; עֵינֵי גַבְהוּת אָדָם שָׁפֵל *the lofty looks of man shall be brought low* Jes. 2, 11; וְאוֹר עֵינַי גַּם הֵם אֵין אִתִּי *as for the light of mine eyes, it also is gone from me* Ps. 38, 11.

2) With two or more subjects connected by the conjunction וְ the predicate generally stands in the plur., provided it follows the subject; e. g. זֶרַע וְקָצִיר .... לֹא יִשְׁבֹּתוּ *seedtime and harvest ..... shall not cease* Gen. 8, 22; וְאַבְרָהָם וְשָׂרָה זְקֵנִים *now Abraham and Sarah were old* Gen. 18, 11; בָּנֶיךָ וּבְנוֹתֶיךָ נְתֻנִים *thy sons and thy daughters shall be given* Deut. 28, 32.[1]) If however the predicate precedes, then it generally agrees in number and gender with the subject which stands nearest to it; e. g. וַיָּבֹא נֹחַ וּבָנָיו *and Noah and his sons went in* Gen. 7, 7; וַיֹּאמֶר אָחִיהָ וְאִמָּהּ *and her brother and mother said* Gen. 24, 55; וַתִּגַּשׁ גַּם לֵאָה וִילָדֶיהָ *and Leah also and her children came near* Gen. 33, 7; וַיָּבֹא יְהוּדָה וְאֶחָיו *and Judah and his brethren came* Gen. 44, 14; יָשִׁיר מֹשֶׁה וּבְנֵי יִשְׂרָאֵל *Moses and the children of Israel sang* Ex. 15, 1; וַתְּדַבֵּר מִרְיָם וְאַהֲרֹן *and Miriam and Aaron spoke* Num. 12, 1; וַיִּשָּׂאֵם דָּוִד וַאֲנָשָׁיו *and David and his men took them away* 2 Sam. 5, 21.

---

1) In Ex. 21, 4 הָאִשָּׁה וִילָדֶיהָ תִּהְיֶה *the wife and her children shall be*, הָאִשָּׁה is evidently considered as the principal person.

Rem. 3. The predicate occasionally stands in the plur. even when it precedes; e. g. וְהָאֹפֶה ...... מַשְׁקֵה חָטְאוּ *the butler and the baker committed offence* Gen. 40, 1; נְמֹגִים אֶרֶץ וְכָל יֹשְׁבֶיהָ *the earth and all the inhabitants thereof are dissolved* Ps. 75, 4; יִגְאָלֻהוּ חֹשֶׁךְ וְצַלְמָוֶת *let the darkness and shadow of death claim it for their own* Job 3, 5. On the other hand the predicate rarely stands in the sing. when it follows; e. g. שֶׁמֶן וּקְטֹרֶת יְשַׂמַּח לֵב *ointment and perfume rejoice the heart* Prov. 27, 9, in which case also the masc. form is evidently preferred to the fem.

3) The deviations from the natural construction in the case of more than one subject, are restricted to the first predicate, for when more predicates follow, these stand in the plur. e. g. וַיָּקָם אֲבִימֶלֶךְ וּפִיכֹל ....וַיָּשֻׁבוּ *and Abimelech and Picol rose up and returned* Gen. 21, 32; וַתָּקָם רִבְקָה וְנַעֲרֹתֶיהָ וַתִּרְכַּבְנָה *and Rebekah and her damsels rose up and rode* Gen. 24, 61; וַתַּעַן רָחֵל וְלֵאָה וַתֹּאמַרְנָה *and Rachel and Lea answered and said* Gen. 31, 14; וַתִּגַּשׁ גַּם לֵאָה וִילָדֶיהָ וַיִּשְׁתַּחֲווּ *and Leah also and her children came near and bowed themselves* Gen. 33, 7. (Conf. § 37, 2).

CHAPTER XII. — SEQUENCE OE THE DIFFERENT PARTS OF THE SENTENCE.

§ 39. **Place of the Subject and of the Predicate.**

1) The Hebrews are fond of placing the principal idea or word at the *beginning* of the sentence. The other portions of the sentence follow according to the greater or less value which they have in the opinion of

§ 39. PLACE OF THE SUBJECT AND OF THE PREDICATE. 145

the speaker or writer, so that the relative preference given to the various portions of the sentence may serve as a standard for estimating the importance or value which the speaker or writer assigns to them.

Rem. 1. The portion of the sentence, on which the greatest emphasis rests, is seldom placed at the end; e. g. וְהָיוּ הַדְּבָרִים הָאֵלֶּה... עַל־לְבָבֶךָ *and these words shall be upon thine heart* Deut. 6, 6; and in order to strengthen the emphasis, the subject already expressed is repeated even after one single intermediate sentence; e. g. הָאָרֶץ אֲשֶׁר ..... טוֹבָה הָאָרֶץ מְאֹד מְאֹד *the land which we passed through ..... is an exceedingly good land* Num. 14, 7.

2) According to the principle of n°. 1 the verb generally stands first in verbal sentences; the more so, because the subject is already implied in the form of the verb. Yet even in nominal sentences the nomen expressing the predicate frequently precedes the subject, because the predicate may in many cases be considered as the principal word.

3) The subject, however, generally takes the first place in proverbial language and in comparisons; e. g. בֵּן חָכָם יְשַׂמַּח אָב *a wise son maketh a glad father* Prov. 10, 1; מַלְכוּתְךָ מַלְכוּת כָּל־עֹלָמִים *thy kingdom is an everlasting kingdom* Ps. 145, 13; כָּמוֹךָ כְּפַרְעֹה *for thou art even as Pharao* Gen. 44, 18.

4) The subject stands first also in verbal sentences, which serve to communicate something which is necessary to the context, but for which no fit opportunity has yet presented itself (*pluperfect*), or shall present

itself in the continuation of the narrative; e. g. וּמַלְכַּת
שְׁבָא שָׁמְעָה *now the queen of Sheba had heard* 1 Kings
10, 1; פַּרְעֹה מֶלֶךְ מִצְרַיִם עָלָה *Pharaoh, king of Egypt had
gone up* 1 Kings 9, 16; וְהָאָרֶץ הָיְתָה תֹהוּ וָבֹהוּ *for the earth
was waste and formless* Gen. 1, 2.

Sentences with the adverb טֶרֶם may fitly be added
to this group; e. g. וְכֹל שִׂיחַ הַשָּׂדֶה טֶרֶם יִהְיֶה בָאָרֶץ *no plant
of the field was yet on the earth* Gen. 2, 5; וּשְׁמוּאֵל טֶרֶם
יָדַע *now Samuel did not yet know the Lord* 1 Sam. 3, 7.

5) The subject, further, naturally stands first whenever
it forms the principal part of the narrative, or when for
some other reason it requires to be prominently set forth;
e. g. וְהַמַּיִם גָּבְרוּ *now the waters had increased exceedingly*
Gen. 7, 19 (the narrator commences to describe the particulars of the flood, and especially the fall of water).
וְנֹחַ מָצָא חֵן *now Noah found grace in the eyes of the
Lord* Gen. 6, 8 (Noah will be the chief person in the
subsequent history). הַנָּחָשׁ הִשִּׁיאַנִי *the serpent* (therefore
no human being) *beguiled me* Gen. 3, 13; אַבְרָם יָשַׁב
Abram dwelled in the land of Canaan Gen. 13, 12 (in
contrast with Lot).

Relative and interrogative pronouns when subjects
also stand first. (Conf. § 40, 3).

6) The predicate, if an adjective, participle or pronoun,
stands first in nominal sentences; e. g. רַב מְאֹד מַחֲנֵהוּ Joel
2, 11; מֵתָה אָנֹכִי *or else I die* Gen. 30, 1; יָרֵא אָנֹכִי אֹתוֹ
for I fear him Gen. 32, 12; זֶה הַדָּבָר *this is the thing*
Ex. 16, 16; אֵלֶּה הַדְּבָרִים *these are the words* Deut. 1, 1.

If, however, the predicate is a noun then the subject

stands first; e. g. שֵׁם הָאֶחָד פִּישׁוֹן *the name of the first is Pishon* Gen. 2, 11; except when special emphasis is to be laid on the predicate; e. g. עָפָר אַתָּה *dust thou art* Gen. 3, 19; אֲחֹתִי אָתְּ Gen. 12, 13; וּבֹסֶר גֹּמֵל יִהְיֶה נִצָּה *and a ripening grape the flower becometh* Jes. 18, 5; אִם כֹּחַ אֲבָנִים כֹּחִי *is my strength then of stone* Job 6, 12.

Rem. 2. Expressions such as פֶּה לָהֶם *they have a mouth* Ps. 115, 5; מַה לָּךְ *what ailest thou?* belong to the same class. With this kind of sentence, the predicate of which is merely expressed by לְ with a suffix, the Hebrew writers even went further, and joined the subject with the predicate into one word, by appending to the noun of the predicate a suffix; e. g. יְדֵיהֶם Ps. 115, 7 = יָדַיִם לָהֶם; רַגְלֵיהֶם = רַגְלַיִם לָהֶם; וּפִילַגְשׁוֹ = וּפִילֶגֶשׁ לוֹ *and he had a concubine* Gen. 22, 24; נְבִיאֲכֶם = נָבִיא לָכֶם *if ye have a prophet* Num. 12, 6.[1]

Rem. 3. Concerning the place of the attributive adjective see § 4, 10 and Rem. 3.

§ 40. The places of the other parts of the sentence.

1) The copula in nominal sentences stands generally last, when it is a pers. pron. of the third pers., (See § 31, 2; § 37, 1 *d*) but it precedes the predicate when the copula is the verb הָיָה. For examples see § 31, 3.

The object in verbal sentences has its place after the subject and predicate.

Adverbial determinations, chiefly those of place and

---

[1] On the other hand some writers sever the suffix from its noun, and place it separately, after having connected it with a letter preposition; e. g. מִצָּרָתִי = מִצָּרָה לִי *out of mine affliction* Jonah 2, 3. Conf. the author's Essay, Darche Hannesigah, L. B. 1881, § 60, 2.

time, stand by preference as near as possible (either before or after) to the predicate.

The negation however stands immediately before the predicate.

Rem. 1. The *object* is seldom placed between the negation and the verb; e. g. לֹא מַיִם עָיֵף תַּשְׁקֶה *thou hast not given water to the weary to drink* Job 22, 7; וְהוּא לֹא פָנִים קִלְקַל *and one do not whet the edge* Eccl. 10, 10; seldom also the subject; e. g. לֹא ה' שְׁלָחָנִי *the Lord hath not sent me* Num. 16, 29; לֹא לִבִּי הָלַךְ *mine heart went not* 2 Kings 5, 26; כִּי לֹא לְפָנָיו חָנֵף יָבוֹא *a godless man shall not come before him* Job 13, 16; or a determination; e. g. אַל לְאֶרֶךְ אַפְּךָ תִּקָּחֵנִי *take me not away in thy long suffering* Jer. 15, 15; אַל בְּאַפְּךָ תוֹכִיחֵנִי *rebuke me not in thine anger* Ps. 6, 2; לֹא בְמוֹתוֹ יִקַּח הַכֹּל *when he dieth he shall carry nothing away* Ps. 49, 18; לֹא עַל זְבָחֶיךָ אוֹכִיחֶךָ *I will not rebuke thee for thy sacrifices.* Ps. 50, 8; לֹא עַל אִישׁ יָשִׂים עוֹד *for he needeth not further to consider a man* Job 34, 23, Conf. § 25 Rem. 8.

2) The deviations from the rule stated in n°. 1 have their ground in the greater emphasis the writer wishes to lay upon one or other part of the sentence. Hence:

(*a*) the object in verbal sentences sometimes stands before the subject; e. g. וְכָתַב אֶת הָאָלֹת הָאֵלֶּה הַכֹּהֵן *and the priest shall write these curses in a book* Num. 5, 23; תְּמוֹתֵת רָשָׁע רָעָה *evil shall slay the wicked* Ps. 34, 22; or even before the verb; e. g. וְהָרְכֻשׁ קַח לָךְ *and take the goods unto thyself* Gen. 14, 21; אִם אֶת הַדָּבָר הַזֶּה תַּעֲשֶׂה *if thou shalt do this thing* Ex. 18, 23; סֵפֶר הַתּוֹרָה מָצָאתִי *I have found the book of the law* 2 Kings 22, 8; כַּאֲשֶׁר אֲבֵלִים יְנַחֵם *as one that comforteth the mourners* Job. 29, 25.

Rem. 2. The arrangement: object, subject, verb, is very rare; e. g. דָּבָר גָּדוֹל הַנָּבִיא דִּבֶּר *if the prophet had imposed on thee some great thing* 2 Kings 5, 13; and that of: subject, object, verb, equally rare and only poetical; e. g. גָּמוּל יָדוֹ הָדָה *the weaned child shall put its hand* Jes. 11, 8; וּקְשָׁתוֹת נְעָרִים תְּרַטַּשְׁנָה *and bows shall dash the young men in pieces* Jes. 13, 18; ה' תְּפִלָּתִי יָקָּח *the Lord will receive my prayer* Ps. 6, 10; ה' צַדִּיק יִבְחָן *the Lord trieth the righteous* Ps. 11, 5.

(*b*) the adverbial determination stands before the verb; e. g. בְּרֵאשִׁית בָּרָא אֱלֹהִים Gen. 1, 1.

3) A few adverbs of time, such as אָז, עַתָּה almost always stand at the beginning of the sentence; others such as עוֹד, תָּמִיד generally stand after the verb.

All particles of interrogation and אֲשֶׁר invariably stand at the beginning of the sentence.

§ 41. Case absolute.

The greatest emphasis, which can be given to an idea, is obtained by placing it first (*absolute*), quite indepently of the place it should naturally have in the sentence, and by repeating it in the subsequent sentence; viz. by means of a pronoun when it is subject, and otherwise by means of a pronominal suffix (conf. *c'est moi, qu'on a accusé*). This subsequent sentence should then be considered not so much as a new sentence, but as the predicate of the idea which has been placed first. This predicate may be expressed in the form of a nominal sentence, the examples of which have been already given in § 30, 3 and Rem. 2, or by a verbal sentence; e. g. בִּרְכַּת ה' הִיא תַעֲשִׁיר *the blessing of the Lord, it maketh rich* Prov. 10, 22; conf. v. 24; שָׂרַי אִשְׁתְּךָ לֹא תִקְרָא אֶת שְׁמָהּ שָׂרָי *Sarai thy wife, thou shalt not call her name Sarai* Gen. 17, 15; אָנֹכִי בַּדֶּרֶךְ נָחַנִי *as for me, the Lord has led me on the way* Gen. 24, 27; וְגַם אֶת בֶּן הָאָמָה לְגוֹי אֲשִׂימֶנּוּ *and also of the son of the bondwoman will I make a nation* Gen. 21, 13; וְאֶת הָעָם הֶעֱבִיר אֹתוֹ לֶעָרִים *and as for the people, he removed them to the cities* Gen. 47, 21; שְׁכֶם בְּנִי חָשְׁקָה נַפְשׁוֹ בְּבִתְּכֶם *Shechem, my son, he longeth for your daughter* Gen. 34, 8; שֹׁרֶשׁ יִשַׁי ..... אֵלָיו גּוֹיִם יִדְרֹשׁוּ *the root of Jesse ..... of him the nations shall anxiously inquire* Jes. 11, 10; וְהֵמָּה דַרְכָּם לֹא יִתָּכֵן *but as for them, their way is not right* Ez. 33, 17; קַיִץ וָחֹרֶף אַתָּה יְצַרְתָּם *summer and winter, thou hast made them* Ps. 74, 17 (conf. § 10, 1).

Rem. 1. We occasionally find such a casus absolutus introduced by לְ; e. g. לִקְדוֹשִׁים אֲשֶׁר בָּאָרֶץ הֵמָּה וְאַדִּירֵי כָּל־חֶפְצִי־בָם *as for the saints that are in the land, they are the excellent in whom is all my delight* Ps. 16, 3. 4; sometimes even when it expresses the subject; e. g. וּלְשָׂרִים לְמִשְׁפָּט יָשֹׂרוּ *and as for princes, they shall rule according to judgment* Jes. 32, 1; לְכֶלֶב חַי הוּא טוֹב מִן הָאַרְיֵה הַמֵּת *as for a living dog, it is better than a dead lion* Eccl. 9, 4; וְלִבְנֵי יִשָּׂשכָר תּוֹלָע *and as for the sons of Issachar, Thola and Puah* etc. 1 Chr. 7, 1; לְכֹל עֹבֵר עָלָיו יִשֹּׁם *every one that passeth by it shall be astonished* 2 Chr. 7, 21.

The *casus absolutus* is now and then also introduced by אֶת; e. g. וְאֵת כָּל מִבְרָחָיו ..... בַּחֶרֶב יִפֹּלוּ *and as for all his fugitives* .....

§ 41. CASE ABSOLUTE. 151

they shall fall by the sword Ez. 17, 21; אֶת עַמּוּד הֶעָנָן לֹא סָר *as for the pillar of cloud, it departed not* Nehem. 9, 19. This אֶת is sometimes also placed before that part of the sentence which is repeated *after* the whole sentence has been already pronounced, for the purpose of bringing it forward more prominently; e. g. אֲשֶׁר הֲבֵאתִי ..... אֵת כָּל אֲשֶׁר הֲבֵאתִי עָלֶיהָ *concerning the evil that I have brought upon Jerusalem, yea as regards all that I have brought upon her* Ez. 14, 22; conf. Judges 20, 44. 46. אֶת with the signification *as regards* is very clear in Jer. 23, 33. אֶת מַה מַשָּׂא *thou shalt say unto them; as regards (your question) What burden! I will cast you off* etc.

We have however already seen (§ 10 Rem. 7) that generally certain words, or ideas, which have already been indicated by a suffix, are purposely repeated to revive the reader's attention.

2) In § 30 Rem. 2, we have seen that with sentences of this kind the suffix referring to the main word may sometimes be omitted. Examples of such an omission are Michah 7, 11 יוֹם הַהוּא יִרְחַק חֹק instead of חֻקּוֹ *as for that day, its decree shall be far removed*; Ps. 9, 7. הָאוֹיֵב תַּמּוּ חֳרָבוֹת לָנֶצַח instead of חָרְבוֹתָיו or חָרְבוֹתֶיךָ *the enemy are come to an end, his ruins are for ever*; or *O thou enemy ... thy ruins* etc. In this case the predicate is frequently introduced by וְ (the so called וְ *apodosis*); e. g. מִסְפַּר שָׁנָיו וְלֹא חֵקֶר (namely לָהֶן) *the number of his years is unsearchable* Job 36, 26; ··· הַבַּיִת הַזֶּה ···וְשָׁכַנְתִּי בְּתוֹךְ בְּנֵי יִשְׂרָאֵל (namely בּוֹ) *as for this house ... ... I will dwell (in it) amongst the children of Israel* 1 Kings 6, 12; מִצְוַת שְׂפָתָיו וְלֹא אָמִישׁ (namely אוֹתָהּ) *as for the commandment of his lips, I did not reject it* Job 23, 12.

Rem. 2. The וְ *apodosis*, however, appears also where the suffix has not been omitted; e. g. מְשַׂנְאַי וָאַצְמִיתֵם *as for those that hate me, I will cut them off* 2 Sam. 22, 41; וְתוֹרָתִי וַיִּמְאָסוּ בָהּ *and as for my law, they have rejected it* Jer. 6, 19; chiefly when the casus absolutus indicates the subject, and is introduced by another word; e. g. וַיְהִי הַנִּשְׁאָרִים וַיָּפֻצוּ *and as for them who were left, they were scattered* 1 Sam. 11, 11; וְעַתָּה הַבְּרָכָה..... וְנִתְּנָה *and now as for this present ..... let it be given* 1 Sam. 25, 27.

3) When such a *casus absolutus* is expressed by a participle, it not unfrequently contains a conditional sentence; e. g. כָּל הֹרֵג קַיִן שִׁבְעָתַיִם יֻקָּם *if anyone slayeth Cain, vengeance shall be taken on him sevenfold* Gen. 4, 15; אֲשֶׁר כָּל שֹׁמְעוֹ תְּצִלֶּינָה שְׁתֵּי אָזְנָיו *at which, if anyone heareth it, both his ears shall tingle* 1 Sam. 3, 11, conf. 2 Kings 21, 12; יוֹלֵד חָכָם וְיִשְׂמַח בּוֹ *if one begetteth a wise child, he shall have joy of him.* Prov. 23, 24. (In Keri ויולד......ישמח *and he that begetteth a wise child shall have joy of him*). כָּל אִישׁ זֹבֵחַ זֶבַח וּבָא נַעַר הַכֹּהֵן *when any man offered, the priest's servant came.* 1 Sam. 2, 13. Conf. § 28, 2 e.

INDEX OF PASSAGES QUOTED.

Gen. 1, 1.	§ 16, 3		Gen. 3, 13.	§ 11, 3 c
	§ 32, 2			§ 39, 5
	§ 40, 2 b		3, 15.	§ 33, 4
1, 2.	§ 4, 7		3, 16.	§ 28, 2 b
	§ 31, 3		3, 19.	§ 39, 6
	§ 39, 4		3, 22.	§ 5 Rem. 4
1, 4.	§ 32, 12			§ 16, 1
1, 6.	§ 17, 3 a		3, 22.	§ 25 Rem. 12
1, 11.	§ 32, 5			§ 27, 6 C α
1, 14.	§ 37, 1 a		4, 2.	§ 6, Rem. 1
	§ 37, 2			§ 6, 4
1, 16.	§ 8, 2		4, 4.	§ 28, 2 b
1, 26.	§ 27, 6 A γ		4, 7.	§ 32 Rem. 5
1, 30.	§ 12, 1			§ 37 Rem. 3
2, 5.	§ 15, 7		4, 9.	§ 26, 3
	§ 39, 4		4, 10.	§ 38, 1
2, 7.	§ 33, 3		4, 13.	§ 8, 3
2, 10.	§ 15, 5		4, 14.	§ 16, 2.
	§ 30, 2		4, 15.	§ 9, 9
2, 11.	§ 12, 1			§ 41, 3
	§ 39, 6		4, 18.	§ 34, 1 c
2, 12.	§ 31, 1		4, 20.	§ 32, 8 c
2, 16.	§ 15, 6		4, 26.	§ 10, 1
2, 18.	§ 22, 3			§ 19, 4 c
	§ 30, 5		5, 3.	§ 27, 6 A γ
2, 19.	§ 10 Rem. 7		5, 5.	§ 38, 1
2, 23.	§ 30 Rem. 1		5, 23.	§ 37, 1 d
2, 24.	§ 15, 5		5, 24.	§ 25, 2 C γ
3, 1.	§ 28, 5 A β		6, 2.	§ 32, 12
	§ 31, 3		6, 8.	§ 39, 5
3, 4.	§ 22 Rem. 2		6, 13.	§ 33, 3
3, 5.	§ 28, 2 e			§ 34, 2
3, 11.	§ 25, 3 d		6, 16.	§ 33, 3

Gen. 6, 17. § 23 Rem. 2
7, 1. § 27, 6 D α
7, 2. § 31, 2
7, 4. § 23, 3
7, 7. § 38, 2
7, 9. § 14. 1
§ 9, 8 b
7, 19. § 24, 2
§ 39, 5
7, 21. § 27, 6 A α
8, 4. § 2, 9
8, 7. § 22, 4
8, 8. § 26, 6
8, 17. § 27, 6 A α
8, 22. § 38, 2
9, 2. § 10. 5
9, 3. § 31, 2
9. 4. § 27, 6 A η
9, 6. § 34, 2
9, 7. § 19. 5
9, 9. § 30, 3
9, 10. § 27, 6 A α
9, 11. § 34, 2
9, 14. § 32, 5
9, 20. § 21, 2 C α
9, 29. § 38 Rem. 1
11, 3. § 32, 5
11, 4. § 27, 6 A ζ
11, 7. § 15, 2
§ 28, 4 e
11, 9. § 19, 4 a
11, 10. § 16, 3
11, 27. § 32, 2
11, 28. § 6, 4
11, 30. § 25 Rem. 8
12, 4. § 9, 5
12, 5. § 6 Rem. 1 . 3
§ 35, 2
12, 11. § 4, 15
12, 12. § 16, 2
12, 13. § 18, 2 a
§ 28, 7 c
§ 39, 6
12, 14. § 27, 6 F β
§ 32, 12
12, 17. § 32, 5.
13, 2. § 3, 1a.
13, 8. § 6, 1

Gen. 13, 9. § 28, 2 e
13, 11. § 13, 7 c
13, 12. § 39, 5
13, 13. § 30, 2
14, 1. § 16, 5
14, 4. § 32, 10
14, 10. § 2, 6
§ 5 Rem. 1
14, 18. § 30 Rem. 1
14, 19. § 34, . 2
14, 21. § 40, 2 a
14, 23. § 19, 5.
15, 2. § 28, 2 f
15, 3. § 23, 3 . 6
§ 32, 13
15, 4. § 23, 3
15, 13. § 12, 5
15, 14. § 23, 3
§ 27, 6 A η
15, 15. § 19, 5
15, 17. § 16, 5
§ 37 Rem. 3
15, 19. § 28, 2 a
15, 20. § 28, 2 a
16, 2. § 27, 6 C γ
16, 12. § 6 Rem. 2
17, 4. § 30, 3
17, 5. § 33, 3.
§ 34, 1 c
17, 8. § 4, 3.
17, 10. § 5 Rem. 5
17, 11. § 34, 1 b
17, 14. § 34, I b
17, 15. § 41, 1
17, 17. § 26 Rem. 4.
17, 18. § 28, 5 F α
17, 24. § 34, 1 b
17, 25. § 34, 1 b
18, 1. § 23, 3
18, 6. § 21. 3
18, 7. § 10 Rem. 6.
18, 10. § 27, 6 F β
18, 11. § 38, 2
18, 14. § 13, 4
§ 27, 6 C γ
18, 18. § 28, 4 d
18, 20. § 28, 4 c
18, 24. § 9, 3 a

INDEX OF PASSAGES QUOTED.   155

Gen. 18, 24.	§ 32 Rem. 5
18, 25.	§ 27, 6 F α
18, 26.	§ 32 Rem. 5
18, 28.	§ 27, 6 A ε
	§ 32, 8 b
19, 1.	§ 28, 2 f
19, 2.	§ 28, 4 d
19, 8.	§ 13, 4
19, 11.	§ 3, 1 c
19, 14.	§ 6 Rem. 3
19, 15.	§ 28, 5 C α
19, 16.	§ 22, 2
19, 17.	§ 15, 4.
19, 18.	§ 25, 2 B β
19, 33.	§ 3 Rem. 5
20, 2.	§ 27, 6 D α
20, 3.	§ 28, 2 f
20, 7.	§ 18, 3
20, 9.	§ 15, 6
20, 17.	§ 37 Rem. 3.
21, 5.	§ 34, 1 c
21, 12.	§ 27, 6 A γ
	§ 27, 6 B β
21, 13.	§ 41, 1
21, 16.	§ 27, 6 A ζ
21, 25.	§ 14, 1
21, 32.	§ 38, 3
22, 1.	§ 16, 5
22, 3.	§ 35, 5.
22, 4.	§ 16, 3
	§ 28, 2 e
22, 12.	§ 28, 2 g
22, 16.	§ 14, 2 b
22, 20.	§ 16, 5
22, 21.	§ 28, 2 a
22, 22.	§ 28, 2 a
22, 24.	§ 16, 4 b
	§ 39 Rem. 2
23, 1.	§ 9, 5.
23, 4.	§ 1 Rem. 2
23, 6.	§ 25 Rem. 3
	§ 27, 6 C γ
23, 13.	§ 17, 4 b
	§ 18, 2 b
24, 6.	§ 25, 3 b
24, 8.	§ 3 Rem. 5
	§ 17. 3 b
24, 18.	§ 21, 2 C α

Gen. 24, 21.	§ 26, 6
24, 23.	§ 11, 5
24, 25.	§ 28, 5 A α
24, 27.	§ 41, 1
24, 30.	§ 4, 3
24, 31.	§ 23 Rem. 3
	§ 35, 2
24, 40.	§ 16, 1
24, 44.	§ 28, 5 A α
24, 55.	§ 38, 2
24, 58.	§ 26, 9
24, 61.	§ 38, 3
24, 63.	§ 1, 1
25, 1.	§ 21, 2 C γ
25, 19.	§ 16, 2
25, 21.	§ 34, 2
25, 25.	§ 19, 4 b
25, 26.	§ 22, 2
25, 34.	§ 32, 1
26, 7.	§ 19 Rem. 2.
26, 10.	§ 13, 3 c
26, 12.	§ 9, 4
26, 13.	§ 22, 4.
27, 1.	§ 22, 3.
27, 9,	§ 33, 3
27, 11.	§ 4, 8
27, 13.	§ 10, 5
27, 20.	§ 21, 2 b
27, 21.	§ 26, 5
27, 22.	§ 30, 4.
27, 24.	§ 11, 3 c
	§ 26, 5 . 9
27, 29.	§ 36, 5
27, 30.	§ 28, 2 e
27, 33.	§ 23. 4 e
	§ 26 Rem. 10
	§ 32, 5.
27, 34.	§ 10, 1.
	§ 27, 6 F β
27, 36.	§ 11, 3 b
27, 37.	§ 33, 2
27, 42.	§ 23 Rem. 2
	§ 34, 1 c
27, 44.	§ 13, 8
27, 45.	§ 28, 5 A α
	§ 32, 8 b
28, 9.	§ 27, 6 B β
28, 18.	§ 33, 3

INDEX OF PASSAGES QUOTED.

Gen.	28. 22.	§ 37 Rem. 1
	29, 2.	§ 19, 4 *b*
	29, 5.	§ 26, 9
	29, 6.	§ 26, 9
	29, 7.	§ 22, 3
	29, 9.	§ 7, 1
		§ 28, 2 *e*
	29. 17.	§ 36, 6.
	29, 25.	§ 16, 5
	29, 26.	§ 8, 2
		§ 15, 5.
	29, 30.	§ 28, 5 A α
	29, 32.	§ 28, 4 *a*
	30. 1.	§ 39, 6
	30, 3.	§ 28, 2 *k*
	30, 31.	§ 21, 2 C δ
	30, 34.	§ 17, 3 *a*
	30, 38.	§ 28, 4 *b*
		§ 36, 2
	30, 39.	§ 37, 2
	31, 9.	§ 10 Rem. 5
	31, 13.	§ 3, 9.
	31, 14.	§ 38, 3.
	31, 27.	§ 21, 2 B
	31, 28.	§ 21, 2 A.
	31, 29.	§ 25, 2 C α
	31, 30.	§ 22, 4.
	31, 31.	§ 25, 3 *b*
	31, 32.	§ 12 Rem. 1
	31. 37.	§ 28, 2 *k*
	31, 42.	§ 14, 3
	31, 50.	§ 27, 6 B β
	32, 6.	§ 17, 2
	32, 7.	§ 23 Rem. 3
	32, 8.	§ 19, 3
	32, 9.	§ 37 Rem. 1.
	32, 11.	§ 27, 6 A η
	32, 12.	§ 6, 4.
		§ 23, 3.
		§ 27, 6 B β
		§ 39, 6.
	32, 13.	§ 27, 6 C ε
	32, 16.	§ 1, 1
	32, 19	§ 6, 4
	32, 20.	§ 28, 5 A α
	33, 7.	§ 38, 2 . 3
	33, 13.	§ 1, 1
	33, 18.	§ 28, 7 *a*

Gen.	33, 18.	§ 25, 2 B β
	34, 8.	§ 41, 1
	34, 30.	§ 36 Rem. 2
	35, 11.	§ 36 Rem. 1
	36, 24.	§ 28, 2 *a*
	37, 2.	§ 3 Rem. 5
	37, 3.	§ 8, 4 *a*
	37, 5.	§ 21, 2 A
	37, 7.	§ 32, 5
	37, 8.	§ 22, 4.
	37, 15.	§ 15, 5
		§ 23 Rem. 3
	37, 18.	§ 32, 14
	37, 21.	§ 33, 4.
	37, 23.	§ 33, 1
	37, 29.	§ 25, 2 C α
	33.	§ 22 Rem. 1
	37, 33.	§ 26, 9
	38, 17.	§ 10, 6
		§ 28 Rem. 11
	38, 24.	§ 27, 6 C δ
		§ 23 Rem. 3
		§ 28, 2 *k*
	38, 28.	§ 13, 3 *d*
	38, 29.	§ 28, 5 C ε
	39, 11.	§ 3, 1 *d*
	39, 20.	§ 5, 4
	39, 22.	§ 23 Rem. 3
	40, 1.	§ 38 Rem. 3
	40, 5.	§ 7, 1
	40, 8.	§ 25 Rem. 8.
	40, 9.	§ 28, 2 *e*
	40, 10.	§ 28, 5 C ε
	40, 14.	§ 28 Rem. 15
	40, 20.	§ 34, 1 *c*
	41, 1.	§ 23 Rem. 1
		§ 27, 6 B δ
	41, 4.	§ 4, 15
		§ 32, 9
	41, 14.	§ 19, 4 *b*
	41, 15.	§ 28, 7 *c*
	41, 25.	§ 23, 2
	41, 26.	§ 3 Rem. 4
		§ 31, 2
	41, 34.	§ 16, 1
	41, 39.	§ 28, 5 C δ
	41, 42.	§ 33, 1
	41, 43.	§ 22, 5 A δ

INDEX OF PASSAGES QUOTED. 157

Gen. 42, 10.	§ 25, 2 A γ	
	§ 28 Rem. 3	
42, 13.	§ 25, 2 C γ	
42, 15.	§ 28, 5 F δ	
42, 18.	§ 18, 3	
42, 19.	§ 3 Note 2	
42, 28.	§ 21, 3	
42, 35.	§ 13. 1.	
42, 38.	§ 16, 7	
43, 3.	§ 22, 4	
43, 5.	§ 31, 4	
43, 7.	§ 15, 6	
43, 14.	§ 3 Note 2	
	§ 14, 1	
43, 16.	§ 12, 4.	
43, 25.	§ 15, 1	
43, 27.	§ 4, 7.	
	§ 12, 2	
43, 33.	§ 21, 3	
44, 2.	§ 10 Rem. 1	
44, 4.	§ 32, 6.	
44, 5.	§ 27, 6 A β	
44, 14.	§ 38, 2	
44, 18.	§ 15, 3	
	§ 27, 6 F α	
	§ 39, 3.	
45, 4.	§ 12, 3	
45, 6.	§ 12, 2	
45, 8.	§ 27. 7	
45, 12.	§ 3 Rem. 6	
45, 18.	§ 18, 2 a	
45, 19.	§ 18, 1	
46, 15.	§ 5 Note 1.	
46, 27.	§ 3, 13	
47, 3.	§ 37, 1 c	
47, 21.	§ 41, 1	
47, 24.	§ 37 Rem. 3.	
48, 6.	§ 36, 2	
48, 19.	§ 14, 2a	
48, 21.	§ 23, 4 b	
49, 4.	§ 30 Rem. 3	
49, 8.	§ 10, 1	
49, 15.	§ 32, 12	
49, 22.	§ 36, 5	
49, 24.	§ 4, 9	
Ex. 1, 2.	§ 28, 2 a	
1, 3.	§ 28, 2a	

Ex. 1, 6.	§ 34, 1 c	
1, 7.	§ 28, 6	
1, 9.	§ 8, 1	
1, 12.	§ 28, 5 H α	
1, 14.	§ 27, 6 A ε	
2, 2.	§ 32, 12	
2, 6.	§ 10 Rem. 7.	
3, 1.	§ 23, 3.	
3, 3.	§ 3, 10	
3, 20.	§ 15, 1	
4, 9.	§ 32, 6	
4, 10.	§ 4, 8	
4, 13.	§ 12, 5	
4, 18.	§ 17, 1b	
5, 4.	§ 35, 2	
5, 8.	§ 28, Rem. 1	
5, 10.	§ 25, 2 C β²	
5, 16.	§ 25, 2 C β²	
5, 22.	§ 11, 3 c.	
6, 3.	§ 27, 6 A δ	
7, 20.	§ 35, 6	
8, 17.	§ 25, 2 C β²	
8, 22.	§ 26, 5	
9, 22.	§ 27, 6 B δ	
9, 27.	§ 3 Rem. 6.	
10, 1.	§ 3 Rem. 5	
10, 2.	§ 5 Note 1	
10, 8.	§ 11, 4	
	§ 34, 1 c	
10, 15.	§ 25, 2 A β	
12, 16.	§ 25, 2 A β	
12, 33.	§ 1 Rem. 4	
12, 43.	§ 27, 6 A ζ	
12, 49.	§ 37 Rem. 3	
12, 51.	§ 27, 6 B β	
13, 1.	§ 16, 3	
13, 3.	§ 22, 5 B γ	
13, 17.	§ 28 Rem. 7	
14, 11.	§ 25, 4	
14, 13.	§ 28, 6	
15, 1.	§ 15, 7	
	§ 38, 2	
15, 4.	§ 38, 1	
15, 5.	§ 35, 4	
15, 15.	§ 38, 1	
15, 22.	§ 35, 2	
16, 3.	§ 17 4 a	
16, 4.	§ 26, 6	

Ex. 16, 4.	§ 35, 6	Ex. 32, 22.	§ 30 Rem. 4.
16, 16.	§ 39, 6		§ 32, 12
16, 27.	§ 13, 8	32, 27.	§ 18, 4
16, 29.	§ 13, 3 a	32, 31.	§ 32, 5
16, 32.	§ 39, 6	32, 33.	§ 11 Rem. 3
17, 1.	§ 22, 3	33, 16.	§ 26 Rem. 10
17, 4.	§ 16, 1.	33, 4.	§ 36 Rem. 3
	§ 28, 7 a	36, 4.	§ 13, 1
17, 5.	§ 13, 8	38, 3.	§ 33, 3
18, 17.	§ 23. 3	38, 27.	§ 9, 4
18, 23.	§ 16, 1	39, 10.	§ 6, 3
	§ 21, 2 A		
	§ 40, 2 a	Lev. 1, 2.	§ 13, 3 b
19, 1.	§ 16, 3		§ 27, 6 C α
19, 5.	§ 27, 6 C α	1, 15.	§ 32, 2
20, 3.	§ 15, 4	2, 1.	§ 37 Note 1
20, 20.	§ 10, 5	2, 12.	§ 34 Rem.
	§ 15, 2	4, 2.	§ 27 Rem. 5
21 .	§ 28 Note 1.	4, 22.	§ 28 Rem. 6
21, 4.	§ 36, 3	5, 1.	§ 37 Note. 1
	§ 38 Note 2	5, 2.	§ 13 4
21, 15.	§ 28, 2 a	6, 3.	§ 6, 2.
21, 28.	§ 32 Rem. 1	6, 7.	§ 22 Rem. 5
21, 29.	§ 2, 1 e	8, 14.	§ 32, 2
	§ 36, 3.	11. 10.	§ 25 Rem. 8
21, 36.	§ 28, 5 B α	13, 9.	§ 38, 1
21, 37.	§ 1, 1	13, 45.	§ 35, 3
	§ 2, 1 a	13, 46.	§ 5, 4
22, 5.	§ 32, 5	13, 52.	§ 19, 4 d
22, 10.	§ 5, 4	13, 55.	§ 19, 4 d
22, 12.	§ 22 Rem. 1	13, 57.	§ 19, 4 d
22, 22.	§ 28 Rem. 11	19, 20.	§ 22 Rem. 1 and 2.
23, 1.	§ 15, 4	22, 11.	§ 27, 6 A ζ
23, 9.	§ 28, 2 g	22, 13.	§ 35, 4
23, 30.	§ 24, 2	24, 5.	§ 33, 3
24, 5.	§ 6, 1	25, 14.	§ 22, 5 A γ
24, 10.	§ 13, 5	25, 46.	§ 32, 14
24, 14.	§ 11 Rem. 3	26, 21.	§ 32, 9
25, 40.	§ 34, 1 a	26, 24.	§ 9, 9
26, 16.	§ 31, 1	26, 37.	§ 35 Rem. 1
26, 30.	§ 34, 1a	26, 42.	§ 10, 7
28, 2.	§ 4, 5.	26, 43.	§ 28, 6
28, 3.	§ 33, I	26, 44.	§ 28, 5 A β
28, 11.	§ 27, 6 B β	27, 2.	§ 19, 4 d
28, 17.	§ 6, 2		
29, 12.	§ 27, 6 C α	Num. 1, 1.	§ 7, 2 c
30, 25.	§ 33, 3.		§ 9 Rem. 1
31, 14.	§ 36, 5	1, 2.	§ 2 Rem. 4

INDEX OF PASSAGES QUOTED. 159

Num.	3, 46.	§ 9, 7
	5, 3.	§ 27, 5 b
	5, 23.	§ 40, 2 a
	6, 9.	§ 13, 3 a
		§ 23, 5.
	6, 26.	§ 17, 3a
	7, 87.	§ 9, 2.5
	9, 15.	§ 22, 2.
	11, 17.	§ 27, 6 A δ
	12, 1.	§ 38, 2
	12, 6.	§ 39 Rem. 2
	12, 14.	§ 28, 2 i
	13, 18.	§ 26, 6
	13, 2.	§ 17 Rem. 2
		§ 28, 5 F α
	14, 7.	§ 39 Rem. 1
	14, 20.	§ 14, 2 b
	14, 32.	§ 10, 1
	14, 42.	§ 25, 2 C α
	15, 6.	§ 28, 5 B α
	15, 15.	§ 3, 5
	15, 24.	§ 27, 6 C γ
	15, 35.	§ 22, 5 A γ
		§ 22 Rem. 5.
	16, 6.	§ 18, 4
	16, 9.	§ 8, 3
	16, 11.	§ 28, 2 i
	16, 15.	§ 17, 3 b
	16, 29.	§ 40 Rem. 1
	17, 3.	§ 15, 2
	17, 21.	§ 9, 2
	17, 28.	§ 28, 5 F ε
	18, 7.	§ 27, 5 b
	18, 23.	§ 13, 5
	19, 2.	§ 6 Rem. 4
	20, 13.	§ 28 Rem. 8
	20, 17.	§ 17, 1 a
	20, 18.	§ 1 Rem. 4
		§ 25 Rem. 13
	22, 6.	§ 21 Rem. 6
	22, 19.	§ 28, 5 k
	22, 30.	§ 12, 3
	22, 33.	§ 10, 3 a
		§ 14, 3
	23, 3.	§ 13, 4
	23, 13.	§ 25, 2 A β
	24, 11.	§ 28, 5 k
	28, 2.	§ 16, 1
Num.	28, 2.	§ 18, 1
	28, 4.	§ 3 Note 2
	28, 6.	§ 24, 1 b
	30, 10.	§ 5 Rem. 1
	32, 5.	§ 34, 1 c
	32, 27.	§ 23, 2
	35, 5.	§ 9 Rem. 3
	35, 19.	§ 22, 2
	36, 2.	§ 34, 2
Deut.	1, 1.	§ 39, 6
	1, 5.	§ 21 Rem. 4
	1, 19.	§ 32, 4
	1, 23.	§ 9, 2.8 c
	1, 27	§ 22, 2
	1, 32.	§ 25, 2 C β²
	1, 46.	§ 32, 10 a
	2, 24.	§ 21, 2 C δ
	2, 25.	§ 21, 2 A
	3, 24.	§ 19, 5.
		§ 28. 4 c
	4, 3.	§ 23, 3
	5; 12.	§ 22, 5 B γ
	5, 26.	§ 17, 4 a
	6, 3.	§ 28, 4 e
	6, 6.	§ 39 Rem. 1
	6, 10.	§ 16, 2
	8, 12.	§ 24, 3
	8, 16.	§ 33, 1
	9, 16.	§ 33, 4
	9, 25.	§ 32, 10 a
	9, 26.	§ 17, 3 b.
	10. 17.	§ 3. 10
	11, 13.	§ 16, 2
	11, 27	§ 28 Rem. 6.
	12, 30.	§ 15, 2
	14, 22.	§ 34 Rem.
	15, 18.	§ 30, 5
	16. 6.	§ 27, 6 D β
	16, 20.	§ 28, 6
	19, 17.	§ 12, I
	20, 15	§ 31, 2
	21, 10.	§ 37, 3
	22, 2.	§ 10, 4
	22, 6.	§ 27, 6 B β
	22, 8.	§ 19. 4 b
		§ 23, 5.
	22, 26.	§ 33, 4

Deut. 23, 5.	§ 27. 6 A η	
23, 15.	§ 13, 4	
24, 11.	§ 12, 1	
28, 32.	§ 38, 2	
28, 35.	§ 35, 7	
28, 43.	§ 24, 2	
28, 56.	§ 21, 2 a	
	§ 22, 2	
28, 48.	§ 37, 3	
28, 67.	§ 17. 4 a	
29, 9.	§ 10 Rem. 4	
29, 20.	§ 4, 10	
31, 12,	§ 21, 2 C β^1	
32, 11.	§ 25, 2 A δ	
	§ 28 Rem. 14	
32, 15.	§ 19 Rem. 2	
32, 17.	§ 19 Rem. 2	
32, 39.	§ 31, 2	
33, 11.	§ 28, 5 E γ	
	§ 33, 1	
33, 29.	§ 14, 3	
Jos. 1, 2.	§ 10 Rem. 7	
2, 7.	§ 28, 5 C δ	
2, 8.	§ 28, 2 a	
2, 10.	§ 28, 3	
3, 7.	§ 28, 4 e	
3, 12.	§ 9, 8 a	
3, 14.	§ 3 Rem. 2	
3, 16.	§ 21 Rem. 4	
4, 16.	§ 28, 2 k	
5, 1.	§ 16, 5	
5, 13.	§ 16, 5	
6, 13.	§ 22, 4	
7, 7.	§ 21, 2 C β^2	
7, 21.	§ 3 Rem. 1	
9, 2.	§ 32, 9	
9, 5.	§ 31, 3	
9, 12.	§ 23, 3	
13, 14.	§ 37, 1 d	
14, 11.	§ 27, 6 F α	
15, 19.	§ 10, 2.	
19, 51.	§ 7, 2 b	
22, 29.	§ 10 Rem. 7	
24, 19.	§ 2, 2 e	
Judges 1, 7.	§ 31, 3	
1, 22.	§ 36, 2	

Judges 1, 28.	§ 22, 4 Rem. 2	
4, 20.	§ 18 Rem.	
5, 8.	§ 28, 5 F ε	
5, 10.	§ 5, 5.	
5, 17.	§ 32, 8 c	
5, 24.	§ 27, 6 C δ	
5, 27.	§ 28 Rem. 1	
5, 29.	§ 8, 4 d	
6, 25.	§ 3 Rem. 4	
6, 36.	§ 31, 4	
7, 3.	§ 11. Rem. 3.	
9, 17.	§ 27, 6 B γ	
9, 28.	§ 11, 4	
9, 29.	§ 17, 4 a	
9, 45.	§ 33, 2	
9, 48.	§ 28, 7 c	
9, 55.	§ 36, 2	
11, 23.	§ 26, 5.	
12, 7.	§ 2, 9	
13, 11.	§ 26, 9	
13, 12.	§ 28, 7 a	
13, 16.	§ 27, 6 A ζ	
14, 15.	§ 26 Rem. 7	
15, 1.	§ 27, 6 A η	
15, 12.	§ 19, 5	
15, 13,	§ 22 Rem. 2.	
15, 18.	§ 19 5	
16, 14.	§ 3 Rem. 2	
16, 15.	§ 28, 2 f	
19, 5.	§ 33, 2	
19, 6.	§ 21, 2 C α	
19, 22.	§ 32, 14	
20, 44 46.	§ 41 Rem. 1	
21, 2.	§ 37, 1 a	
I. Sam. I. 1.	§ 13 Rem. 1	
1, 10.	§ 27, 6 B δ	
1, 13.	§ 36, 6	
1, 16.	§ 4, 8	
1, 22.	§ 32, 14	
2, 3.	§ 21, 2 C δ	
	§ 25, 5.	
2, 4.	§ 38 Rem. 2	
2, 13.	§ 41, 3	
2, 19.	§ 16, 6	
2, 27.	§ 26, 3	
2, 28.	§ 10, 4.	
	§ 22, 5 A α	

INDEX OF PASSAGES QUOTED. 161

1. Sam.	2, 28.	§ 27, 6 C α
	2, 33.	§ 36, 2
	3, 2.	§ 21, 2 D
	3, 7.	§ 25, 2 D
		§ 39, 4
	3, 11.	§ 41, 3
	4, 15.	§ 36, 6
	9, 9.	§ 19, 4 e
	9, 24.	§ 3, 13
	10, 27.	§ 27, 6 F γ
	11, 11.	§ 41 Rem. 2
	11, 12.	§ 26, 5
	12, 4. 5.	§ 26, 9
	12, 23.	§ 3 Note 1
	14, 14.	§ 35 Rem. 1
	14, 45.	§ 13, 4
	15, 20.	§ 28, 4 a
	15, 23.	§ 16, 4 a
		§ 27, 6 C γ
	15, 32.	§ 32, 9
	16, 16.	§ 21, 2 D
	17, 8.	§ 7, 2 a
	17, 34.	§ 28, 2 b
	17, 39.	§ 21, 2 b
		§ 28 Rem. 7
	17, 40.	§ 4 Rem. 3
	17, 46.	§ 36, 2
	18, 18.	§ 11, 4
	19, 13 16.	§ 2, 2 e
	19, 22.	§ 3 Rem. 4
	19, 23.	§ 10, 1
	20, 16.	§ 32 Rem. 5
	20, 19.	§ 21 Rem. 5
	21, 9.	§ 25 Rem. 11
	22, 7.	§ 24, 3
	22, 15.	§ 26, 5
	23, 11.	§ 26 Rem. 7
		§ 26, 9
	24, 11.	§ 28, 3
	24, 12.	§ 28, 5 A a
	24, 14.	§ 3, 4
	24, 18.	§ 33, 2
	24, 19.	§ 28, 3
	25, 22.	§ 28, 5 F δ
	25, 24.	§ 10, 1
	25, 26.	§ 32, 11
	25, 27.	§ 41 Rem. 2
	25, 33.	§ 32, 11
I. Sam.	27, 10.	§ 26 Rem. 9
	28, 3.	§ 28, 2 b
	28, 7.	§ 6, 3
	28, 16.	§ 28, 2 i
	30, 6.	§ 19, 3
II. Sam.	1, 4.	§ 30 Rem. 4
	1, 22.	§ 25 Rem. 5
	2, 8.	§ 7, 1
	2, 23.	§ 35, 7
	3, 25.	§ 32, 12
	3, 27.	§ 33, 4
	3, 30.	§ 35, 1
	3, 35.	§ 28 Rem. 12
	4, 7.	§ 28, 2 f
	5, 21.	§ 38, 2
	6, 6.	§ 32 Rem. 5
	7, 5.	§ 26, 3
	7, 18.	§ 11, 4
	10, 3.	§ 28, 5 E a
	10, 9.	§ 36, 3
		§ 38, 1
	12, 4.	§ 3 Rem. 4
	12, 6.	§ 9, 9
	13, 15.	§ 32, 5
	13, 39.	§ 6 Rem. 1
	14, 6.	§ 13, 7 b
	15, 4.	§ 17, 4 a
	15, 23.	§ 32, 11
		§ 36, 2
	15, 25.	§ 10, 3 b
	17, 8.	§ 32, 12
	17, 9.	§ 23, 5
	18, 4.	§ 9, 8 c
	18, 11.	§ 27, 6 B a
	18, 12.	§ 11 Rem. 3
	18, 22.	§ 11 Rem. 3
		§ 13, 4
	18, 29.	§ 26, 5
	19, 2.	§ 16, 6
	19, 27.	§ 1 Rem. 2
	21, 11.	§ 34, 1 c
	21, 20.	§ 9, 8 b
	22, 1.	§ 28, 2 b
	22, 38.	§ 17, 1 c
	22, 41.	§ 41 Rem. 2
	23, 4.	§ 4, 4
	24, 3.	§ 28 Rem. 4

11

INDEX OF PASSAGES QUOTED.

II. Sam. 24, 9. § 5 Rem. 2

I. Kings 1, 2. § 19, 4 b
§ 26 Rem. 3
1, 6. § 27, 6 C a
1, 12. § 18, 3
2, 21. § 34, 1 c
2, 22. § 28, 2 c
2, 31. § 24, 1 b
2, 39. § 7, 2 a
3, 8. § 27, 6 C ε
3, 27. § 22 Rem. 2
5, 1. § 16, 3
5, 9. § 24, 1 a
5, 11. § 8, 4 a
5, 17. § 32, 12
6, 12. § 41, 2
6, 19. § 28, 5 E β
6, 23. § 37, 3
8, 5. § 36, 2
8, 6. § 27 Rem. 1
8, 24. § 28, 6
8, 30. § 27, 6 D β
8, 33. § 28, 4 b
8, 64. § 8, 3
9, 16. § 39, 4
9, 23. § 23, 6
9, 26. § 1 Rem. 3
10, 1. § 39, 4
10, 21. § 25, 4
10, 23. § 27, 6 E β
10, 24. § 36, 2
13, 30. § 29, 1
13, 31. § 28, 7 a
15, 3. § 5, 4
15, 23. § 33, 4
15, 30. § 27, 6 B β
18, 5. § 27, 6 C a
18, 13. § 34, 1 c
18, 32. § 33, 3
19, 11. § 4, 11
§ 37 Rem. 1
20, 20. § 36, 2
20, 36. § 3, 1 c
21, 7. § 19, 5
22, 3. § 26, 3
22, 7. § 28, 2 k
22, 15. § 26, 2

I. Kings 22, 20. § 28, 2 k
22, 27. § 5 Rem. 4
22, 28. § 18, 4
22, 48. § 31, 1

II. Kings 1, 2. § 26, 6
1, 8. § 4, 8
1, 16. § 25, 4
2, 10. § 21, 2 B
2, 16. § 28, 5 B a
2, 24. § 1 Rem. 1
3, 3. § 36, 4
3, 16. § 2, 6
4, 16. § 27, 6 F β
4, 41. § 28, 2 H
4, 43. § 22, 5 B β
5, 13. § 40 Rem. 2
5, 26. § 40 Rem. 1
6, 21. 22. § 26, 9
7, 13. § 28, 2 H
8, 22. § 15, 7
8, 25. § 9, 6
10, 10. § 13, 8
10, 23. § 25, 3 b
11, 15. § 27, 5 b
12, 17. § 5, 1
13, 14. § 32, 5
15, 21. § 26, 3
16, 14. § 3 Rem. 1
20, 20. § 26, 3
22, 1. § 9, 1 c
22, 8. § 40, 2 a
23, 17. § 3, 9
24, 7. § 19, 2

Jes. 1, 1. § 28, 2 b
1, 4. § 29, 1
1, 5. § 13, 2
1, 6. § 25 Rem. 8
1, 7. 9. § 27, 6 F γ
1, 11. § 32, 14
1, 14. § 21, 2 A. § 27, 6 B a
1, 15. § 36, 6
1, 16. § 4, 6
1, 18. § 3, 1 b
§ 28, 5 G a
1. 20. § 34, 2
1, 26. § 35 Rem. 1

INDEX OF PASSAGES QUOTED.

Jes. 1, 29. § 19 Rem. 2
2, 1. § 28, 2 b
2, 4. § 36 Rem. 1
2, 9. § 32 Rem. 5
2, 11. § 38 Rem. 2
2, 17. § 37, 1 a
2, 22. § 27, 6 E γ
3, 7. § 32 Rem. 5
3, 8. § 1 Rem. 4
3, 10. § 32, 12
3, 12. § 36, 5
3, 14. § 28, 2 i
4, 4. § 14, 1. § 28, 5 C a
5, 1. § 4, 8
5, 2. § 33, 2
5, 6. § 32, 7
5, 8. § 19 Rem. 2
5, 9. § 25, 4
5, 11. § 21 Rem. 5.
5, 14. § 25, 2 F. § 35, 6
5, 17. § 35, 4
5, 26. § 37, 3
6, 2. § 9, 8 a
6, 3. § 13, 7 a
§ 28, 6
6, 8. § 32, 2
6, 9. § 22, 4
6, 10. § 19, 3
6, 11. § 27 Rem. 5
6, 13. § 21, 2 C a
7, 2. § 1 Rem. 4
7, 7. § 15, 1
§ 19, 2
7, 8. § 27, 6 C γ
7, 21. § 19, 4 e
8, 4. § 19, 4 a
8, 7. § 28 Rem. 4
8, 19. § 21, 3
8, 23. § 5, 4
9, 1. § 5, 5
9, 8. § 36, 2
9, 10. § 16, 6
9, 12. § 3 Rem. 1
10, 10. § 8 Rem. 1
10, 15. § 26, 4
10, 22. § 28, 5 G a
§ 32, 7
10, 30. § 32, 11

Jes. 11, 2. § 5 Note 1. Rem. 2
11, 8. § 40 Rem 2
11, 9. § 22, 2
11, 10. § 21, 3
§ 41, 1
12, 6. § 1, 3 b
13, 8. § 21, 3
13, 18. § 40 Rem. 2
14, 2. § 32, 14
14, 3. § 27, 6 A ε
§ 34 Note 2
14, 6. § 32, 5
14, 9. § 37 Rem. 1
14, 17. § 21, 3
14, 19. § 3, 1 b
§ 5, 5
15, 8. § 27, 7
16, 4. § 36, 2
16, 10. § 23, 5
17, 1. § 27, 6 C γ
17, 4. § 4, 6
17, 6. § 4, 9
17, 10. § 33, 2
18, 5. § 37, 1 d
§ 39, 6
19, 4. § 2, 2 e
§ 4, 13
19, 11. § 6, 3
19, 14. § 2 Rem. 2
19, 22. § 22, 4
21, 2. § 34 Note 2
21, 7. § 32, 5
21, 17. § 5, 3
§ 38, 1
22, 1. § 26, 7
22, 3. § 27, 6 C β
22, 14. § 28, 5 F ε
22, 16. § 8 Rem. 2
23, 1. § 27, 6 C γ
23, 4. § 25, 5
23, 5. § 27, 6 F a
23, 8. § 8, 4 d
24, 2. § 27, 6 F a
24, 10. § 27, 6 C γ
24, 12. § 34, 1 c
24, 13. § 28, 5 C a
24, 22. § 22, 5
26, 2. § 2 Rem. 2

Jes.	26,	3.	§ 23 Rem. 3
	26,	4.	§ 27, 6 A δ
	27,	5.	§ 28, 5 B a
	27,	11.	§ 36, 2
	27,	12.	§ 5 Rem. 4
	27,	13.	§ 16, 2
	28,	4.	§ 4, 5
			§ 23, 5
	28,	6.	§ 27, 7
	28,	9.	§ 5, 5
	28,	24.	§ 23, 5
	29,	16.	§ 26 Rem. 3
	29,	19.	§ 8, 4 d
	30,	16.	§ 4, 9
	30,	23.	§ 33, 2
	30,	26.	§ 30, 4
	31,	2.	§ 31, 1
	32,	1.	§ 41 Rem. 1
	32,	11.	§ 18 Rem.
	33,	1.	§ 21, 2 D
	33,	5.	§ 23 Rem. 3
	33,	9.	§ 37 Rem. 1
	33,	15.	§ 27, 6 C γ
	33,	16.	§ 32, 8 c
	33,	22.	§ 30, 2
	34,	4.	§ 3, 1 b
	34,	13.	§ 32, 7
			§ 36, 4
	36,	9.	§ 27, 6 E β. 6 E γ
	37,	11.	§ 26, 5
	37,	24.	§ 4, 6
	37,	30.	§ 18, 3
	38,	10.	§ 34, 1 a
	38,	15.	§ 28, 5 A a
	38,	18.	§ 23 Rem. 5
	40,	9.	§ 27, 6 E γ
	40,	10.	§ 27, 6 A δ
	40,	29.	§ 25, 2 C δ
	41,	1.	§ 21, 3
	41,	8.	§ 12, 3
	41,	23.	§ 1, 3 a
	42,	21.	§ 21 Rem. 5
	42,	22.	§ 2 Rem. 4
	42,	24.	§ 21, 2 A
	44,	21.	§ 10, 2
	45,	12.	§ 10, 1
	45,	17.	§ 32, 5
	45,	21.	§ 25 Rem. 10

Jes.	47,	1.	§ 21 Rem. 6
	47,	8.10.	§ 25, 1
	47,	12.	§ 12 Rem. 1
	48,	8.	§ 28, 7 c
	48,	9.14.	§ 27, 7
	48,	10.	§ 27, 6 A γ
	48,	18.	§ 17 Rem. 2
	48,	19.	§ 30, 4
	49,	11.	§ 37 Rem. 3
	49,	23.	§ 12, 3
	50,	2.	§ 26, 8
			§ 27, 6 C γ
	50,	10.	§ 2 Rem. 2
	51,	21.	§ 5 Rem. 4
	52,	8.	§ 38, 1
	52,	15.	§ 12, 4
	53,	9.	§ 28, 5 G β
	54,	9.	§ 27, 6 C γ
	55,	9.	§ 28, 5 H a
	56,	4.	§ 12 Rem. 1
	57,	8.	§ 19, 1
			§ 37 Rem. 1
	58,	9.	§ 24, 3
	59,	10.	§ 25, 2 C δ
	59,	20.	§ 5, 4
			§ 23 Rem. 5
	60,	2.	§ 3, 1 c
	60,	14.	§ 32, 9
	61,	7.	§ 19 Rem. 2
			§ 27, 7
	62,	5.	§ 32, 5
	62,	6.	§ 25 Rem. 5
	63,	2.	§ 30. 4
	64,	10.	§ 28 Rem. 8
			§ 38 Rem. 1
	65,	6.	§ 28, 5 I β
Jer.	2,	22.	§ 28, 5 I β
	2,	35.	§ 22, 3
	3,	5.	§ 19, 1
			§ 32 Rem. 5
			§ 37 Rem. 1
	3,	8.	§ 28, 5 D a
	4,	5.	§ 21, 2 C δ
	4,	22.	§ 31, 2
	5,	29.	§ 26, 4
	6,	6.	§ 1, 3 b
	6,	19.	§ 16, 4 b

Jer.			Ezech.		
		§ 41 Rem. 2			§ 37 Rem. 1
8,	9.	§ 11, 5	6,	10.	§ 24 Rem. 1
9,	1.	§ 17, 4 *a*	10,	15.	§ 27, 6 A ζ
9,	2.	§ 27, 6 E β	11,	13.	§ 32, 11
		§ 33 Note 1	13,	3.	§ 25, 3 *a*
9,	17.	§ 32, 7	13,	10.	§ 33, 2
9,	22.	§ 19, 4 *b*	14,	1.	§ 37, 2
10,	3.	§ 37, 1 *d*	14,	22.	§ 41 Rem. 1
10,	7.	§ 19, 2	17,	21.	§ 41 Rem. 1
10,	20.	§ 25, 2 C γ	18,	7.	§ 10 Rem. 2
10,	22.	§ 38, 1	18,	10.	§ 27 Rem. 5
10,	25.	§ 25, 4	18,	20.	§ 27, 6 A ζ
12,	8.	§ 35, 6	18,	32.	§ 28, 2 *h*
13,	16.	§ 37, 1 *a*	21,	32.	§ 28, 6
13,	17.	§ 32, 7	22,	4.	§ 37 Rem. 1
13,	18.	§ 21, 2 C δ	23,	28.	§ 12, 4
14,	15.	§ 28, 2 *f*	23,	32.	§ 37 Rem. 1
15,	15.	§ 40 Rem. 1	23,	49.	§ 19, 1
17,	11.	§ 28, 7 *b*	24,	17.	§ 32, 9
17,	16.	§ 27, 6 C γ	26,	3.	§ 27, 6 E ε
18,	16.	§ 35, 6	27,	24.	§ 4, 2
19,	5.	§ 19, 2	31,	16.	§ 5 Rem. 2
22,	16.	§ 22, 2	33,	17.	§ 41, 1
22,	29.	§ 28, 6	37,	11.	§ 27, 6 E γ
23,	14.	§ 25, 3 *a*	39,	27.	§ 3 Rem. 5
23,	17.	§ 22, 4	40,	1.	§ 28, 5 C δ
23,	23.	§ 24, 1 *b*	41,	22.	§ 30, 4
23,	33.	§ 41 Rem. 1	47,	4.	§ 5, 4
25,	13.	§ 32, 14			
28,	4.	§ 4, 14	Hosea 1,	7.	§ 27, 6 A ε
30,	14.	§ 28 Rem. 10	2,	11.	§ 21, 2 C β¹
31,	5.	§ 19, 4 *b*	3,	2.	§ 27, 6 A ε
33,	20.	§ 10, 7	4,	2.	§ 22, 5 B *a*
33,	22.	§ 23 Rem. 4	4,	9.	§ 27, 6 F *a*
		§ 28, 48 *f*	6,	1.	§ 17, 3 *e*
35,	7.	§ 23, 2	6,	2.	§ 27, 6 C δ
38,	5.	§ 25 Rem. 7	8,	5.	§ 22 Rem. 3
40,	8.	§ 28, 5 A *a*	8,	7.	§ 28, 5 B *a*
41,	12.	§ 27, 6 D β	8,	14.	§ 37, 3
44, 7. 8.		§ 27, 6 E β	9,	6.	§ 28, 7 *a*
48,	2.	§ 27, 6 C γ	9,	9.	§ 21, 2 C δ
48,	32.	§ 3, 9	9,	12.	§ 28, 5 F *a*
48,	36.	§ 5, 4	10,	14.	§ 27, 6 B β
49,	24.	§ 36, 4	12,	1.	§ 2, 2 *e*
50,	9.	§ 30, 4	12,	15.	§ 32, 9
50,	11.	§ 4 Rem. 2	13,	4.	§ 25 Rem. 10
			13,	8.	§ 1, 2
Ezech. 2,	9.	§ 1 Rem. 5	14,	1.	§ 37 Rem. 3

Hosea	14, 4.	§ 34, 2	
	14, 5.	§ 32, 9	
	14, 7.	§ 37, 1 a.	
Joel	1, 2.	§ 3, 5	
		§ 26 Rem. 4	
	1, 6.	§ 25, 2 C δ	
	2, 2.	§ 30 Rem. 4	
	2, 13.	§ 25 Rem. 5	
	2, 16.	§ 39, 6	
	2, 22.	§ 19, 1	
	2, 23.	§ 16, 6	
	2, 26.	§ 21 Rem. 2	
	4, 14.	§ 30 Rem. 3	
	4, 18.	§ 32, 7	
Amos	1, 1.	§ 27, 6 A a. 6 C a.	
	1,3.6.9.13.	§ 28, 2 c	
	1,5.8.	§ 36, 2	
	5, 14.	§ 25 Rem. 5	
	6, 6.	§ 27, 6 A β	
	6, 10.	§ 13 Rem. 2	
	6, 13.	§ 25, 2 A δ	
	9, 1.	§ 23, 5	
	9, 8.	§ 22 Rem. 2	
	9, 13.	§ 32, 7	
Obadja	10.	§ 5, 4	
	16.	§ 28, 5 H a	
Jona	1, 7. 8.	§ 7 Rem. 1	
		§ 26 Rem. 2	
	2, 3.	§ 39 Note 1	
	4, 6.	§ 32, 5	
	4, 10.	§ 4, 8	
	4, 11.	§ 26, 5	
Micha	1, 13.	§ 18 Rem.	
	1, 16.	§ 2 Rem. 2	
	2, 3.	§ 32, 9	
	2, 6.	§ 37, 1 a.	
	2, 13.	§ 16, 6	
	4, 3. 11.	§ 36 Rem. 1	
	4, 14.	§ 27, 6 A s	
		§ 35, 7	
	5, 1.	§ 13, 8	
		§ 27, 6 C a	
	5, 4.	§ 6 Rem. 2	
Micha		§ 28, 2 c	
	6, 3.	§ 28, 4 d	
	6, 8.	§ 21, 2 A	
	7, 8.	§ 1, 3 b	
Nahum	3, 15.	§ 37 Rem. 2	
Hab.	1, 5. 2. 10.	§ 23 Rem. 3	
	2, 19.	§ 25 Rem. 3. § 26, 5	
	3, 9.	§ 22 Rem. 1	
	3, 17.	§ 36, 3	
Zeph.	2, 2.	§ 25, 4. § 28, 5 C δ	
	2, 12.	§ 31, 2	
	2, 15.	§ 25, 1	
	3, 9.	§ 32, 9	
Haggai	1, 4.	§ 10, 1	
	1, 6.	§ 10 Rem. 8. § 21, 3	
	2, 3.	§ 30 Rem. 4	
Zech.	1, 14.	§ 32, 5	
	1, 15.	§ 32, 5. § 28, 4 c	
	3, 9.	§ 1 Rem. 5	
	7, 5.	§ 10, 2	
	8, 6.	§ 26, 5	
	9, 11.	§ 24, 3	
	12, 10.	§ 22, 5 A β	
	14, 10.	§ 3 Note 1	
Mal.	2, 15.	§ 19 Rem. 2	
Psalms	1, 1.	§ 14, 2 c	
	1, 3.	§ 27, 6 B δ	
	2, 6.	§ 19, 5. § 28, 2 i	
	2, 10. 24.	§ 15, 5	
	3, 5.	§ 16, 6. § 32, 11	
	3, 6.	§ 17, 2	
	3, 8.	§ 33, 4	
	4, 4.	§ 28, 2 h	
	4, 8.	§ 10 Rem. 8	
	5, 5.	§ 23, 6. § 32, 8 c	
	5, 10.	§ 1, 3 a § 25 Rem. 8	
	5, 13.	§ 33, 2	
	6, 2. 6.	§ 25 Rem. 8	
	6, 2.	§ 40 Rem. 1	
	6, 10.	§ 40 Rem. 2	
	7, 4. 5. 6.	§ 28, 5 F β	

Psalms 7, 10. § 28, 2 g
7, 12. § 3 Rem. 3
8, 6. § 33, 1
9, 7. § 41, 2
9, 16. § 11, 2
9, 21. § 28, 7 c
11, 5. § 40 Rem. 2
12, 4. § 1, 3 a
12, 5. § 27, 6 E β
12, 8. § 3 Rem. 5
14, 3. § 25 Rem. 8
14, 4. § 28, 7 b
14, 5. § 32, 5
16, 3. 4. § 41 Rem. 1
17, 10. 13. § 32, 11
18, 17. § 32 Rem. 5
18, 28. § 4, 12
18, 30. § 27, 6 A ε
18, 31. § 30, 3
18, 33. § 33, 1
19, 14. § 25 Rem. 1
22, 8. § 35, 6
22, 13. § 4, 9
22, 16. § 1 Rem. 5
22, 22. § 21, 3
22, 32. § 23, 2
25, 19. § 32, 12
27, 7. § 32, 11
29, 4. § 4 Rem. 1
29, 26. § 15, 5
31, 7. § 14, 2 a
32, 2. § 25 Rem. 8
32, 6. § 24, 3
32, 9. § 25, 2 E
34, 22. § 40, 2 a
35, 16. § 35, 6
35, 19. § 10 Rem. 2
37, 20. § 27, 6 A γ
37, 23. § 34, 2
38, 11. § 36, 6. § 38 Rem. 2
39, 7. § 27, 6 A γ
40, 6. § 1, 3 a § 21 Rem. 3
41, 9. § 13, 4
42, 2. § 1 Rem. 2 § 28 Rem. 14
43, 1. § 25, 2 A δ
44, 5. § 31, 2
44, 6. § 27, 6 A ε
44, 20. § 35, 6

Psalms 44, 21. § 28, 5 F β
45, 7. § 10 Rem. 3. § 30, 4
45, 8. § 33, 2
45, 9. § 28, 2 a
45, 10. § 27, 6 E δ
45, 13. § 8, 4 d
48, 6. § 28, 5 H a
49, 8. § 22 Rem. 2
49, 18. § 40 Rem. 1
50, 3. § 19, 2
50, 8. § 40 Rem. 1
50, 12. § 28, 5 F a
51, 4. § 21, 2 C δ
51, 14. § 33, 2
54, 2. § 26, 3
55, 18. § 32, 10 b
55, 19. § 27, 6 A δ
58, 9. § 5 Rem. 4
60, 7. § 32, 11
60, 13. § 28, 2 g
63, 3. § 27, 6 E β
65, 5. § 29, 2
65, 14. § 32, 8 a
66, 16. § 17, 1 a
66, 17. § 32, 11
68, 5. § 27, 6 A δ
68, 7. § 23, 4 a
69, 5. § 10, 7
69, 6. § 27, 6 E ε
69, 11. § 2 Rem. 2
73, 15. § 28, 5 F β
73, 20. § 27, 6 C δ
74, 7. § 21 Note 3
74, 17. § 41, 1
75, 4. § 38 Rem. 3
76, 7. § 28, 2 a
77, 3. § 21 Rem. 3
78, 18. § 27, 6 E β
78, 26. 30. 45. 52. § 16 Rem.
78, 31. § 27, 6 A a
80, 11. § 34, 1 a
81, 9. § 17, 4 b
81, 14. § 14, 3. § 17, 4 b
83, 2. § 25 Rem. 5
83, 5. § 27, 6 C γ
83, 12. § 10 Rem. 7
85, 14. § 4 Rem. 2
86, 8. § 13 Rem. 2

Psalms 87, 5. § 13, 1
88, 5. § 25, 2 C δ
88, 6. § 23 Rem. 5
89, 2. § 35, 6
89, 40. § 21 Note 3
90, 4. § 27, 7
90, 16. § 15, 3
92, 7. § 32, 2
99, 6. § 27, 6 A δ
101, 8. § 27, 6 E β
102, 4. § 27, 6 A γ
102, 19. § 23, 2
102, 28. § 13, 6
103, 9. § 32 Rem. 5
104, 2. § 32, 8 a
104, 8. § 11, 2
104, 17. § 30, 3
104, 18. § 3 Rem. 4
104, 20. § 17, 3 c
104, 25. § 11, 3 a
105, 12. § 27, 6 F γ
105, 24. § 8, 1
106, 13. § 21, 2 C δ
107, 23. § 5, 4
108, 7. § 32, 11
109, 3. § 32, 14
109, 4. § 4 Rem. 2
109, 29. § 32, 8 a
109, 30. § 35, 6
112, 9. § 21, 2 C δ
115, 5. 7. § 39 Rem. 2
116, 16. § 27, 6 E ε
118, 21. § 15, 5
119, 14. § 35 Rem. 1
119, 41. § 32, 6
119, 86. § 32, 9
119, 137. 155. § 37, 1 b
120, 5. § 32, 8 c
120, 7. § 4, 7
125, 1. § 28 Rem. 14
129, 6. § 28, 5 C δ
130, 3. § 15, 6
132, 11. § 13, 8
136, 19. 20. § 27, 6 E ε
137, 5. § 28, 5 F β
137, 8. 9. § 29, 2
139, 2. § 19, 5
139, 8. § 28, 5 F a

Psalms 139, 19. § 17, 4 b
142, 2. § 32, 11
144, 1. § 3, 13
144, 3. § 16, 7
144, 14. § 1, 2
145, 13. § 30, 3. § 39, 3
145, 14. § 27, 6 E ε
147, 14. § 23, 4 d
149, 2. § 2, 2 e

Prov. 1, 28. § 24, 3
2, 4. § 4, 5
2, 21. § 6, 2
2, 22. § 19 Rem. 1
3, 10. § 32, 8 b
3, 18. § 36, 5
3, 26. § 27, 6 A δ
6, 6. § 18, 3
6, 16. § 28, 2 c
6, 24. § 4, 5
9, 10. § 2, 2 e
10, 1. § 39, 3
10, 4. § 32, 11
10, 22. § 41, 1
10, 24. § 41, 1
12, 21. § 25, 2 A β
13, 21. § 32 Rem. 1
14, 20. § 34, 2
15, 20. § 6 Rem. 2
16, 2. § 38 Rem. 1
17, 3. § 28, 2 d
17, 8. § 4, 3
17, 12. § 1, 2. § 22 Rem. 5
18, 5. § 30, 5
18, 22. § 28, 7 a
21, 9. 19. § 30, 5
21, 20. § 6 Rem. 2
21, 27. § 36, 5
22, 17. § 15, 3
22, 19. § 10, 1
22, 23. § 33, 2
23, 24. § 41, 3
24, 27. § 28, 2 e
24, 28. § 24, 1 b
24, 31. § 32, 7
25, 3. § 25, 2 C δ § 28, 2 d
25, 12. 26. § 28 Rem. 2
25, 25. § 28, 2 d

INDEX OF PASSAGES QUOTED. 169

Prov. 27, 7. § 30 Rem. 2
27, 8. § 3, 1 b
27, 9. § 38 Rem. 3
27, 24. § 26 Rem. 4
28, 1. § 36, 5
30, 18. § 28, 2 c
30, 30. § 25, 2 A β

Job. 1, 5. § 32, 9
1, 6. § 27, 6 B δ
1, 14. § 27, 6 B δ § 36, 2
2, 3. § 26, 3
2, 9. § 26, 5
3, 4. § 4, 7
3, 5. § 37 Rem. 3
3, 8. § 21 Rem. 3
3, 26. § 14, 2 a
4, 2. § 26, 8
4, 5. § 19, 2
4, 17. § 26, 4
5, 2. § 27, 6 E ε
5, 5. § 27, 5 b
5, 7. § 28, 2 d
5, 19. § 28, 2 c
6, 5. § 26, 4
6, 12. § 4, 2 § 26 Rem. 3. 8.
       § 30, 4. § 39, 6
6, 28. § 21 2 C δ
7, 3. § 19 Rem. 1 § 34, 1 a
7, 13. § 27, 6 A ζ
7, 18. § 13, 2
7, 20. § 27, 6 B a § 28, 7 a
8, 3. § 26, 4
8, 9. § 30 Rem. 4
8, 11. § 26 Rem. 6
9, 15. § 28, 5 G a
10, 4. § 26, 4
10, 7. § 28, 5 G β
10, 17. § 28, 2 b
11, 2. 7. § 26, 4
11, 15. § 27, 6 C β
12, 11. § 28, 2 d
12, 17. 19. § 23, 4 f
13, 7. § 26 Rem. 6
13, 13. § 21, 3
13, 16. § 40 Rem. 1
13, 28. § 19 Rem. 2
14, 14. § 26, 3

Job. 15, 3. § 27, 7
15, 7. § 26 Rem. 6
15, 24. § 21 Rem. 1
16, 3. § 26 Rem. 5
16, 4. 9. 10. § 35, 6
16, 6. § 17, 1 c
16, 7. § 19 Rem. 2
16, 17. § 28, 5 G β
17, 10. § 18, 4. § 21, 2 C γ
17, 15. § 26, 7
18, 21. § 5, 4
19, 9. § 35, 3
19, 16. § 35, 6
19, 23. § 17, 4 a
19, 26. § 27, 6 C β
20, 4. § 26, 3
20, 19. § 28 Rem. 1
20, 26. § 37 Rem. 1
20, 33. § 35, 6
21, 4. § 26 Rem. 4
21, 9. § 25 Rem. 2. § 27, 6 C β
21, 12. § 23, 4 c
21, 21. § 38, 1
21, 25. § 27, 6 A ζ
21, 34. § 32, 9
22, 3. § 26, 4
22, 7. § 40 Rem. 1
22, 9. § 34 Note 2
22, 12. § 28, 2 g
22, 20. § 28, 5 F ε
22, 30. § 25 Rem. 11
23, 2. § 27, 6 B a
23, 3. § 17, 4 a § 21, 2 C β²
23, 6. § 25, 2 A γ
23, 12. § 41, 2
23, 13. § 27, 6 A ζ
24, 5. § 5, 5
24, 19. § 28, 7 b
24, 25. § 25, 1
26, 2. § 4, 4
26, 5. § 27 Rem. 3
27, 6. § 27, 6 C a
27, 7. § 27, 6 F γ
28, 17. § 25, 5
29, 10. § 38, 1
29, 23. § 35 Note 4
29, 25. § 40, 2 a
31, 15. § 23, 6

Job. 31, 18. § 28, 4 *d*
32, 7. § 38, 1
32, 22. § 21 Rem. 5
33, 13. § 25, 2 A β
34, 3. § 28, 2 *d*
34, 10. § 27, 7
34, 17. § 26 Rem. 4
34, 23. § 40 Rem. 1
34, 27. § 28 Rem. 9
35, 15. § 25 Rem. 10
36, 26. § 41, 2
37, 14. § 32, 14
37, 16. 18. § 26 Rem. 6
38, 4, 5, 18. § 28 Rem. 6
38, 12. § 27, 6 C *a*
38, 21. § 38, 1
38, 30. § 35, 4
38, 32. § 37, 3
39, 13. § 36, 3
39, 15. § 36, 4
39, 17. § 27, 6 A ζ
40, 8. 9. § 26 Rem. 4
40, 23. § 27, 6 D *a*
40, 29. § 35, 4
41, 7. § 32, 9
41, 20. § 4, 8
42, 7. § 28, 5 C δ
42, 8. § 28 Rem. 15
42, 15. § 37, 1 *a*

Cant. 1, 4. § 17, 1 *b*
1, 6. § 7 Rem. 1
1, 15. § 30, 4
2, 3. § 21, 2 C *a*
2, 7. § 19, 1
2, 11. § 28 Rem. 1
2, 17. § 27, 6 E γ
3, 7. § 7 Rem. 1 § 10 Rem. 7
3, 8. § 23 Rem. 1
5, 6. § 28 Rem. 1
6, 1. § 8, 4 *b*
6, 8. § 10 Rem. 5
6, 9. § 37 Rem. 3
7, 12. § 32, 6
7, 13. § 26, 6
8, 6. § 35, 4

Ruth 1, 8. § 19, 1

Ruth 1, 13. § 25, 2 B β
Lam. 1, 5. 9. § 32, 9
1, 8. § 32, 5
1, 14. § 12, 5
1, 16. § 32, 7
1, 17. § 35, 6
3, 23. § 13, 2
3, 38. § 26, 5
3, 48. § 32, 7
5, 16. § 29, 1

Eccl. 1, 9. § 25 Rem. 3
1, 16. § 19, 5
2, 7. § 37 Rem. 3
2, 11. § 19, 5
2, 19. § 26 Rem. 5
3, 11. § 25, 4
4, 1. 7. § 21, 2 C β²
5, 15. § 28, 5 H β
5, 18. § 31, 2
7, 26. § 3, 4
8, 15. § 19, 5
9, 4. § 41 Rem. 1
10, 10. § 40 Rem. 1
12, 9. § 36, 3

Esther 1, 3. § 9 Rem. 1
1, 5. § 4, 14
1, 8. § 13, 1
1, 20. § 19, 1
2, 11. § 35, 5
3, 13. § 22, 5 A *a*
4, 1. § 32, 5
4, 2. § 21 Rem. 1
4, 14. § 26 Rem. 1
4, 16 § 24 Rem. 1
7, 2. § 17, 3 *a*
7, 4. § 28, 5 F *a*
7, 5. § 11, 3 *c*
8, 1. § 13, 3 *a*
8, 8. § 22 Rem. 4
9, 1. § 13, 5
10, 2. § 26, 3

Daniel 1, 3. § 28, 2 *b*
2, 30. § 19 Rem. 1
5, 2. § 26, 6 A β

Daniel	5. 3.	§ 19 Rem. 1
	8, 13.	§ 28, 2 a
	9, 17.	§ 5, 2
	9, 23.	§ 4 Rem. 2
	9, 24.	§ 34 Note 2
	9, 25.	§ 21, 2 C β¹
	9, 26.	§ 9, 5
	11, 7.	§ 13, 8. § 27, 6 C a
Ezra	7, 8.	§ 9 Rem. 1
	8, 16.	§ 27, 6 E ε
	8, 29.	§ 3, 9
	8, 35.	§ 9, 5
	10, 13.	§ 30, 4
Neh.	2, 12.	§ 24, 1 a
	3, 20.	§ 21 Rem. 4
	3, 37.	§ 27, 6 B γ
	4, 4.	§ 27, 6 A ζ
	4, 17.	§ 25 Rem. 9
	5, 2. 3. 4.	§ 13, 8
	5, 5.	§ 25, 2 C a
	7, 2.	§ 27, 6 F γ
	9, 19.	§ 41 Rem. 1
	9, 28.	§ 4 Rem. 3
	9, 35.	§ 3 Rem. 4

I. Chron.	7, 1.	§ 41 Rem. 1
	9, 13.	§ 5 Rem. 3
	13, 2.	§ 21 Rem. 4
	17, 4.	§ 26, 3
	19, 3.	§ 28, 5 E a
	27, 24.	§ 34 Rem.
	29, 9.	§ 32, 5
II. Chron.	3, 3.	§ 9, 3 b
	7, 21.	§ 41 Rem. 1
	9, 20.	§ 25, 4
	11, 21.	§ 9, 3 a. b
	16, 12.	§ 33, 4
	16, 14.	§ 28, 2 b
	17, 7.	§ 27, 6 E ε
	21, 4.	§ 27, 6 C a
	26, 15.	§ 21 Rem. 1
	26, 18.	§ 28, 5
	27, 7.	§ 26, 3
	31, 2.	§ 27, 6 E ε
	31, 10.	§ 34, 1 c
	32, 15.	§ 25, 2 A β
	32, 32.	§ 26, 3

Messrs. LUZAC & Co.'s
PUBLICATIONS CONCERNING „WESTERN ASIA".

(Includ. Books on the Old Testament).

Publishers to the India Office, the Asiatic Society of Bengal, the University of Chicago, etc.

Assab'iniyya. A Philosophical Poem in Arabic by MUSA B. TUBI. Together with the Hebrew Version and Commentary styled Batte Hannefes by SOLOMON B. IMMANUEL DAPIERA. Edited and Translated bij HARTWIG HIRSCHFELD. 8vo. pp. 61. 2s. 6d.

Babylonian (The) and Oriental Record. A Monthly Magazine of the Antiquities of the East. Edited by Prof. TERRIEN DE LACOUPERIE. Published Monthly.
Single Numbers, 1s. 6d. each. Annual Subscription, 12s. 6d.

Bezold, Ch. Oriental Diplomacy: being the Transliterated Text of the Cuneiform Despatches between the Kings of Egypt and Western Asia in the 15th century before Christ, discovered at Tell-el-Amarna, and now preserved in the British Museum. With full Vocabulary, Grammatical Notes, &c., by CHARLES BEZOLD. Post 8vo. Cloth. pp. XLIV, 124. 18s.

Biblia. A Monthly Magazine devoted to Biblical Archæology and Oriental Research. Published Monthly. Annual Subscription. 5s.

Biblical World (The). Continuing the Old and New Testament Student. Editor, WILLIAM R. HARPER. Published Monthly. Annual Subscription. 9s.

Blackden, M. W. and Fraser, G. W. Collection of Hieratic GRAFFITI from the Alabaster, Quarry of Hat-Nub, situated near Tell-el-Amarna, found December 28th 1891, copied September, 1892. Oblong. pp. 10. 10s.

LUZAC & CO., 46, GREAT RUSSELL STREET, LONDON, W.C.

LUZAC & Co's Publications.

Budge, E. A. Wallis. — Oriental with and Wisdom; or The Laughable Stories collected by Bar-Hebraeus. The Syriac Text with an English Translation, by E. A. WALLIS BUDGE, Litt. D., F. S. A., Keeper of the Department of Egyptian and Assyrian Antiquities, British Museum. (Vol. I of Luzac's Semitic Text andTranslation Series). 8vo. Cloth. pp. XXVII, 204, 166. 25*s*.

Harper, Robert Francis. Assyrian and Babylonian Letters, belonging to the K Collection of the British Museum. By ROBERT FRANCIS HARPER, of the University of Chicago. Parts I to IV. Post 8vo. Cloth. £ 1. 5*s*. each Part.

Hebraica. A Quarterly Journal in the interests of Semitic Study. Edited by WILLIAM R. HARPER and the Staff of the Semitic Department of the University of Chicago. Published Quarterly.
Annual Subscription. 14*s*.

Jastrow's Dictionary of the Targumim, the Talmud Bablii and Yerushalmi, and the Midrashic Literature. Compiled by M. JASTROW, Ph. D. Parts I to VIII. 4to. pp. 480. 5*s*. each Part.

King, Leonard W. Babylonian Magic and Sorcery. Being "The Prayers of the Lifting of the Hand." The Cuneiform Texts of a Group of Babylonian and Assyrian Incantations and Magical Formulæ, edited with Transliterations, Translations, and Full Vocabulary from Tablets of the Kuyunjik Collection preserved in the British Museum. By LEONARD W. KING, M. A., Assistant in the Departement of Egyptian and Assyrian Antiquities, British Museum. Roy. 8vo. Cloth. pp. XXXII, 199 and 76 Cuneiform-Plates. 18*s*. net.

Luzac's Oriental List. Containing Notes and News on, and a Bibliographical List of, all new Publications on Africa and the East. Published Monthly. Annual Subscription, 3*s*. Vol. I to VII (1890—1896) are still to be had (with Index, half-bound).
Price of Vols. I—III 6*s*. each. IV—VII 5*s*. each.

Luzac's Semitic text and translation series. Vol. I. Containing Dr. E. A. WALLIS BUDGE's Edition and Translation of Bar-Hebraeus' Laughable Stories. 21*s*.

Margoliouth, D. S. Arabic Papyri of the Bodleian Library, reproduced by the Collotype Process. With Transcription and Translation. Text in 4to. pp. 7 and 2 Facsimiles in large folio. 5*s*.

Margoliouth, D. S. Chrestomathia Baidawiana. The Commentary of El-Baidáwi on Sura III. Translated and explained for the use of Students of Arabic. By D. S. MARGOLIOUTH, M. A. Laudian Professor of Arabic in the University of Oxford, etc. etc. Post 8vo. Cloth. pp. XVI, 216. 12*s*. net.

LUZAC & Co., 46, GREAT RUSSELL STREET, LONDON, W.C.

LUZAC & Co's Publications.

Muallakat. The Seven Poems suspended in the Temple at Mecca. Translated from the Arabic. By Capt. F. E. JOHNSON. With an Introduction by Shaikh TAIZULLABHAI. 8vo. pp. XXIV, 238. 7s. 6d.

Ruben (Paul). Critical Remarks upon some passages of the Old Testament, by PAUL RUBEN, Ph. D. 4to. Cloth. pp. II, 23, 14. 3s. 6d.

Sacred Books of the Old Testament. A critical edition of the Hebrew Text. Printed in Colours, with Notes. Prepared by eminent Biblical Scholars of Europe and America. Under the Editorial Direction of PAUL HAUPT, Professor in the John Hopkins University, Baltimore. Edition de luxe, in 120 numbered copies only. Subscription price for the complete Work (20 parts). £ 20.
Prospectuses sent on application.

Sayce, A. H. Address to the Assyrian Section of the Ninth International Congress of Orientalists. 8vo, pp. 32. 1s.

Tiele, C. P. Western Asia, according to the most Recent Discoveries. Rectorial Address on the occasion of the 318th Anniversary of the Leyden University, 8th February, 1893. Translated by ELIZABETH J. TAYLOR. Small 8vo. Bound. pp. 36. 2s. 6d.

Transactions of the Ninth International Congress of Orientalists. (Held in London, 5th to 12th September, 1892). Edited by E. DELMAR MORGAN. 2 Vols. Roy. 8vo, cloth. £ 1. 15s.
Vol. I. contains: Indian and Aryan Sections. £ 1. 1s.
Vol. II. contains: Semitic, Egypt and Africa, Geographical, Archaic Greece and the East, Persia and Turkey, China, Central Asia and the Far East, Australasia, Anthropology and Mythology Sections. £ 1. 1s.

Wijnkoop, J. D. — Manual of Hebrew Syntax. Translated from the Dutch by C. VAN DEN BIESEN. 8vo. Cloth. pp. XXII, 152 and Index. 5s.

Wildeboer, G. The Origin of the Canon of the Old Testament. An Historico-Critical Enquiry. Translated by WISNER BACON. Edited, with Preface, by Professor GEORGE F. MOORE. Roy. 8vo. Cloth. pp. XII, 132. 7s. 6d.

Winckler, H. — The Tell-El-Amarna Letters. Transliteration, *English translation*, Vocabulary, etc. Roy. 8vo. Cloth. pp. XLII, 416, and Registers 50 pages. £ 1. 1s.

—— The same. In Paper Covers. £ 1.

LUZAC & Co., 46, GREAT RUSSELL STREET, LONDON, W.C.

A COMPLETE LIST OF

BOOKS & PERIODICALS,

PUBLISHED AND SOLD BY

LUZAC and Co.,

Publishers to the India Office, the Asiatic Society of Bengal, the University of Chicago, etc.

(With Index)

1740

LONDON:
LUZAC & Co.
46, GREAT RUSSELL STREET (OPPOSITE THE BRITISH MUSEUM).
1898.

Messrs. **LUZAC & Co.** having been appointed **OFFICIAL AGENTS FOR THE SALE OF INDIAN GOVERNMENT PUBLICATIONS** and **PUBLISHERS TO THE SECRETARY OF STATE FOR INDIA IN COUNCIL,** are able to supply at the shortest notice all Works published by the **GOVERNMENT OF INDIA.**

They have also been appointed **OFFICIAL ENGLISH AGENTS AND PUBLISHERS** to the **ASIATIC SOCIETY OF BENGAL,** and **THE UNIVERSITY OF CHICAGO,** and keep all Works published by the above Society and University in stock.

ORIENTAL STUDENTS are invited to submit to **Messrs. LUZAC & Co,** their **MANUSCRIPTS** for publication before sending them elsewhere.

Messrs. LUZAC and Co. are able to Supply, at the Shortest Notice and most favourable Terms, **all English, Foreign,** and **Oriental Books** and **Periodicals. Monthly Lists** Issued Regularly and Sent Gratis on Application.

Messrs. LUZAC and Co. have a Large Stock of New and Second-hand Oriental Works, of which they issue regularly Lists and Catalogues, which are to be had on application.

COMPLETE LIST OF
BOOKS AND PERIODICALS,

PUBLISHED AND SOLD BY

LUZAC and Co.

American Journal of Theology. Edited by Members of the Divinity Faculty of the University of Chicago. Vol. I. (Vol. II in progress). Quarterly. Annual Subscription. 14s. 6d.

"The theologians of America are attempting to supply a real need... it aims at a complete presentation of all recent theological work ... we give it a hearty welcome, as a scheme likely to prove of real utility to theological students and to the cause of truth." — *Guardian*.

American Journal of Semitic Languages and Literatures (continuing Hebraica). Edited by WILLIAM R. HARPER and the Staff of the Semitic Department of the University of Chicago. Vol. I—XIII. (Vol. XIV in progress). Published quarterly. Annual subscription. 14s.

American Journal of Sociology. Vol. I—III. (Vol. IV in progress). Published quarterly. Annual subscription. 10s. 6d.

Anandás'rama Sanskrit Series. — Edited by Pandits of the Ánandás'rama. Published by Mahádeva Chimnáji Ápte, B.A., LL.B., Pleader High Court, and Fellow of the University of Bombay. Nos. 1 to 35. In 42 Vols. Royal 8vo. Price of the set £ 16. Single Vols. at different prices.

Asiatic Society of Bengal, Journal of. Messrs Luzac and Co are the sole agents for Great Britain and America of the Asiatic Society of Bengal and can supply the continuation of the Journal at 3*s.* each No., of the Proceedings at 1*s.* each No. As they keep a large stock of the Journal and Proceedings, they can also supply any single No. at the published price.

Assab'iniyya. — A philosophical Poem in Arabic by Mūsā B. Tūbi. Together with the Hebrew Version and Commentary styled Bāttē Hannefeš by Solomon Immānuēl Dapiera. Edited and translated by HARTWIG HIRSCHFELD. 8vo. pp. 61. 2*s.* 6*d.* net.

Assyrian and Babylonian Letters. 4 vols. See: Harper.

Aston (W. G.) — A Grammar of the Japanese Written Language. Second Edition, enlarged and improved. Roy. 8vo. Cloth. pp. 306. (Published 28*s.*) Reduced-Price, 18*s.*

Aston (W. G.) — A Short Grammar of the Japanese Spoken Language. Fourth Edition. Crown 8vo. Cloth. pp. 212. (Published 12*s.*) Reduced-Price, 7*s.* 6*d*

Babylonian and Oriental Record. (The) — A Monthly Magazine of the Antiquities of the East. Edited by Prof. TERRIEN DE LACOUPERIE. Vol. I—VI. (Vol. VII in progress). Published monthly. Single Numbers, 1*s.* 6*d.* each.

Babylonian Magic and Sorcery. See: King.

Bāna's Kadambari. Translated, with Occasional Omissions, with a full Abstract of the Continuation of the Romance by the Author's Son Bhushanabhatta, by C. M. RIDDING. 8vo. Cloth. pp. XXIV, 232. 10*s.*

Bāna's Harsa Carita. An Historical Work, translated from the Sanskrit, by E. B. Cowell and F. W. Thomas. 8vo. Cloth. pp. XIV, 284. 10*s.*

Bezold (Ch.) — **Oriental Diplomacy**: being the transliterated Text of the Cuneiform Despatches between the King of Egypt and Western Asia in the XVth. century before Christ, discovered at Tell el Amarna, and now preserved in the British Museum. With full Vocabulary, grammatical Notes, &c., by CHARLES BEZOLD. Post 8vo. Cloth. pp. XLIV, 124. 18s. net.

"For the Assyriologist the book is a servicable and handy supplement to the British Museum volume on the Tell El-Amarna tablets. The author is specially skilled in the art of cataloguing and dictionary making and it is needless to say that he has done his work well". — *The Academy.*

"Die in dem Hauptwerke (The Tell el Amarna Tablets in the British Museum with autotype Facsimiles, etc.) vermisstte Transcription des Keilschrifttextes der Tafeln, sowie ein sehr ausführliches, mituntur die Vollständigkeit einer Concordanz erreichendes Vocabulary bietet die Oriental Diplomacy von C. Bezold, das eben deshalb gewissermassen als Schlüssel zu dem Publicationswerke betrachtet werden kann." —
Liter. Centralblatt.

„Wichtig und sehr nützlich vor allem wegen der Einleitung und des Wörterverzeichnisses... Transkription und kurze Inhaltsangabe der Briefe sehr zweckmässig.... eine anerkennenswerthe Leistung."
Deutsche Litteraturzeitung.

Biblia. — **A Monthly Magazine**, devoted to Biblical Archaeology and Oriental Research. Vol. I—X. (Vol. XI in progress). Published monthly. Annual Subscription, 5s.

Biblical World (The) — Continuing the Old and New Testament Student. Edited by WILLIAM R. HARPER. New Series. Vol. I—X. (Vol. XI and XII in progress). Published monthly. Annual Subscription, 10s. 6d.

"The Biblical World makes a faithful record and helpful critic of present Biblical Work, as well as an efficient practical and positive independent force in stimulating and instructing the student, preacher and teacher"

Bibliographical List of Books on Africa and the East. Published in England. 2 Vols. Vol. I. Containing the Books published between the Meetings of the Eighth Oriental Congress at Stockholm, in 1889, and the Ninth Congress in London in 1892. Vol. II. Containing the Books published between the Meetings of the Ninth Oriental Congress in London, in 1892, and the Tenth Oriental Congress at Geneva, in 1894. Systematically arranged, with Preface and Author's Index, by C. G. Luzac. 12mo. each Vol. 1s.

Bibliotheca Indica. — Messrs Luzac & Co. are agents for the sale of this important series and keep most of the numbers in stock.

Blackden (M. W.) and G. W. Frazer. — Collection of Hieratic Graffiti, from the Alabaster Quarry of Hat-Nub, situated near Tell El Amarna. Found December 28th. 1891, copied September, 1892. Obl. pp. 10. 10s.

Buddhaghosuppatti; or, Historical Romance of the Rise and Career of Buddaghosa. Edited and translated by JAMES GRAY, Professor of Pali. Rangoon College. Two Parts in one. Demy 8vo. Cloth. pp. VIII, 75 and 36. 6s.

Budge (E. A. Wallis) — The Laughable Stories collected by Bar-Hebraeus. The Syriac Text with an English Translation, by E. A. WALLIS BUDGE, Litt. D., F. S. A., Keeper of the Department of Egyptian and Assyrian Antiquities, British Museum. 8vo. Cloth. 21s. net. [Luzac's Semitic Texts and Translation Series, Vol. I].

"Dr. BUDGE's book will be welcome as a handy reading book for advanced students of Syriac, but in the mean time the stories will be an addition to the literature of gnomes and proverbs, of which so many are found in India, and in Persian, Hebrew and Arabic, although not yet published. We are happy to say that Dr. BUDGE's new book is well edited and translated as far as we can judge". — *Athenæum.*

"The worthy Syrian Bishops idea of humour may excite admiration when we hear that he collected his quips in the grey dawn of the middle ages". — *Pall Mall Gazette.*

"Man sieht, das Buch ist in mehr als einer Hinsicht interessant, und wir sind Budge für die Herausgabe aufrichtig dankbar. — *Lit. Centralb.*

"Sous le titre de *Récits amusants*, le célèbre polygraphe syrien Barhébraeus a réuni une collection de sept cent vingt-sept contes, divisés en vingt chapitres et renfermant des aphorismes, des anecdotes et des fables d'animaux ayant un caractère soit moral, soit simplement récréatif. Le livre nous était connu par quelques spécimens publiés précé-

dement. M. BUDGE, qui a déja rendu tant de services aux lettres syriaques, vient d'éditer l'ouvrage entier avec une traduction anglaise.....
En tous cas, M. B. a eu raison de ne pas faire un choix et de donner l'ouvrage en son entier.... Les aphorismes, écrits dans un style concis et avec, une pointe dont la finesse n'est pas toujours sensible, présentent des difficultés de traduction dont M. B. a généralement triomphé." —
Revue Critique.

"È questo un libro singolare, appartemente ad un genere assai scarso nella letteratura siriaca, quantunque così ricca, cioè a quello dell'amena letteratura. Bar Ebreo scrisse questo libro nella vecchiaia, o forse allora mise insieme e ordinò estr atti che avea prese nelle lunghe letture da lui fatte, di tanto opere e cosi svariate.... I cultori degli studi siriaci saranno assai grati al Dr. Budge per questo suo novello contributo; l'edizione per carte e per tipi è veramente bellissima." — *La Cultura*.

Budge, see Luzac's Semitic Text and Translation Series. Vols. I, III, V and VII.

Cappeller (Carl) — A Sanskrit-English Dictionary. Based upon the St. Petersburg Lexicons. Royal 8vo. Cloth. pp. VIII, 672 [Published £ 1. 1s]. Reduced to 10s. 6d.

"Linguistic and other students should hail with satisfaction the publication of a cheap and handy Sanskrit-English Dictionary, such as is now to be found in the new English edition of Prof. CAPPELLER's Sanskrit-German 'Wörterbuch,' recently published by Messrs. Luzac. The book is well adapted to the use of beginners, as it specially deals with the text usually read in commencing Sanskrit; but it will be of use also to philological students — or such as have mastered the Nāgari character — as it includes most Vedic words, a great desideratum in many earlier dictionaries, especially such as were founded on native sources. The basis of the present work is, on the contrary, the great lexicon of Boethlingk and Roth with the addition of compound forms likely to be of service to beginners." — *Athenæum.*

"The English edition of Prof. CAPPELLER's Sanskrit Dictionary is something more than a mere translation of the German edition. It includes the vocabulary of several additional texts; many compounds have been inserted which are not given in the Petersburg lexicons; and some improvements have been made in the arrangement. The errors enumerated by the reviewer of the *Academy* have for the most part been corrected, though a few still remain..... The book is certainly the cheapest, and, for a beginner, in some respects the best, of existing Sanskrit-English dictionaries." — *Academy.*

"Professor CAPPELLER furnishes the Student of Sanskrit, if not with a complete Lexicon, — for that he tells us, was not his object, — still with a handy and yet very full vocabulary of all the words occurring in the texts which are generally studied in that language. His plan is to avoid all unnecessary complications, to give each word in such a manner as to show its formation, if it is not itself a stem. It is not merely an English version of the author's Sanskrit-German Dictionary, nor merely an enlarged edition of the same; it is a new work, with a distinct plan and object of its own. We can recommend it to the Sanskrit student as a sufficient dictionary for all practical purposes, which will enable him to dispense with larger and more costly and complicated Lexicons till he has acquired a considerable proficiency in this difficult and scientific language." — *Asiatic Quarterly Review.*

Ceylon. A Tale of Old..... See: Sinnatamby.

Chakrabarti (J. Ch.) — The Native States of India. 8vo. Cloth. pp. XIV, 274. With Map. 5s. net.

Cool (W.) — With the Dutch in the East. An Outline of the Military Operations in Lombock, 1894, Giving also a Popular Account of the Native Characteristics, Architecture, Methods of Irrigations, Agricultural Pursuits, Folklore, Religious Customs and a History of the Introduction of Islamism and Hinduism into the Island. By Capt. W. COOL (Dutch Engineer), Knight of the Order of Orange Nassau; decorated for important War Services in the Dutch Indies; Professor at the High School of War, the Hague. Translated from the Dutch by E. J. Taylor. Illustrated by G. B. HOOYER. Late Lieut. Col. of the Dutch Indian Army; Knight of the Military Order of William; decorated for important War Services in the Dutch Indies. Roy. 8vo. Cloth. 21s.

"There are, it is to be feared, but few books published in this country from which English readers can obtain information as to the doings of the Dutch in their Eastern colonies. — For this reason we are glad that Capt. Cool's account of the Lombock expedition has been translated." — *Athenæum.*

"The book contains an interesting account of the Balinese and Sassak customs, and throws some light on the introduction of the Mahomedan and Hindu religions into Lombock... The translation by Miss E. J. Taylor is satisfactory, and some of the illustrations are excellent." — *The Times.*

"Lombock forms a small link in the long chain of volcanic lands... To folklorists and students of primitive religions it has always presented many attractive features... They will be much interested in the local traditions recorded in the volume before us. Miss Taylor's version deserves a word of recognition, and the general equipment of the book is creditable to the Amsterdam press. There is a good index." — *Academy.*

"The author not only describes the military operations, but gives a full history of Lombock and its people. Much curious information as to a land very much out of the way and little known to English readers is given. In addition the account of the actual warfare is full of incident. The book is freely illustrated." — *Yorkshire Daily Post.*

"This is a work which will no doubt attract considerable attention, both in the West and throughout the East. Miss Taylor has acquitted herself as a translator with rare ability and taste, and the comprehensive and excellent way in which the work is illustrated adds an additional charm to what is at once the most entertaining and most attractive chapter of Netherlands Indian history." — *European Mail.*

"Besides containing a great deal of information concerning this hitherto very slightly known island and its inhabitants, Captain Cool's volume is profusely and excellently illustrated... Miss Taylor's translation of it is fluent and thoroughly readable." — *Glasgow Herald.*

Cowell, E. B., See: Bāna's Harsa Carita.

Cowper (B. H.) Principles of Syriac Grammar. Translated and abridged from the work of Dr. HOFFMANN. 8vo. Cloth. pp. 184. 7s. 6d.

Cust (R. N.) — The Gospel Message or Essays, Addresses, Suggestions and Warnings of the different aspects of Christian Missions to Non Christian Races and peoples. 8vo. pp. 494. Paper 6s. 6d. Cloth. 7s. 6d.

".... There are few objects of controversy in missionary matters which are not very fully discussed by Dr. CUST, and if we not infrequently differ from him we gladly thank him for copious information and the benefits of his long experience". — *Guardian.*

"It is a big book. it ranges over a very wide field, and it is never dull or dry". — *Expository Times.*

"The scheme is so comprehensive as to include almost every detail of the missionary enterprise. Every essay is stamped, of course with the personality of its author, whose views are expressed with characteristic force and clearness". — *The Record.*

Cust (R. N.) — Essay on the Common Features which appear in all Forms of Religious belief. Post 8vo. Cloth. pp. XXIV, 194. 5s.

"Dr. CUST has put his very considerable knowledge to excellent purposes in this modest little publication. He seems most at home with the faiths of the East, but even the most elementary of savage creeds have not escaped him". — *Pall Mall Gazette.*

Cust (R. N.) — Essay on Religious Conceptions. Post 8vo. Cloth. pp. V, 148. 5s.

Cust (R. N.) — Linguistic and Oriental Essays.
Fourth Series. From 1861 to 1895. 8vo. pp. XXV, 634. Paper Covers. 16s., Cloth. 17s. 6d.

Dawlatshah's Lives of the Persian Poets. Edited by EDWARD G. BROWNE, Lecturer in Persian in the University of Cambridge. Vol. 1. Tadhkirátu'sh Sh'ará. 8vo. Cloth. 18s. net.

Edkins (Joseph) — China's Place in Philology. An Attempt to show that the Languages of Europe and Asia have a common Origin. Demy 8vo. Cloth. pp. XXIII, 403. (Published 10s. 6d.) 7s. 6d.

Edkins (Joseph) — Introduction to the Study of the Chinese Characters. Royal 8vo. Boards. pp. XIX, 211, 101. (Published 18s.) 12s. 6d.

Edkins (Joseph) — Nirvana of the Northern Buddhists. 8vo. pp. 21. Reprint. 6d.

Edkins (Joseph) — Chinese Architecture. Contents. — 1. Classical Style. — 2. Post-Confucian Style. — 3. Buddhist Style. — 4. Modern Style. 8vo. pp. 36. 1s.

Edkins (Joseph) — Chinese Currency. Roy. 8vo. pp. 29. 1s.

Edkins (Joseph) — Ancient Symbolism among the Chinese. Cr. 8vo. pp. 26. 6d.

Efes Damîm. — A Series of Conversations at Jerusalem between a Patriarch of the Greek Church and a Chief Rabbi of the Jews, concerning the Malicious Charge against the Jews of using Christian Blood. By J. B. LEVINSOHN. Translated from the Hebrew by Dr. L. LOEWE. Roy. 8vo. Cloth. pp. XVI, 208. (Published 8s.) Reduced Price 2s. 6d.

Eitel (E. J.) — Europe in China. The History of Hongkong. From the Beginning to the year 1882. 8vo. Cloth. pp. VII, 575. With Index. 15s. net.

"His work rises considerably above the level commonly attained by colonial histories written from a colonial point of view". — *Times.*

"His painstaking volume is really a detailed history of the colony and of the adminstration of successive governors from 1841 down to the present day". — *Daily Telegraph.*

"This is an interesting book. The subject is full of matter, and Dr. EITEL has, as a rule, treated it successfully. — *Athenæum.*

".... The student will find Dr. EITEL's book a very storehouse of information.... has told it with a mastery of fact that vouches for his industry and perseverance". — *Saturday Review.*

Gladstone (Right Hon. W. E.) — Archaic Greece and the East. 8vo. pp. 32. 1s.

Gribble (J. D. B.) — A History of the Deccan.
With numerous Illustrations, Plates, Portraits, Maps and Plans. Vol. I. Roy. 8vo. Cloth. 21s.

„In a style easy and pleasant the author tells the story of the Mohammedan occupation of the Deccan .... the general style of the book and the admirable photographs and drawings with which it is enriched leave nothing to be desired". — *Athenæum.*

"Mr. J. D. B. GRIBBLE has accomplished a difficult task. He has constructed from original materials a continuous narrative of one of the most confused periods of Indian history. He has also presented it with a lucidity of style which will go far to render it acceptable to the reading public.... The book is illustrated by a number of interesting reproductions of scenery and architecture in Southern India. These and the maps, plans, and clear genealogical tables reflect credit both upon the author and the publisher". — *Times.*

"Mr. GRIBBLE has brought great industry and knowledge of the country to this compilation .... The work is of some historical importance". — *Saturday Review.*

Gray (James). See Buddhaghosuppatti.

Gray (James). See Jinalankara.

Guide to the Dutch East Indies. By Dr. J. F. van BEMMELEN and G. B. HOOYER. Trans. from the Dutch by the Rev. B. J. BERRINGTON B.A., with 16 Plates, 13 Maps and Plans, and a copious index. Sm. 8vo. pp. 202. 1s. 6d.

"For any one going in that direction this remarkably complete little work is indispensable". — *Pall Mall Gazette.*

"The guide book omits nothing needed by the traveller. It describes the necessary outfit, customs afloat and ashore, mode of living, how to dress, how often to bathe, who to tip, and how much". — *The Shipping World.*

Guirandon (F. G. de) — Manuel de la langue foule, parlée dans la Sénégambie et le Soudan. Grammaire textes, vocabulaire. 8vo. Cloth. pp. 144. 6s.

Halcombe (Charles J. H.) — **The Mystic Flowery Land.** A Personal Narrative. By CHARLES J. H. HALCOMBE. Late of Imperial Customs. China, 8vo. Cloth. gilt. pp. 226. 16s.

"This valuable and handsome volume contains thirty long chapters, a frontispiece of the Author and his wife — the latter in her Oriental costume — numerous fine reproductions from photographs, and several beautiful coloured pictures representing many scenes and phases of Chinese life, etchings and comprehensive notes by the Author.

"His pages are full of incident and his narrative often vivid and vigorous". — *Times.*

"The illustrations are good and numerous. Many are facsimiles of coloured Chinese drawings showing various industrial occupations: others are photogravures representing buildings and scenery". — *Morning Post.*

"Handsomely attired in red, yellow and gold, with Chinese characters to give further appropriateness to the outer garb, is this volume of freely illustrated personal experience in China.... Mr. HALCOMBE gives a graphic description of places and peoples, with their manners and customs". — *Liverpool Courier.*

"The illustrations are all good, and the Chinese pictures reproduced in colours interesting. We have not seen any of them before". — *Westminster Review.*

Hansei Zasshi. Monthly. Vol. I—XII. (Vol. XIII in progress). Annual subscription. 6s.

Hardy (R. Spence) — **The Legends and theories of the Buddhists.** Compared with History and Science. 8vo. Cloth. pp. 244. 7s. 6d.

Harîri. — The Assemblies of al Harîri. Translated from the Arabic with an Introduction and notes, Historical and Grammatical, by TH. CHENERY and F. STEINGASS. With Preface and Index, by F. F. ARBUTHNOT, 2 Vols. 8vo. Cloth. pp. X, 540 and XI, 395. £1.10s.

Harper (Robert Francis) — **Assyrian and Babylonian Letters,** belonging to the K. Collection of the British Museum. By ROBERT FRANCIS HARPER, of the University of Chicago. Vols. I to IV. Post 8vo. Cloth. Price of each Vol. £1. 5s. net.

"The Assyriologist, will welcome them with gratitude, for they offer him a mass of new material which has been carefully copied and well printed, and which cannot fail to yield important results." — *Athenæum*.

"The book is well printed, and it is a pleasure to read the texts given in it, with their large type and ample margin." — *Academy*.

Hebraica. — A Quarterly Journal in the Interests of Semitic Study. Edited by WILLIAM R. HARPER and the Staff of the Semitic Department of the University of Chicago. Vol. I—XI. Published quarterly. Annual Subscription. 14s.

See American Journal of Semitic Languages, etc.

India. (The Native States of). See: Chakrabarti.

India. (The Armenians in). See: Seth.

Indian Antiquary (The) — A Journal of Oriental Research in Archaeology, Epigraphy, etc. etc. Edited by R. C. TEMPLE. Vol. I—XXVI. (Vol. XXVII in progress). Annual Subscription, £1. 16s.

Indian Terms. (A Glossary of). See: Temple.

Indian Wisdom. See: Monier-Williams.

Jastrow's Dictionary of the Targumim, the Talmud Babli and Yerushalmi, and the Midrashic Literature. Compiled by M. JASTROW, Ph. D. Parts I to IX. 4to. pp. 480. 5s. each Part.

"This is the only Talmudic dictionary in English, and all students should subscribe to it. The merits of this work are now too well known to need repetition." — *Jewish Chronicle*.

Jinalankara or **"Embellishments of Buddha"**, by Buddharakkhita. Edited with Introduction, Notes and Translation, by JAMES GRAY. Two Parts in one. Demy 8vo. Cloth. 6s.

"The commendable care with which the volume has been prepared for the use of students is evident throughout its pages. — *Athenæum*.

Johnson (Capt. F. N). — The Seven Poems etc. See: Muallakat.

Johnston (C.) Useful Sanskrit Nouns and Verbs. In English Letters. Compiled by CHARLES JOHNSTON,

Bengal Civil Service, Dublin University Sanskrit Prizeman, India Civil Service Sanskrit Prizeman. Small 4to. Boards. pp. 30. 2s. 6d.

Johnston (C.) — **The Awakening to the Self.** Translated from the Sanskrit of Shankara the Master. Oblong 8vo. Paper covers. 2s.

Journal of the Buddhist Text Society of India. Edited by Sarat Candra Das, C. J. E. Vols. I to IV. 8vo. Calcutta, 1893—1897. £1. 10s.

Messrs. Luzac & Co. are the English agents for the above and can supply the Continuation. Subscription. 10s. each Vol.

Judson (A.) — **English-Burmese Dictionary.** Fourth Edition. Royal 8vo. Half bound. pp. 1752. £1. 12s.

Judson (A.) — **Burmese-English Dictionary.** Revised and enlarged by ROBERT C. STEVENSON. Royal 8vo. Paper covers. pp. 1192.

Kathákoça. See Tawney.

King (Leonard W.) — **Babylonian Magic and Sorcery.** Being "The Prayers of the Lifting of the Hand". The Cuneiform Texts of a Group of Babylonian and Assyrian Incantations and magical Formulae, edited with Transliterations, Translations, and full Vocabulary from Tablets of the Kuyunjik Collection preserved in the British Museum. By LEONARD W. KING, M. A., Assistant in the Department of Egyptian and Assyrian Antiquities, British Museum. Roy. 8vo. Cloth. 18s. net.

"We cannot pretend to form an adequate judgment of the merits of Mr. KING's work, but it is manifestly conceived and executed in a very scholarly spirit." — *Times.*

"Mr. KING's book, will, we believe be of great use to all students of Mesopotamian religions, and it marks an era in Assyriological studies in England.... A word of special praise is due to Mr. KING for the excellence of his autograph plates of text." — *Athenæum.*

"The work will be found a valuable addition to our knowledge of Babylonian history, and to the study of comparative philology."
Morning Post.

King, L. W. See: Luzac's Semitic Text and Translation Series, Vols. II, IV and VI.

Kittel (Rev. F.) — **A Kannada-English Dictionary.** By Rev. F. KITTEL, B. G. E. M. Royal 8vo. Half-Bound. pp. L. 1725. £1. 12s.

Korean Repository. Vols. I to III. Annual Subscription 15s. Post free.

Land (J. P. N.) — **The Principles of Hebrew Grammar.** By J. P. N. LAND, Professor of Logic and Metaphysics in the University of Leyden. Translated from the Dutch by REGINALD LANE POOLE, Balliol College, Oxford. Demy 8vo. Cloth. pp. XX, 219 (Published 7s. 6d.) Reduced price 5s.

Lives of the Persian Poets Series. See Dawlatshah.

Loewe (L.) — **A Dictionary of the Circassian Language.** In two Parts. English—Circassian—Turkish, and Circassian—English—Turkish. 8vo. Cloth. (Published 21s.) Reduced price 6s.

Loewe (L.) Efes Damim. See: Efes.

Luzac's Oriental List. — Containing Notes and News on, and a Bibliographical List of all new Publications on Africa and the East. Published Monthly. Annual Subscription, 3s. Vols. I to VIII (1890—1897) are still to be had (with Index, half-bound), at £2. 15s.

Vols. I to IV are nearly out of print and can only be sold in the set. Vols V to VIII are still to be had at 5s. each vol.

"It deserves the support of Oriental students. Besides the catalogue of new books published in England, on the Continent, in the East, and in America, it gives, under the heading of "Notes and News" details about important Oriental works, which are both more full and more careful than anything of the sort to be found elsewhere." — *Academy*.

"A bibliographical monthly publication which should be better known."
The Record.

Luzac's Semitic Text and Translation Series.
Vol. I: See: Budge.

Vol. II. The Letters and Despatches of Hammurabi king of Babylon about B. C. 2250, to Sin-idinnam, King of Larsa, together with other royal and official correspondence of the same period: the Cuneiform texts edited with an Introduction and short descriptions by L. W. King, M. A.

This volume will contain about 100 letters relating to a variety of official subjects, and their contents are of great importance for the study of the history of Babylonia, Elam and the neighbouring districts about the time of the patriarch Abraham. These letters reveal the system by which Hammurabi maintained his rule in the remote provinces of his newly acquired empire, and contain some of the orders and directions, which he issued for the movements of troops, for the building of canals and waterways, for the food-supply of his capital, and for the regulation of legal tribunals. The letters of Hammurabi are the oldest Babylonian despatches extant. — *Ready in June.*

Vol. III. The History of the Blessed Lady Mary the Virgin, and the History of the Image of Christ, which the men of Tiberias made to mock at; the Syriac text edited, with an English translation, by E. A. WALLIS BUDGE, Litt. D., D. Lit., etc. — *Ready in October.*

This Life of the Virgin is the fullest known to exist in Syriac, and varies in many important particulars from the versions of which fragments have already been published. The Life has been copied from an ancient Nestorian MS., to the text of which have been added all the variants found in the XVIth century MS. in the possession of the Royal Asiatic Society of Great Britain.

Vol. IV. The Letters and Despatches of Hammurabi together with other official and private correspondence of the same period, by L. W. KING, M. A.

This volume will contain a number of transliterations and translations of the texts of the 100 letters and despatches which are printed in volume 2; to these will be added indexes of proper names etc. and a List of Characters. An attempt will be made to give a description of the circumstances under which these letters were written, and short notes on points of grammar, history, etc. will be added. — *In the Press.*

Vol. V. The History of Rabban Hormizd by Mâr Simon, the disciple of Mâr Yôzâdhâk; the Syriac text edited, with an English translation by E. A. WALLIS BUDGE, Litt. D., D. Lit., etc.

The text describes the life of this famous Nestorian anchorite, the building of his monastery, and the struggle which went on in the VIIth century between the rival sects of Jacobites and Nestorians in Mesopotamia. This prose version of the life of Rabban Hormizd is, probably, the source from which the metrical versions were drawn; and it is of great importance for the study of the second great development of monasticism in Mesopotamia. — *In the Press.*

Vol. VI. Babylonian Private Letters written during the period of the First Dynasty of Babylon; the Cuneiform texts edited with Introduction and short descriptions by L. W. KING, M. A.

This volume will contain about 200 letters of a private nature which reveal the social condition of the country and incidentally throw much light upon the civilization of the period. From grammatical and lexicographical points of view these texts are of considerable importance, for they afford numerous examples of unusual words and forms of expression. — *In the Press.*

Vol. VII. The Life of Rabban Bar-Idtâ by John his disciple; The Syrac text edited, with an English translation, by E. A. WALLIS BUDGE, Litt. D., D. Lit., etc.

Bar-Idtâ was the founder of a famous rule and monastery in Mesopotamia in the VIIth century, and the author of a very valuable work on monastic history which is quoted with respect by Thomas, Bishop of Margâ. He was a contemporary of Babhai of Mount Izlâ, and of Jacob of Bêth Abbê.

Volumes 5, 6, and 7 will, it is hoped be ready early next year.

Macnaghten (Sir W. Hay) — Principle of Hindu and Mohammedan Law.
Republished from the Principles and Precedences of the same. Edited by the late H. H. WILSON. 8vo. Cloth. pp. 240. 6s.

Margoliouth (D. S.) — Arabic Papyri of the Bodleian Library
reproduced by the Collotype Process. With Transcription and Translation. Text in 4to. pp. 7 and 2 Facsimiles in large folio. 5s.

Margoliouth (D. S.) — Chrestomathia Baidawiana.
The Commentary of El-Baidâwi on Sura III. Translated and explained for the Use of Students of Arabic. By D. S. MARGOLIOUTH, M. A., Laudian Professor of Arabic in the University of Oxford, etc. etc. Post 8vo. Cloth. 12s.

"The book is as scholarly as it is useful. Of particular importance are the numerous grammatical annotations which give the beginner an insight into the method of the Arabic national grammarians, and which form an excellent preparatory study for the perusal of these works in the original..... The introduction and the remarks in particular show how well Mr. MARGOLIOUTH has mastered the immense literatures of Moslim Tradition, Grammar and Kalaïm.... The perusal of the book affords pleasure from beginning to end." — *Journal Royal Asiatic Society*.

Mirkhond. — The Rauzat-us-Safa; or, Garden of Purity.
Translated from the Original Persian by E. REHATSEK; edited by F. F. ARBUTHNOT. Vols. I to V. 10s. each Vol.

Vols. 1 and 2 contain: The Histories of Prophets, Kings and Khalifs.
Vols. 3 and 4 contain: The life of Muhammad the Apostle of Allah.
Vol. 5 contains: The Lives of Abú Bakr, O'mar, O'thmàn, and Ali'; the four immediate successors of Muhammad the Apostle.

Monier-Williams (Sir Monier) — Indian Wisdom; or Examples of the religious, philosophical, and ethical Doctrines of the Hindus, with a brief History of the chief Departments of Sanskrit Literature, and some account of the past and present Condition of India, moral and intellectual. By Sir MONIER MONIER-WILLIAMS, K. C. I. E., M. A., Hon. D. C. L., Oxford. Fourth Edition, enlarged and improved. Post 8vo. Cloth. pp. 575. £1. 1s.

"His book.... still remains indispensable for the growing public, which seeks to learn the outline of Indian literature and thought in a simple and readable form. We are glad to welcome the fourth edition of this eminently readable book." — *Daily Chronicle.*

"The learned professor's thorough mastery of his subject enables him to deal effectively with his difficult task..... He omits nothing that enters the scope of his work : he is choice in his selections and accurate in his comments, and the result is a work as instructive and sound as it is pleasant to read." — *Asiatic Quarterly Review.*

"For all students of the philosophy of religion, as well as for all especially interested in Indian literature and thought, the work is one of very great value." — *Glasgow Herald.*

"It is a fine volume and contains valuable additions by the author.... this edition will be more than ever prized by students of Indian lore."
Scotsman.

Muallakat. — **The Seven Poems suspended in the Temple at Mecca.** Translated from the Arabic. By Capt. F. E. JOHNSON. With an Introduction by Shaikh Taizullabhai. 8vo. pp. XXIV, 238. 7s. 6d.

"This handy volume decidedly supplies a great want for those who make a serious study of Arabic.... The grammatical, historical, geographical and other notes comments and explanations are ample and thorough". — *Imperial and Asiatic Quarterly Review.*

Müller (F. Max) — **Address** delivered at the Opening of the Ninth International Congress of Orientalists, held in London, Sept. 5, 1892, 8vo. pp. 66. 1s. 6d.

Mystic Flowery Land. See: Halcombe.

Oriental Translation Fund (New), See: Mirkhond, Tawney, Bana, and Harîri.

Oudemans Jzn. (A. C.) — **The Great Sea-Serpent.** An historical and critical Treatise. With the Reports of 187 Appearances (including those of the Appendix), the Suppositions and Suggestions of scientific and non-scientific Persons, and the Author's Conclusions. With 82 Illustrations. Royal 8vo. Cloth. pp. XV, 592. £1. 5s. net.

"The volume is extremely interesting". *Athenaeum.*

Reis Sidi Ali. The Travels and Adventures of the Turkish Admiral. In India, Afghanistan, Central Asia and Persia 1553—1556. Translated from the Turkish into English with notes. By H. VAMBERY. — *In the Press.*

Ridding (C. M.) — See: Bana's Kadambari.

Rosen (F.) — **A Modern Persian Colloquial Grammar,** containing a short Grammar, Dialogues and Extracts from Nasir Eddin Shah's Diaries, Tales, etc. and a Vocabulary. Cr. 8vo. Cloth. pp. XIV, 400. 10s. 6d,

"Dr. ROSEN's learned work will be useful to all who have occasion to go to Persia, Baluchistan, and Afghanistan. The Vocabulary will be a boon to students, especially as it is in the same volume with the grammar and the dialogues." — *Publ. Circular.*

"Very useful to students." — *Westminster Review.*
"Excellent Guide to the acquisition of Persian." — *Asiatic Quarterly Review.*

Rosthorn (A. de) — **On the Tea Cultivation in Western Ssüch'uan and the Tea Trade with Tibet via Tachienlu.** 8vo. pp. 40. With Sketch Map. 2s. net.

Ruben (Paul) — **Critical Remarks upon some Passages of the Old Testament,** by PAUL RUBEN, Ph. D. 4to. Cloth. pp. II. 24, 14. 3s. 6d.

"It may suffice to congratulate ourselves that a scholar of vigorous mind and accurate philological training is devoting his leisure to a subject worthy of attention.... Very many of the notes are in a high degree stimulating and suggestive. The get up of the book is excellent".
Academy.

"Dr. RUBEN shows much originality, a wide knowledge of authorities, and a true grasp of critical principles". — *Jewish Chronicle.*

Sacred Books of the Old Testament. — A critical Edition of the Hebrew Text, Printed in Colours, with Notes. Prepared by eminent Biblical Scholars of Europe and America. Under the editorial direction of PAUL HAUPT, Professor in the John Hopkins Univ. Baltimore. **Edition de Luxe,** in 120 numbered Copies only. 4to. Subscription price for the complete Work (20 Parts), £ 20.

> Prospectuses sent on application. The following Parts have already been issued:
> Part   1: **Book of Genesis,** by C. J. Ball. pp. 120. London. 1896. £ 2.
> Part   3: **Leviticus,** by Prof. S. R. Driver. pp. 32. 1894. 16s.
> Part   6: **Joshua,** by Prof. W. H. Bennet. pp. 32. 1895. £ 1.
> Part   8: **Samuel,** by Prof. K. Budde. pp. 100. 1894. £ 1. 10s.
> Part 11: **Jeremiah,** by Prof. C. H. Cornill. pp. 80. 1895. £ 1.
> Part 14: **Psalms,** by J. Wellhausen, pp. 96. 1895. £ 1. 10s.
> Part 18: **Book of Daniel,** by A. Kamphausen, 4to. pp. 44. 1896. £ 1.
> Part 20: **Chronicles,** by R. Kittel. pp. 82. 1895. £ 1. 10s.

A valuable "Edition de Luxe" in 120 numbered copies only, and which may be described as the most splendidly got up Hebrew work in existence.

Each single part is numbered and signed by the editor with his own hand. The single parts will be issued in highly elegant covers. After the conclusion of the work a handsome binding cover will be supplied.

Sankaranarayana (P.) — English-Telugu Dictionary, by P. SANKARANARAYNA M. A., M. R. A. S., Tutor to their Highnesses the Princes of Cochin. 8vo. Cloth. pp. 61, 756, 10s. 6d.

Sanskrit Phonetics. A Manual of. See: Uhlenbeck.

Sanskrit Nouns and Verbs. See: Johnston.

Sayce (A. H.) — Address to the Assyrian Section of the Ninth International Congress of Orientalists. 8vo. pp. 32. 1s.

Sauerwein (G.) — A Pocket Dictionary of the English and Turkish Languages. Small 8vo. Cloth. limp. pp. 298. 3s. 6d.

Scholia on passages of the Old Testament. By MAX JACOB Bishop of Edessa. Now first edited in the original Syriac with an English translation and notes by G. PHILLIP. DD. 8vo. Paper Covers. 5s.

Seth (Mesrovb J.) — History of the Armenians in India. From the earliest Times to the present Day. 8vo. Cloth. pp. XXIV, 199. 7s. 6d. net.

"The subject is invested with peculiar interest at the present time by recent events in Asia Minor.... his unpretending little work is a valuable reportory of original information never before accessible in print and scarcely even known to exist." — *Times*.

"The book is happily distinguished among the number of books recently issued concerning Armenia in that it deals strictly with fact..... The volume deserves the attention of every one interested in the history of India and of the hardly treated race which seems to flourish better there than in its own country." — *Scotsman*.

"Sinnatamby". Letchimey. A Tale of Old Ceylon. 8vo. pp. III, 54. With Photogr. Plates and Illustrations. *In the Press*.

Stein (M. A.) — Catalogue of the Sanskrit MSS. in the Raghunata Temple Library of His Highness the Maharaja of Jammu and Kashmir. 4to. Cloth. pp. 423. 12s.

Steele's (R.) The Discovery of Secrets, attributed to Geber from the MS Arabic text. 8vo. 1s.

Stoffel (C.) Studies in English, Written and Spoken. For the Use of continental Students. With Index. First Series. Roy. 8vo. Cloth. pp. XII, 332. 7s. 6d.

Suhrillekha (The); or "Friendly Letter;" written by Lung Shu (Nàgàrjuna), and addressed to King Sadvaha. Translated from the Chinese Edition of I-Tsing, by the late Rev. SAMUEL BEAL, with the Chinese Text. 8vo. pp. XIII, 51. 5s.

Swami Vivekananda's Addresses. See: Vivekananda.

Tawney (C. H.) — The Kathákoça; or Treasury of Stories. Translated from Sanskrit Manuscripts. With Appendix, containing Notes, by Prof. ERNST LEUMANN. 8vo. Cloth. pp. XXIII, 260. 10s.

Temple (G.) — A Glossary of Indian Terms relating to Religion, Customs, Government, Land, and other Terms and Words in Common Use. To which is added a Glossary of Terms used in District Work in the N. W. Provinces and Oudh., and also of those applied to Labourers. With an Appendix giving Computation of Time and Money, and Weights and Measures, in British India, and Forms of Address. Roy. 8vo. Cloth. pp. IV, 332. 7s. 6d.

"The book is moderate in price and clear in print." — *Athenæum.*

"The book is handy, well printed and well got up and no student of Indian subjects should be without it." — *Asiatic Quarterly Review.*

"Students of Oriental travel may find something serviceable in its pages; and those who are engaged in trade in the East Indies might occasionally turn to the volume, with profit, if it were on the office shelf." — *The Nation.*

Temple (Major R. C.) — **Notes on Antiquities in Ramannadesa.** (The Talaing Country of Burma.) 4to. pp. 40. With 24 Plates and a Map. 18s.

Thomas, F. W., See: Bāna, Harsa Carita.

Tiele (C. P.) — **Western Asia,** according to the Most Recent Discoveries. Rectorial Address on the Occasion of the 318th Anniversary of the Leyden University, 8th February, 1893. Translated by ELIZABETH J. TAYLOR. Small 8vo. Bound. pp. 36. 2s. 6d.

"An authoritative summary of the results of recent Oriental research and discovery." — *The Times.*

"The address presents a graphic picture of the political situation in Western Asia in the fifteenth and fourteenth centuries B. C."
Morning Post.

"The professor's grasp of his subject is very evident, and his deductions from the materials commented on worthy of all attention."
Imperial and Asiatic Quarterly Review.

T'oung Pao. — **Archives pour servir à l'étude de l'histoire,** des langues, de la géographie et de l'ethnographie de l'Asie orientale. (Chine, Japon, Corée, Indo-Chine, Asie Centrale et Malaise.) Rédigées par MM. G. SCHLEGEL et H. CORDIER. Vol. I—VIII. Vol. IX in progress). Annual Subscription. £ 1.

Transactions of the Ninth International Congress of Orientalists. London, 5th to 12th September, 1892.) Edited by E. DELMAR MORGAN. 2 Vols. Roy. 8vo. Cloth. £1. 15s.

Vol. I. contains: Indian and Aryan Sections. £1. 1s.

Vol. II. contains: Semitic, Egypt and Africa, Geographical, Archaic Greece and the East, Persia and Turkey, China, Central Asia and the Far East, Australasia, Anthropology and Mythology Sections. £1. 1s.

Uhlenbeck. (C. C.). A Manual of Sanskrit Phonetics. In comparison with the Indogermanic mother-language, for students of Germanic and classical philology. 8vo. pp. 115. 6s.

Ummagga Yataka. See: Yatawara.

Usha. — The Dawn. A Vedic Periodical, edited by Pandit Satya Vrata Samasrami. 8vo. Published monthly. Annual subscription. £1. 1s.

Valmiki. — The Ramayan of Valmiki. Translated into English Verse, by R. T. H. GRIFFITH, M. A., C. I. E. Complete in one Volume. 8vo. Cloth. pp. IX, 576. 7s. 6d.

Vambery, see: Reis Sidi Ali.

Vivekânanda (Swami). — Lectures delivered in London. Nos. 1—12. 6d. each.

Vivekânanda (Swami). — Madras Lectures. 8vo. 1s. 6d.

Vizianagram Sanskrit Series. — Under the Superintendence of ARTHUR VENIS, M.A., Oxon, Principal, Sanskrit College, Benares. Different Prices.

West (Sir Raymond) — Higher Education in India: Its Position and Claims. 8vo. pp. 61. 1892. 1s.

Wildeboer (G.) — The Origin of the Canon of of the Old Testament. An historico-critical Enquiry. Translated by WISNER BAÇON. Edited with

Preface by Prof. GEORGE F. MOORE. Royal 8vo. Cloth. pp. XII, 182. 7s. 6d.

"We will only add that we cordially echo the professor's hope that his book may not only be read by professed students but that it may come also into the hands of such as have already left the University."
Guardian.

"The method adopted is that of historical investigation: the student is thus enabled to see how the results of critical inquiry have been obtained .... he accompanies a guide who is familiar with the way which leads to them." — *Academy.*

"The first thing to notice is the translation. This is how a book ought to be translated .... The book must be used, not read merely ... it is independent, painstaking, farseeing." — *Expository Times.*

Winckler (H.) — The Tell-El-Amarna Letters.
Transliteration, English Translation, Vocabulary, etc. Roy. 8vo. Cloth. pp. XLII, 416, and Registers 50 pages. £ 1. 1s. net.
The same. In Paper Covers. £ 1.

With the Dutch in the East. See: Cool.

Wright (W.) — The Book of Jonah in four Semitic versions. Chaldee, Syriac, Aethiopic and Arabic. With corresponding glossaries. 8vo. Cloth. pp. 148. 4s.

Wynkoop (J. D.) — Manual of Hebrew Syntax.
Translated from the Dutch by C. VAN DEN BIESEN. 8vo. Cloth. pp. XXII, 152 and Index. 2s. 6d. net.

"It is a book, which every Hebrew student should possess, ... we recommend it for general usefulness, and thank Dr. van den Biesen for giving it to the English reader." — *Jewish World.*

"It is one of those books which will become indispensable to the English student who will desire to become acquainted with the construction of Hebrew syntax .... this takes a high rank and will undoubtedly become a general text book on the subject in many colleges and universities."
American Hebrew News.

Wynkoop (J. D.) — Hebrew Grammar. Translated from the Dutch by C. VAN DEN BIESEN. 8vo. Cloth. 2s. 6d. net.

Yatawara (J. B.) — The Ummaga Yataka, translated into English. *In the Press.*

FOREIGN AND ORIENTAL BOOKS.

Messrs. LUZAC & Co. having Agents in all the principal Towns of the Continent, America and the East, are able to supply any Books not in stock at the shortest notice and at the most reasonable terms.

Subscriptions taken for all Foreign, American and Oriental Periodicals.

LIST OF
INDIAN GOVERNMENT PUBLICATIONS.

Messrs. LUZAC & Co. are Official Agents for the sale of the Indian Government Publications.

Acts of the several Governments in India. Different dates and prices.
Aden Gazetteer. By Captain F. M. Hunter. 1877. 5*s*.
Adi Granth. By E. Trumpp. 1877. £ 1.
Agriculture, Report on Indian. By J. A. Voelcker, Ph. D. 1893. 3*s*. 6*d*.
Annals of the Calcutta Botanic Gardens:
    I. Monograph on Ficus. Part 1. 1887. £ 1 5*s*.
        „   „   Part 2. 1888. £ 2.
        „   „   Appendix. 1889. 10*s*. 6*d*.
    II. Species of Artocarpus, &c. 1889. £ 1 12*s* 6*d*.
    III. Species of Pedicularis, &c. 1891. £ 3 10*s*.
    IV. Anonaceæ of British India. 1893. £ 3 10*s*.
    V., Part 1. A Century of Orchids. Memoir of W. Roxburgh. 1895. £ 3 3*s*. coloured, £ 1 12*s*. 6*d*. uncoloured.
    V., Part 2. A Century of New and Rare Indian Plants. 1896. £ 1 12*s*. 6*d*.
    VI., Part 1. Turgescence of Motor Organs of Leaves. Parasitic species of Choanephora. 1895. £ 1 10*s*.
    VII. Bambuseæ of British India. 1896. £ 2.
Anwar-i-Soheli. By Colonel H. S. Jarrett. 1880. 15*s*.
Archæological Survey of India. (New Series):
    IX. South Indian Inscriptions. By E. Hultzsch, Ph.D. Vol. I. 1890. 4*s*.
    X.   „   „   „   „   Vol. II, Part. 1. 1891. 3*s*. 6*d*.

South Indian Inscriptions. By E. Hultzsch, Ph.D. Vol. II, Part 2. 1892. 3s. 6d.
South Indian Inscriptions. By E. Hultzsch, Ph.D. Vol. II, Part 3. 1895. 5s. 6d.
XI. Sharqî Architecture of Jaunpur. By A. Führer, Ph.D. 1889. £1 1s. 6d.
XII. Monumental Antiquities in the North-West Provinces. By A. Führer, Ph.D. 1891. 13s. 6d.
XV. South Indian Buddhist Antiquities. By A. Rea. 1894. 12s. 6d.
XVII. Architectural, &c. Remains in Coorg. By A. Rea. 1894. 2s.
XVIII. The Moghul Architecture of Fatehpur Sikri. By E. W. Smith. Part 1. 1894. £1 5s.
The Moghul Architecture of Fatehpur Sikri By E. W. Smith. Part 2. 1896. 17s. 6d.
XXI. Châlukyan Architecture. By A. Rea. 1896. £1 2s.
XXIII. Muhammadan Architecture in Gujarat. By J. Burgess, C.I.E., LL.D. 1896. £1.

Army List, The Indian. Quarterly. 4s.
Art Ware, Photographs of Madras and Burmese. 1886. £1 15s.
Arzis: Bengali, Canarese, Hindi, Mahratta, Malayalam, Tamil, Telugu, and Urdu. 7s. 6d. each.
Translations of the above (except Hindi). 7s. 6d. each.

Beer Casks, Destruction of, by a Boring Beetle. By W. F. H. Blandford. 1893. 6d.
Bibliographical Index of Indian Philosophical Systems. By F. Hall.1859. 9s.
Bihar Peasant Life. By G. A. Grierson, Ph.D., C.I.E. 1885. 6s. 6d.
Bihari Language, Seven Grammars of. By G. A. Grierson, Ph.D. C.I.E. (8 parts). 1883—87. £1.
Bihari, The Satsaiya of. Edited by G. A. Grierson, Ph.D., C.I.E. 1896. 7s. 6d.
Bombay Gazetteer, Edited by J. M. Campbell, LL.D., C.I.E.:
I. (Not yet published). — II. Surat and Broach. 1877. 5s. 6d. — III. Kaira and Panch Mahals. 1879. 2s. 6d. — IV. Ahmedabad. 1879. 3s. — V. Cutch, Palanpur, and Mahi Kantha. 1880. 4s. — VI. Rewa Kantha, Narukot, Cambay, and Surat States. 1880. 3s. — VII. Baroda. 1883. 5s. — VIII. Kathiawar. 1884. 6s. 6d. — IX. (Not yet published). — X. Ratnagiri and Savantvadi. 1880. 5s. — XI. Kolaba and Janjira. 1883. 5s. — XII. Khandesh. 1880. 6s. — XIII. Thana. (2 parts). 1882. 8s. — XIV. Thana: places of interest. 1882. 5s. — XV. Kanara. (2 parts). 1883. 7s. 6d. — XVI. Nasik. 1883. 6s. 6d. — XVII. Ahmadnagar. 1884. 7s. — XVIII. Poona. (3 parts). 1885. 15s. 6d. — XIX. Satara. 1885. 6s. 6d. — XX. Sholapur. 1884. 5s. — XXI. Belgaum. 1884. 6s. — XXII. Dharwar. 1884. 7s. 6d. — XXIII. Bijapur. 1884. 6s. 6d. — XXIV. Kolhapur. 1886. 5s. — XXV. Botany of the Presidency. 1886. 4s. 6d. — XXVI. Materials for a Statistical of Bombay Town and Island, Parts I., II., and III. 1893—94. 5s. each.
British Burma Gazetteer. Edited by H. R. Spearman. (2 vols.) 1879—80. £1 13s. 6d.
Buddha Gaya; the Hermitage of Sakya Muni. By Rajendralal Mitra. 1878. £3.
Burmese, Tables for the Transliteration of, into English. 1896. 1s.

Catalogue of the India Office Library, Vol. I (with Index). 1888. 10s. 6d.
" " " (Supplement). 1895. 5s.
" of the Arabic MSS. in the India Office Library. By O. Loth. 1877. 15s.
" of the Mandalay MSS. in the India Office Library. By V. Fausböll. 1897. 2s.
" of the Pali MSS. in the India Office Library. By H. Oldenberg. 1882. 5s.
" of the Sanskrit MSS. in the India Office Library. By Dr. J. Eggeling. (Parts I to V). 1887—96. 10s. 6d. each.
" of Sanskrit MSS., Bikanir. By Rajendralal Mitra. 1880. 3s.
" " " Tanjore. By A. C. Burnell. 1880. £1 11s. 6d.
" of MSS. in Oudh. By A. Sprenger 1854. 15s.
Chestnuts, Papers on Spanish. With Introduction by Sir George Birdwood, K. C. I., C. S. I. 1892. 1s.
Cholera, What can the State do to prevent is? By Dr. J. M. Cunningham. 1884. 3s.
Coorg Gazetteer. 1884. 5s.
Corpus Inscriptionum Indicarum:
I. Inscriptions of Asoka. By Major-General Sir A. Cunningham, K. C. I. E., C. S. I. 1877. 9s. 6d.
II. (Not yet published.)
III. Inscriptions of the early Gupta King. By J. F. Fleet, C. I. E. 1889. £1 13s. 6d. with plates. £1 without plates.
Covenanted Civil Servants, Manual of Rules applicable to. Second edition. 1891. 2s. 6d.
Dictionary of Indian Economic Products. By Dr. Geo Watt, C. I. E. (6 vols. in 9). 1889—93. £3 3s.
Ditto, Index to. 1896. 3s.
Durga puja. By Pratapa Chandra Ghosha. 1871. 6s.
English-Sanskrit Dictionary. By Sir M. Monier-Williams, K. C. I. E. 1851. £1 10s.

Fibres. Report on Indian. By C. F. Cross, E. J. Bevan, &c. 1887. 5s.
Finance and Revenue Accounts of the Government of India. Annual volumes. 2s. 6d. each.
Forest Working Plans. By W. E. D'Arcy. (Second edition). 1892. 1s. 6d.
Fort St. George Diary and Consultation Books: 1681 (Selection) 1893. 3s. 6d. — 1682. 1894. 4s. — 1683. 1894. 5s. 6d. — 1684. 1895. 5s. 6d. — 1685. 1895. 7s.
Geological Survey Department Publications.
Glossary of Indian Terms. By H. H. Wilson. 1855. £1 10s.
Hastings, Warren, Selections from the Records of the Foreign Department relating to the Administration of. Edited by G. W. Forrest, B. A. (3 vols.) 1890. 16s.
" " The Administration of. (A reprint of the Introduction to the foregoing.) By G. W. Forrest, B. A. 1892. 5s. 6d.
India Office Marine Records, List of. 1896. 5s.
Kachin Language, Handbook of the. By H. F. Hertz. 1895. 1s.

Lansdowne, Lord, The Administration of. By G. W. Forrest, B. A. 1894. 2s. 6d.
Lepcha Grammar. By Colonel G. P. Mainwaring. 1876. 3s.
Lighthouse Construction and Illumination, Report on. By F. W. Ashpitel. 1895. £1 9s. 6d.

Madras District Manuals (revised issues:)
South Canara (2 vols.) 1894. 4s.
North Arcot (2 vols.) 1895. 6s.
Malabar Manual. By W. Logan. (3 vols.) 1891. £1 2s. 6d.
Manava-Kalpa-Sutra. By Th. Goldstücker. 1861. £3.
Manual of Hydraulics. By Captain H. D. Love, R. E. 1890. 5s.
Marathi Dictionary. By J. T. Molesworth. 1857. 16s.
Marathi Grammar. By the Rev. Ganpatrao R. Navalkar. (Third edition.) 1894. 10s. 6d.
Meteorological Department Publications.
Muntakhabat-i-Urdu. (Second edition.) 1887. 1s. 10d.
Mutiny, the Indian, Selections from the Records of the Military Department relating to. Edited by G. W. Forrest, B. A. Vol. I. 1893. 12s. 6d.

North-East Frontier of Bengal, Relations of the Government with the Hill Tribes of the. By Sir Alexander Mackenzie, K. C. S. I. 1884. 6s. 6d.
North-West Provinces Gazetteer:
I. Bundelkhand, 1874. 8s. 6d. — II. Meerut Part. I. 1875. 6s. 6d. — III. Meerut, Part. II. 1876. 8s. 6d. — IV. Agra, Part. I. 1876. 8s. 6d. — V. Rohilkhand. 1879. 8s. 6d. — VI. Cawnpore, Gorakhpur and Basti. 1881. 9s. — VII. Farukhabad and Agra. 1884. 8s. — VIII. Muttra, Allahabad and Fatehpur. 1884. 10s. — IX. Shahjahanpur, Moradabad aud Rampur Native State. 1883. 8s. — X. Himalayan Districts, Part. I. 1882. 13s. — XI. Himalayan Districts, Part. II. 1884. 12s.! 6d. — XII. Himalayan Districts Part. III. 1886. 12s. — XIII. Azamgarh, Ghazipur and Ballia' 1883. 8s. — XIV. Benares, Mirzapur and Jaunpur. 1884. 10s.

Oudh Gazetteer. (3 vols.) 1877—78. £1.

Paintings, &c. in the India Office, Descriptive Catalogue of. By W. Forster. 1893. 1s.
Prakrita Prakasa. By E. B. Cowell. 1854. 9s.
Prem Sagar. By E. B. Eastwick. 1851. 15s.

Rajputana Gazetteer. (3 vols.) 1879—80. 15s.
Rigveda Sanhita. Vols. IV to VI. By Professor Max Müller. 1862—74. £2 12s. 6d. per volume.
Index to ditto. £2 5s.
Rigveda Translations. By H. H. Wilson. Vols I, III and IV. 1850—66. 13s. 6d. per volume.
Vols. V and VI. 1888. 18s. per volume.

Sanskritt MSS. in S. India, First and Second Reports on. By Dr. Hultzsch. 1895—96. 1s. 8d. each.
Scientific Memoirs by Medical Officers of the Indian Army:
Part I. 1885. 2s. 6d. — Part II. 1887. 2s. 6d. — Part III. 1888.

4s. — Part IV. 1889. 2s. 6d. — Part V. 1890. 4s. — Part VI. 1891. 4s. — Part VII. 1892. 4s. — Part VIII. 1893. 4s. — Part IX. 1895. 4s.
Selections from the Records of the Burmese Hluttaw. 1889. 6s.
Sikkim Gazetteer. By H. H. Risley, C. I. E., and others. 1894. 12s. 6d.
Specimens of Languages in India. By Sir G. Campbell, K. C. S. I. 1874. £1. 16s.
Survey Department Publications.
Surveys 1875—90, Memoir on the Indian. By C. E. D. Black. 1891. 7s. 6d.
Tamil Papers. By Andrew Robertson. 1890. 4s.
Technical Art Series of Illustrations of Indian Architectural Decorative Work for the use of Art Schools and Craftsmen: 1886—87. (6 plates.) 2s. — 1888—89. (18 plates.) 6s. — 1890. (12 plates.) 4s. — 1891. (18 plates.) 6s. — 1892. (13 plates.) 4s. 6d. — 1893. (12 plates) 4s. — 1894. (14 plates.) 5s. — 1895. (12 plates.) 4s. — 1896. (15 plates.) 4s.
Telegu Reader. By C. P. Brown. (2 vols.) 1852. 14s.
Textile Manufactures and Costumes of the People of India. By Dr. Forbes. Watson. 1866. £1. 1s.
Tibetan-English Dictionary. By H. A. Jaeschke. 1881. £1.
Timber, Mensuration of. By P. J. Carter. 1893. 1s.
Tobacco. Cultivation and Preparation of, in India. By Dr. Forbes Watson. 1871. 5s.
Tombs or Monuments in Bengal, Inscriptions on. Edited by C. R. Wilson, M.A. 1896. 3s. 6d.
Vikramarka, Tales of. By Ravipati Gurumurti. 1850. 1s.
Yield tables of the Scotch Pine. By W. Schlich, Ph. D. 1889. 1s.

N.B. In addition to the above, a large number of departmental reports, &c., are on sale at the various Government presses in India. These publications are not kept in stock at the India Office; but should copies of them be required, they will be furnished (on payment), as far as possible, from the supply received for official purposes.

In all cases applications for publications must be made through the official agents.

INDEX OF PRIVATE NAMES.

Apte, M. C., 1
Arbuthnot, F. F., 10, 15
D'Arcy, W. E. D., 25
Ashpitel, F. W.; 26
Aston, W. G., 2

Bacon, Wisner, 21
Ball, C. J., 18
Beal, S., 19
Bemmelen, J. F. van, 9
Bennet, W. H., 18
Berrington, B. J., 9
Bevan, E. J., 25
Bezold, C., 3
Biesen, C. van den, 22
Birdwood, Sir G., 25
Black, C. E. D., 27
Blackden, M. W., 4
Blandford, W. F. H., 24
Brown, C. P., 27
Browne, Edward G., 9
Budde, K., 18
Budge, E. A. Wallis 4, 14, 15
Burgess, J., 24
Burnell, A. C., 25

Campbell, J. M., 24
Campbell, Sir G., 27
Cappeller, Carl, 5
Carter, P. J., 27
Chakrabarti J. C., 6
Chenery, J., 10
Cool, W., 6
Cordier, H., 20
Cornill, C. H., 18
Cowell, E. B., 2, 26
Cowper, B. H., 7
Cross, C. J., 25
Cunningham, J. M., 25

Cunningham, Sir A., 25
Cust, R. N., 7, 8

Das, Sarat Candra, 13
Driver, S. R., 18

Eastwick, E. B., 26
Edkins, J., 8
Eggeling, J., 25
Eitel, E. J., 8

Fausböll, V., 25
Fleet, J. F., 25
Forrest, G. W., 25, 26
Forster, W., 26
Frazer, G. W., 4
Führer, A., 24

Ghosha, P. C., 25
Gladstone (W. E.), 9
Goldstücker, J., 26
Gray, J., 4, 11
Gribble, J. D. B., 9
Grierson, G. A., 24
Griffith, R. J. H., 21
Guirandon, F. G. de, 10
Gurumurti, R., 27

Halcombe C. J. H., 10
Hall, F. 24
Hardy, R. S., 10
Harper, W. R., 1, 3, 11
Harper, R. F., 10
Haupt, P., 17.
Hertz, H. F., 25
Hirschfeld, H., 2
Hooyer, G. B., 6, 9
Hultzsch, E., 23, 26
Hunter, F. M., 23

Jacob, Max, 18
Jaeschke, H. A., 27
Jarrett, H. S., 23
Jastrow, M., 11
Johnson, F. E., 16
Johnston, C., 11, 12
Judson, A., 13

Kamphausen, A., 18
King, L. W., 12, 14
Kittel, F., 13
Kittel, R., 18

Lacouperie, T. de, 2
Land, J. P. N., 13
Leumann, E., 19
Levinsohn, J. B., 8
Loewe, L., 8, 13
Logan, W., 26
Loth, O., 25
Love, H. D., 26
Luzac, C. G., 3

Mackenzie, Sir A., 26
Macnaghten, (Sir W. Hay), 15
Mainwaring, G. P., 26
Margoliouth, D. S., 15
Mitra, R., 24, 25
Molesworth, J. T. 26
Monier-Williams, Sir M., 16, 25
Moore, G. F., 22
Morgan, E. Delmar, 21
Müller, F. Max, 16, 26

Navalkar, G. R., 26

Oldenberg, H., 25
Oudemans, A. C., 17

Poole, R. Lane, 13

Rea, A., 24.
Rehatsek, E., 15
Ridding, C. M., 2
Risley, H. H., 27
Robertson, A., 27

Rosen, F., 17
Rosthorn, A. de, 17
Ruben, P., 17

Samasrami, S. V., 21
Sankaranarayna, P., 18
Sauerwein, G., 18.
Sayce, A. H. 18
Schlegel, G., 20.
Schlich, W. , 27.
Seth, Mesrovb J., 19
Smith, E. W., 24
Sprenger, A., 25
Steele, R., 19
Stein, M. A., 19
Steingass, F., 10
Stoffel, C., 19
Swâmi Vivekânanda, 21

Taylor, E. J., 6, 20
Tawney, C. H., 19
Temple, G., 20
Temple, R. C., 11, 20
Thomas, F. W., 2
Tiele, C. P., 20
Trumpp, E., 23

Uhlenbeck, C. C., 21

Vambery, H., 17
Venis, A., 21
Vivekânanda Swâmi, 21
Voelcker, J. A., 23

Watson, F., 27
Watt, G. 25
Wellhausen, J., 18
West, Sir R., 21
Wildeboer, G., 21
Wilson, C. R., 27
Wilson, H. H., 15, 25, 26
Winckler, H., 22
Wright, W., 22
Wynkoop, J. D., 22

Yatawara, J. B., 22

LUZAC'S ORIENTAL LIST.

NOTICE TO OUR READERS.

With this number we enter upon the eighth year of the publication of our «Oriental List." Four years ago in the first number of our fourth volume we thanked our readers for the generous support we had received from various quarters, including some flattering notices in our contemporaries referring to the value of our «List", and we now tender our thanks to an extended circle of readers. Within recent years the number of works on oriental subjects has increased enormously, and our «List" was started with the object of furnishing a record of such works which should be published at regular intervals. Our aim has therefore been to give each month a complete list of oriental books published in England, on the Continent, in the East and in America, while under the heading «Notes and News" we have endeavoured to give a faithful account of the progress made during the month in the various branches of oriental learning, literature and archaeology. The encouragement we have continuously received from the beginning of the undertaking emboldens us to believe that the «List" has really supplied a want on the part of those who from taste or profession are interested in the languages, literatures and antiquities of the East, and we therefore venture to appeal to our readers who are in the habit of consulting our «List" when making out their orders to send them to us direct.

LONDON, Jan. '98.   LUZAC & Co.